WHO KILLED KELSEY?

BRITTEN FOLLETT &
CHEROKEE BALLARD

ISBN-13: 9780692010068
Library of Congress Control Number: 2010902129

To: Mr. Howard Hendrick Oklahoma Department of Human Services Director

"This is Kelsey, the little girl who won our hearts and the one we tried so desperately to keep safe and happy. Please remember her when the next grandmother or family member comes to you. Her life had a purpose and we seek to find out exactly what it was. If it was only to give us love and joy for two short years then she succeeded, however I feel it was more than that. My wish is that no other family feels the pain we are feeling right now."

–Kathie Briggs 10/13/05

"*All that is necessary for evil to flourish is for good people to do nothing.*"*-Edmund Burke*

PROLOGUE

THE BED WAS TOO BIG FOR HER TINY BODY. So were the bruises. A two-year-old's cries had been silenced forever.

A step-father's 9-1-1 call for help pierced the phone lines.

Sirens pierced the silence as an ambulance tore through Meeker, Oklahoma. It was a race against time as the little girl slipped away. Her lips turned blue, her skin pale gray. Her blood drained into her stomach from the blow.

Emergency crews found the girl's lifeless body in her step-father's arms.

Only three people could possibly know what happened that October day. Two are in prison. The other is dead. What happened that afternoon, two people's silence may never fill.

Was the two-year-old left for her step-father to find? Or did he wait until his wife left to do the unthinkable?

Meeker lost its innocence that Indian summer day. It was the day Kelsey Smith-Briggs was murdered.

Face to Face Interrogation

A lens, no bigger than the size of a button, tucked secretly into the side of the wall watched a young man drag a garbage can close to his body to catch the vomit that never came.

Another lens, hidden in the ceiling of the next room, looked down on a young mother who fought to produce tears that never came.

Two days after their daughter's death, Raye Dawn and Michael Porter drove to Oklahoma City together to be interviewed by agents with the Oklahoma State Bureau of Investigation.

They drove together and lied together. In separate rooms.

Michael Porter

The device hidden inside the interrogation room recorded the sounds of Michael Porter's hurried breaths. The lens watched the 25-year-old step-father squirm in his chair as Agent Steve Tanner began asking questions, "Mike I appreciate you coming down and visiting with us again. Bottom line is we're trying to figure out here what happened."

"I understand," replied Porter.

Tanner told Porter he could leave at any time. During the four hours he spent in one room, Porter left his chair only once, to pace the small room.

The agent had not begun asking about the death of his step-daughter, Kelsey Smith-Briggs, when Porter started crying, lifting his arms over his head in anguish. Porter said, "It's like I can't breathe sometimes. It just hurts so bad. She could make you feel like she'd known you her whole life in two minutes. I never had anybody touch me the way she'd done."

Tanner asked, "Have you and Raye had any chance to be alone since this thing happened?"

"I don't know," replied Porter.

"You don't know?" asked Tanner.

"I don't know what I...I don't know what she needs me to do. Sometimes I don't know if she needs to be alone. We're getting to the drained point where we cry for two days straight, and we haven't slept and we haven't eaten."

Tanner asked, "You have both cried about this?"

Porter sobbed as he said, "More than I can tell you. I'm sorry. I was going to try to be composed today."

Raye Dawn Smith

She'd be 26-years-old next month. With baby number three on the way. The first one was a miscarriage. The third one was a trimester along. The second one was murdered before she turned three. And that's why two OSBI agents sat staring at Raye Dawn Smith Porter. In a room just down the hall from Mike, Raye tried to hide her face from the agents. She could not hide from the camera recording her every move.

Raye's straight blonde hair was pulled back into a pony tail. Her cargo pants and a hooded sweatshirt concealed the little one growing inside her. She and Porter just moved into a big house on a hill outside of Meeker. It had enough space for their growing family.

"It's pretty much a Cinderella story, you know. Things are really starting to look good," said Agent Kevin Garrett.

"We just said that the other day," replied Raye.

"Who said that? You and Mike?" asked Garrett.

"He was saying to me, 'What do you do at the age of 25 when you have everything you want?'"

"Was this before Kelsey passed or after?" asked Garrett.

Raye did not answer, she just continued, "We have beautiful kids, a beautiful home..."

Garrett cut her off, "Right. And isn't it amazing how quickly it can change?" Garrett asked, "What do you think Kelsey would tell us if we could talk to her? What do you think she would tell us that happened?"

"I don't know because why wouldn't she tell me if something was wrong? Why wouldn't she tell her mommy?" asked Raye.

"Well maybe she tried and you didn't know exactly what she was trying to say," explained Garrett.

"She always came up and told me. She hugged and she would say, 'Mommy I love you. I love you so much.' And I'd say, 'I love you too honey.'"

"Have you talked to Michael about this?" asked Garrett.

Raye asked, "About what?" Apparently Raye was not sure what he could be referring to.

Garrett quickly clarified, "About Kelsey. Why are we here? We are here talking about Kelsey."

"I knew she...we knew she had seizures. That's all anybody ever assumed."

"But this isn't a seizure related death. She may have had a seizure because of what occurred to her, but that's not what killed her. Any thoughts?"

"I have all kinds of thoughts," retorted Raye.

"*Do you want to share them?*" pressed Garrett.

"*I just have all kinds.*"

"*What kind of thoughts do you have?*"

"*It's just, I'm depressed and. . .*" Raye Dawn trailed off.

Garrett interrupted her thoughts, "*I can relate to that.*"

"*Just all kinds of things that I didn't know you could feel,*" explained Raye.

"*Are you scared?*" asked Garrett.

"*Of what?*"

"*What's going to happen to this?*"

"*That's not even on,*" paused Raye Dawn, "*I don't know how to explain anything.*"

"*I mean does it scare you that we're here having to tell you?*" asked Garrett.

"*Of course. I'm not worried about me,*" explained Raye Dawn.

"*Why not?*"

"*Because I'm here thinking about my daughter. That's the only reason I'm up here.*"

O·N·E

12 MONTHS BEFORE THE YOUNG COUPLE SAT IN THOSE OSBI INTERROGATION ROOMS, MICHAEL PORTER AND RAYE DAWN SMITH MET ON OCTOBER 15, 2004.

October 15, 2005 Kelsey Smith-Briggs was buried.

October 15, 2005 Kathie Briggs should have been celebrating her 50th birthday, not attending her granddaughter's funeral.

There would be two services that day. Two families gathered around one tiny casket.

A soldier sat in the last row. A soldier who leaned on his family to carry his weight. A soldier who begged his entire family to sit with him in the back of the room. Not because he wanted to be far away from his baby's body, but because a soldier always has his back to a wall.

His two-year-old always proudly announced, "Daddy a soldier!" So on the day of her funeral, amid a crowd full of shirts, ties, and pinstripes, SPC Lance Briggs wore his military fatigues for Kelsey.

The sounds of war filled Lance's head, along with sounds of his wife hanging up an ocean away. The loudest were the sounds of his baby's voice that he'd never hear again. They drowned out the sounds that filled the room.

The small, white casket was closed, hiding the body of the blonde two-year-old covered with bruises. Lance ordered it closed. He told his Mom he wanted to remember the Kelsey he left behind, the little girl who was happy. He couldn't handle the images of her body after she had been beaten to death.

Kelsey Smith-Briggs had been dead four days.

Two hundred people packed the Parks Brothers funeral home. Most of the people there had never seen a child's casket before. A glance toward the front of the chapel brought them to tears. It was standing room only.

I

People came to hear a few comforting words in a world where the comforts of home killed.

Outside her funeral, Oklahoma City television and newspaper photographers had been banished to a parking lot across the street. The funeral director demanded the journalists respect the family's privacy. The photographers snapped pictures and recorded video of the Briggs' family and friends walking into the funeral home. Images of the mourners were broadcast on the news that evening.

Inside, a doctor in the Briggs family gave Lance a pill to help get through the last two hours he would ever spend with Kelsey. Pastor Glen Walters struggled to find the words to begin the service.

Walters took a deep breath in hopes of comforting himself first, "It's no secret why we're here. Little Kelsey has passed from amongst us. Kelsey was born, December 28, 2002, to Lance Briggs and Raye Dawn Smith. She died October 11, 2005, at Prague hospital. She loved swinging and gymnastics and riding her John Deer tractor. Kelsey is survived by her father SPC Lance Briggs of Fort Benning, Georgia."

"I stand before you today only as a messenger and a weak one at that. The loss of this child has shaken me to the foundation of my being. And I've had to search my own soul as I hope and pray all of you will. Listen to God's word. When I get to where I can see..." Walters wiped his eyes and shared several Bible passages about the place God prepares in heaven for the little ones.

Lance's sister Jeanna broke down when the notes of a familiar song filled the air. Words that still bring tears to her eyes every time she hears the verse:

Jesus loves me! He who died
Heaven's gate to open wide;
He will wash away my sin,
let His little child come in.

Laughter replaced tears if only for a moment as the pastor continued, "All children develop some habits. Some are not so good; some are cute. Kelsey liked to bite, even her own baby cousin. She loved to swing, but she couldn't say swing. She would say, 'Wing, wing!'"

"'Oh man'. And 'I do it, I do it,' were just a few of her favorite sayings," smiled the pastor.

At the end of the service, the Briggs family could hardly bring themselves to leave. The crowd gave their condolences to the family in the grieving room. When everyone left and the room emptied, Lance and his family approached the little casket. They wrapped their arms around it and sobbed.

Only half of the people who knew Kelsey best attended the 10:00 a.m. service. Television crews rushed to cover Kelsey's second funeral service. The afternoon service was for Kelsey's mom's family.

Less than 24 hours after the death of her daughter, Raye Dawn's hair and make-up were immaculate for her trip to the courthouse. Her first order of business was to open her family's plot at the cemetery. While she was there, Raye Dawn filed paperwork to keep Kathie and Lance away from the Smiths' funeral. She filed a restraining order against the man who was not scheduled to get home from Iraq for a few days.

Still making her rounds, Raye Dawn is said to have told her co-workers she was "all cried out" and "this was probably for the best". It was the only suitable reply for a woman whose eyes were dry the morning after her daughter's death.

Lance desperately wanted to see his daughter's casket. Restraining order aside, he would not go to the Smith family's funeral. Since he couldn't bear to see Porter or Raye Dawn, Lance wanted to have a separate service.

While the wounds over Kelsey's death were still raw, the Briggs were now forced into a legal battle for their last hour with the two-year-old's body. After contacting a lawyer, the District Attorney, and the Sheriff, the Briggs got permission to hold a separate funeral. By this time they only had three hours to write the obituary and get to the funeral home to make the arrangements.

The division between the families spilled into the public eye. The local newspaper printed two obituaries, with two different names, for the same dead baby. As the Briggs family shared the need to make arrangements for "Kelsey Smith-Briggs" with the funeral director, they noticed a look of confusion on his face. He explained Raye Dawn told him "Smith" was Kelsey's legal last name. Even in death, Raye Dawn tried to cut Lance out of Kelsey's life. At that moment they made the decision to refer to her only as Kelsey Briggs.

Kelsey's casket would be opened at the Smith family funeral. Witnesses said Raye Dawn again seemed remarkably composed as she gave a several page speech about her daughter's life. Some people at the service felt the speech centered on Raye Dawn herself rather than Kelsey. The room was filled with people including Michael Porter, the man being investigated for Kelsey's murder. Raye Dawn went to extreme lengths to ban Kelsey's biological father from her funeral but didn't seem at all concerned about Porter's presence.

A friend who saw Kelsey's body that day ran out of the room screaming, "They beat that baby! They beat the baby! You have got to see what they did to her."

Michael Porter

After less than an hour of questioning, OSBI Agent Tanner told Porter, Kelsey was murdered. Tanner said, "The problem we're running into is with the report that the Medical Examiner has given. It appears. . .well, it doesn't appear; it's a fact that there were some internal injuries that Kelsey had that absolutely cannot be caused by chest compressions."

Porter adjusted his collar and looked down as Tanner continued, "They were abdominal injuries that were inflicted on Kelsey to the point of where they were so significant that Kelsey would have been in the fetal position right after they happened, okay."

Porter put his hands over his mouth as Tanner explained, "At 1:30 p.m. was when Jean left, so Kelsey was fine at that point in time. Something happened between the time that Jean left and when the ambulance showed up. That's what we have to try to determine, what happened between that time period because that's when those injuries occurred on Kelsey. The Medical Examiner described the injuries as being non-accidental."

Porter leaned over and put his head in his hands as Tanner said, "Something happened to Kelsey."

Porter interrupted, "I don't think. Neither one of us would hurt her, Steve, neither one of us."

Tanner explained, "The injuries were probably caused during a very short time period, okay. The injuries would have absolutely put Kelsey in a fetal position where the pain would have been so significant that she wouldn't have been able to handle it and still be functional.

"The bottom line is we have to try to determine whether it was caused by Raye Dawn or it was caused by you or if it was caused by both of you guys."

Porter cried, "Neither of us, Steve. Neither one of us."

Tanner continued, "It's not unusual in these types of situations and these types of cases. . . and believe me, we've investigated many, many, many of these and you typically have some people that are pretty good folks, people that love their children."

"No. No," Porter scooted to the edge of his chair and shifted his weight.

Tanner said, "And it just happens."

"No it doesn't."

"Well let me ask you this, Mike. Did you do anything. . ."

"No," replied Porter.

Tanner continued, ". . .to hurt Kelsey?"

"No. No. Never, never, never."

"So who would that leave?" asked Tanner.

Quietly Porter said, "She would never do it."

5

Raye Dawn Smith

One hour and eleven minutes into the interview in the room down the hall, Raye Dawn learned the news that had been broken to her husband a few minutes earlier. Agent Kevin Garrett and a female agent told Raye Dawn her daughter had been murdered. Garrett began, "They're saying your daughter was killed. This is a homicide case. I mean something's happened to her that's not consistent with what you're saying and what Mike's saying." Raye Dawn looked into her lap as he continued, "So what we want to try to do is find out why this could have happened and who could have done it."

Raye mumbled, "No."

"Do you have any idea?" asked Garrett.

With a blend of argumentative disbelief Raye said, "There's no way!"

"Are you sure there's something else that might not have taken place whenever she was with you?"

"There's no way," Raye patronized the agent with years of investigatory experience.

Garrett corrected her, "Well, I'm sorry to say, but there is."

She repeated, "There's no way," and bent over to put her face in her lap.

"Was she crying or something when you were trying to go to sleep?"

Raye Dawn flailed her arms in the air as she said, "No. She just laid beside me and went to sleep."

The mother continued to argue with the agents. She told them she did not believe that something happened to Kelsey besides a seizure, "I don't believe that. I don't believe that," became Raye's response to nearly every supposition the agents made.

"Why do you not believe that? Were you worried about Lance coming back? Was that something that had you kind of stressed out?" pressed Garrett.

Raye began dramatically ranting, "No. I would never hurt my baby!"

T · W · O

"GIVE ME A BABY," RAYE DAWN SHOUTED.

And he did.

Lance has a hunch Kelsey was conceived on the side of a dirt road.

The two went dirt roadin' often. Yes, in Meeker dirt roadin' is a verb.

Four stop signs mark the middle of Meeker. It's small, even by Oklahoma standards. If you stand in the intersection, you're standing at the crossroads of Highways 18 and 62 in Lincoln County. On one corner people fill up with gas and get a cold drink at the Rainbow convenience store. On the other, the Bad Dawg café serves up delicious cheeseburgers with sides of fried okra, the kitty chicken salad, and the town gossip. Lucky customers get serenaded at their red leather booths by men with guitars, fiddles and harmonicas. No invitation necessary.

Most of the residents were either born in Meeker or moved there while they were still in diapers. Like Carl Hubbell, arguably Meeker's most famous resident. The hall of fame baseball player and pitcher for the Giants moved to Meeker as a boy. He helped the Giants win the 1933 World Series. Nestled inside Meeker City Hall, "King Carl" has a museum named after him.

Thirty seconds, going the speed limit, and you've seen Meeker. Inside Studio 62, the dryers drown out the buzz of women's voices sharing the latest family stories. Now the talk is somber as the women share their opinions about what happened to Kelsey. Her story divided the town of 980 people.

These days there are more hot pink, heart shaped stickers in Meeker than people. A sticker order at the local sign shop began as 200 and multiplied to more than 400,000. On them, an innocent smile, baby blue eyes and a message: Justice for Kelsey Briggs. The stickers dot store fronts, office doors, and rear windows of cars. Kelsey Briggs smiles back at you. Yes, you're smiling because her personality is contagious. Her blonde hair barely brushes her shoulders. Ribbon holds a tuft of her golden locks off her face. Her eyes are full of mischief. It's a face hard to forget.

Now, many would say she's Meeker's most famous resident.

Oklahoma fell in love with Kelsey in the days following October 11, 2005.

Kelsey's mom and dad met in high school but didn't start dating until after they graduated. Lance was a football player. Raye Dawn was the captain of the pom squad. During half-time of the football games, the pom girls showed off their high kicks and cute, sexy moves. Raye Dawn strutted her stuff at Bulldog stadium. In classic tradition, one year the football star escorted the pom captain for their homecoming ceremony.

Kathie Briggs never missed a chance to watch her son play and always admired Raye Dawn from the stands. She sure could dance. Kathie always thought the pom captain would make a great daughter in-law someday. Lance knew she slept around. She just hadn't made her way around to him until they graduated. The new Millennium marked the beginning of Lance and Raye Dawn's romance.

One night years after high school, the two ran into each other at a party in Shawnee, a nearby town. Lance walked in with a 12 pack of beer, looked around, and spotted the only open seat. The spot on the couch, next to Raye Dawn, seemed to be waiting for him. He made himself comfortable because he knew he'd be staying awhile.

He had a front row seat to the catch of the party and was carrying a ticket backstage for the night. He had beer and she was happy. Lance says, as they started talking, he found himself getting a little nervous. Hard to understand why, at that point he was feeling good about himself. He had a brand new truck. Now he was talking to Raye Dawn. They talked all night and slipped out the front door together.

The party never ended that night. Lance and Raye Dawn went dirt roadin' until the sun came up. As the red glow of the Oklahoma sky began to match the red dirt on the horizon, he dropped her off at her parents' house.

The sex was good; the partying was better. The beer never forced her out of a size four. Lance and Raye Dawn did not miss a beat.

Raye Dawn was Lance's best accessory. When the two of them walked into a party or a bar, everyone looked. Lance walked with an air about him and Raye Dawn knew she was gorgeous. Her black leather pants, low cut tops, and what Lance called tall hooker boots, caught stares of envious men. Lance knew she'd be a tough one to keep, but he always had a thing for the blonde hair and who she was.

He had the girl everyone wanted to be with. Once she and Lance were married, Lance says she kept up with her reputation.

Lance says he loved Raye Dawn, but in hindsight it was the physical attraction that was addicting. Lance nicknamed her "fish" because she drank constantly. He knew they were so wrong for each other, but it was a magnetic attraction. They partied hard and fought harder.

Lance and Raye Dawn hadn't been dating very long, maybe three or four months. Lance was in love though and wanted to get married. The next step was ring shopping. He wanted his bride-to-be to have the biggest ring money could buy. They stopped by every reputable jewelry store in Shawnee, but Raye Dawn kept going back to one. Lance remembers, "I knew it was the one at the time. I told her, 'We can't do it. I'm sorry,' and made her think she'd have to settle."

Lance made it work. He bought the ring long before his credit went sour. "I charged that sucker! It was a big old ring. It cost $3,500 and I got it for $2,800," Lance says.

Ring in tow, it was time for a romantic proposal. Lance took her to a restaurant on Lake Hefner, in Oklahoma City. He says she knew something was up when he told her they were going out and she had to dress up. They never went out to dinner on a Monday night, but he wanted to surprise her.

The weather was perfect. He reserved a table in the back of the restaurant, overlooking the lake. Lance ordered roses for the table and wine for their glasses. While they were waiting for their food, he asked Raye Dawn to go for a walk, "It was perfect; she loved it. I didn't plan on doing it ever again," laughed Lance.

Raye Dawn always told him she would cry when that special someone proposed. He was disappointed when she did not. He remembers she got a bit emotional but never shed a tear.

Raye Dawn loved the ring, though. She had the ring. Lance says it was almost as if the person did not matter. She had the ring.

Lance watched Raye Dawn flash the investment to everyone. It was a princess cut diamond surrounded by a number of smaller stones. Lance says, "I was proud; it made me feel great when she would show it off."

One afternoon after the couple was engaged, Kathie saw Raye Dawn buying something that caught her eye. It was a pregnancy test. Raye Dawn lied and told Kathie it was for her sister. Lance says he remembers Raye Dawn taking the test a couple of times before she went to the doctor who confirmed she was pregnant.

The buzz around Meeker was quite revealing. A relative says Raye Dawn told her one day, "I can't believe I'm fucking pregnant. I hate fucking kids."

They didn't set the date for the wedding because she got pregnant, but it did speed things up.

In the middle of all of the wedding preparations and bridal showers, an unexpected crisis hit the young couple. A week before the wedding, Kathie says Raye Dawn's grandmother asked her to come over to sit with Raye Dawn because she was having cramps. While Kathie was there, Raye Dawn's dad arrived and asked what was wrong. Kathie remembers staring at her in shock as her future daughter-in-law told him, "I just want to get this kid out of me."

Raye Dawn's pain was so intense her family worried she could have a tubal pregnancy. They rushed her to the emergency room. Lance left work and met them at the hospital. Once Raye Dawn was in the hospital room, Raye Dawn's mother Gayla left abruptly to go back to work. Kathie sat with Lance and Raye Dawn as their fears were confirmed.

Raye Dawn had miscarried. Years later in court she would change the events of the day to say Lance hit her in the stomach to cause her to lose their child.

The following morning, Kathie took Raye Dawn to her follow-up appointment. She asked Kathie to come with her into the examination room. During the appointment, Kathie says Raye Dawn never mentioned a blow to the stomach.

Raye Dawn seemed to get over the loss quickly; she had a wedding to plan.

Lance added another ring to Raye Dawn's hand outside the same house Kelsey would eventually die in. It was Gayla's dream home. Lance loved that house. It sits four miles east of Meeker, perched on a huge hill with a breath-taking view of rural Oklahoma. Hay bales and cattle dot the horizon.

The mature oak trees could not begin to shade the unbearable heat that day. It was too hot for an outdoor wedding. Kathie asked Raye Dawn about the possibility of moving the wedding indoors to escape the extreme Oklahoma heat in the middle of July. Kathie knew the home had recently been moved to the hill and the remodeling process was not complete. The air conditioning had not been installed. Raye Dawn told Kathie she was not concerned about her guests and demanded the outdoor wedding. Raye Dawn always got what she wanted.

Ray Smith walked his daughter down the sidewalk wearing a freshly starched, yellow, cotton, collared shirt with dark blue jeans and mustard cowboy boots. After blessing the marriage of his little girl with a farewell kiss, Ray joined Raye Dawn's mother, Gayla. Gayla wore a short, sleeveless yellow dress to compliment her husband's shirt.

Raye Dawn took the final steps to the makeshift altar at the front door to the home on her own. Her dress clung to her curves, highlighting her thin waist and narrow shoulders. Raye Dawn did not wear a veil. She chose a tiara instead.

Raye Dawn's sister Rachelle Smith was her Maid of Honor. Rachelle would continue to stand up for her sister in the tumultuous years that followed. Lance asked his dad, Royce, to be his best man.

A judge read the couple's vows and pronounced them man and wife. Raye Dawn would stand before the same judge twice and say, "I do." The next time Michael Porter was her groom.

Each family took pictures with Lance and Raye Dawn. Pictures of two families that would develop a deep-seated hatred for each other once the two lovers divorced.

Raye Dawn and Lance drove off to their honeymoon with "Mr. and Mrs." written in shoe polish on the back window of Lance's truck. The couple was off to celebrate the joyous day Raye Dawn became a Mrs. for the first time.

On their honeymoon, the couple got matching tattoos. Raye Dawn picked out a four leaf clover for her left breast. Lance was never crazy about their identical good luck symbols. And he certainly wasn't about to show anyone the "manly" tattoo his wife made him get.

The honeymoon stage did not last long. For Lance and Raye Dawn the only thing that complimented the beer was meth. Their small two bedroom house was a straight shot to the Rainbow convenience store. Everyone knew either Lance or Raye Dawn would be at the Rainbow getting beer at least once a day. Lance says she could drink a 12 pack easily. For a little girl, Raye Dawn could put them away.

Lance and Raye Dawn both quickly became full blown drug addicts. They liked to argue but liked meth more. Once they got hooked, Lance remembers everything spiraling out of control.

The meth replaced food. They didn't eat; they couldn't. Some addicts never lose their appetites, but Lance says it's a good thing they did because their meth habits broke the bank. There was no money for food.

Lance knew Raye Dawn ran with her girlfriends and felt certain she was running around with other guys. She started putting out sexually for drugs and ended up putting out for fun. Long after their divorce one of Raye Dawn's friends told Lance a story he would have rather never heard. She says one night Raye Dawn didn't have any money, but they headed to her dealer's house anyway. On the way, Raye Dawn bragged she got crank from the guy for less than other people paid. Through the window blinds, her friend says she could see Lance's wife get on her knees in front of her dealer's chair. She then walked out with a little baggie full of drugs. When they got home, the girlfriend says Raye Dawn cut lines of crank on a mirror for them.

His parents tried to make them stop. They didn't listen. Raye Dawn worked at the Meeker Nursing Home. The drugs made the late shift her dream job. Lance says she would do a hit before she left for work. It kept her up while she took care of the residents. Lance says a handful of employees did meth with Raye Dawn all night.

Lance does not remember why the nursing home job didn't last. She had already been laid off from a job at a nearby airport. With no job, lying around became Raye Dawn's hobby. When she and Lance would finally go to sleep, Raye Dawn would not get up.

Their attitudes and personalities were explosive. Lance says they pushed each other's buttons and she knew his buttons well. Raye Dawn wasted little time launching the first attack.

The shoves escalated throughout the two years Raye Dawn and Lance were married.

Lance says, "I popped her one time. It wasn't a fist. It was a slap. It was meant to be real hard. It caused a bloody nose and a black eye the next day."

"We were out at the Illinois River and she totally embarrassed me. Someone had promised her some meth and didn't come through. At camp that night with about 10 people around, I was in awe of the way she was screaming and acting about. All because she did not get the drugs she wanted."

Lance felt like he had to take control, "I took her to the tent because I wanted to get her away from the group and calm her down. I tried to get her to be quiet. She kept arguing and I just was fed up with it and I hit her. She came out of the tent with a bloody nose. It was a big arrow at me. Everyone at camp knew who did it."

Then there were the nights Lance left in a fury. Lance says one night, a very drunk Raye Dawn came home with some guys in the middle of the night. Lance had called his mom earlier in the evening saying Raye Dawn was out again. Kathie could tell he was defeated and suggested he come sleep at home for the night. He couldn't because he wanted to make sure she made it home safely.

When she finally walked, or stumbled in, Raye Dawn told Lance to leave her alone and she hadn't done anything wrong. About 3:00 a.m., Kathie and Royce's phone rang. It was Raye Dawn screaming about Lance. Kathie told Royce to get dressed and go over to check on the young couple.

Raye Dawn forgot to hang up the phone, so Kathie sat in bed, listening to the entire fight. She heard her son walk into different rooms, asking his wife to stop hitting him. When Royce arrived, Kathie hung up the phone and called Raye Dawn's dad to tell him his daughter was drunk again and needed him. While Ray was on his way over, his daughter went into the bedroom searching for sympathy. She grabbed red lipstick and decorated her neck with marks saying Lance caused them.

Any marks she had, Lance says she caused herself, as she threw herself all over the floor. She was too inebriated to talk. Her words were slurred as she flung her body around and screamed.

Lance went to the drawer and pulled out a loaded shot gun. "I remember thinking this girl is so crazy she'll shoot herself, if not shoot me."

Lance stood silently and unloaded the gun. Royce watched in awe and began walking toward the door, hoping Lance would follow. Lance tried, but says Raye Dawn screamed and threw herself on the ground grabbing his ankle. He dragged her from the kitchen to the front door, silently trying to slam her body against the door frame as he slowly made his way out of the house. Raye Dawn tried to seek sympathy in her father. When she went outside, her dad carried her back in the house and told Lance he would take Raye Dawn with him if he wanted to stay at home alone. Lance decided to leave his wife to sleep in her marital bed alone.

The family interventions only worked for awhile. Law enforcement got involved in May of 2001. Lance and Raye Dawn had been up for a couple of days on meth. Nothing but sweat filled Lance's week. He worked outside under the boiling Oklahoma sun. It was Friday and he had a paycheck in his hand. When he got home that evening, he says his wife told him she was going to her friend's house. Lance knew she was going to get drugs. He tried to talk her out of it saying they had already been up for a couple of days and they should get some sleep.

Lance says, "She wanted to party the weekend up, and we couldn't afford it, so I took her keys from her."

She was an invincible 5'2", or so she thought. As Lance dangled the keys above Raye Dawn's head, she started screaming at him because she couldn't leave. Lance says Raye Dawn was already high and he was taunting her. The keys were her ticket to more drugs. Lance says, "I never hit her, but I remember taking her arm and holding it against her chest."

Raye Dawn called her dad screaming, and this time he called the cops. Lance knew it was bad when they arrived. He'd never had much luck with the law; and although he knew he had done nothing wrong, she would convince them he had beaten her, just to prove a point. A Meeker cop came over to take pictures of Raye Dawn's "injuries". She told the officer Lance hit her in the chest.

The same officer drove Lance to the Lincoln County Jail in Chandler. In the squad car, the officer told Lance there were no injuries on Raye Dawn.

Later, Raye Dawn called Lance's sister Jeanna and admitted he did not hit her. Lance's wife tried to confess and get Lance out of jail. She called and politely told the cops she did not want to press charges. Their response wasn't so polite. Filing a false police report is a crime. Raye Dawn could have gone to jail. Since that sounded upsetting and inconvenient, Raye Dawn went ahead with the domestic abuse charges.

Lance sat in jail all weekend. It was Monday before he could see a judge. Raye Dawn went to court that day and drove her husband home. Their tumultuous marriage seemed to be doomed.

Lance says he knew Raye Dawn had been cheating on him the last time they slept together. He knew she didn't want to be with him. The fighting was constant. The bill collectors were swallowing them. Loud music and booze on a dirt road drowned out their problems and they began to have sex.

Lance remembers, "She asked for a baby that night. I knew she wasn't on the pill and we were not using condoms, but I did it anyway."

After another knock down, drag out fight a couple of days later, they split up. Raye Dawn took her stuff and left for her mom's house. Lance thought she'd be back in the morning.

She always was.

Day after day passed and time dragged on.

This time she did not come back.

Lance believes her family played a large role in her decision to stay away. When they asked him to move out of the house, he knew it was over.

She filed for divorce, and they began fighting over empty rooms and empty cabinets.

When the divorce papers arrived, Lance refused to sign them. With the papers in hand, Lance drove up the long driveway, stood on the same porch where they recited, "'till death do us part," and banged on the glass door until Raye Dawn and Rachelle answered.

A small pane of glass became a symbolic barrier between the couple who preferred contact fights. Lance screamed, "I'm not signing this until you give me the ring back."

Since he was still paying on that ring, Lance decided to play dirty. He remembers shouting, "I'm going to stay here until your parents get back and spill all about the drugs."

Lance says he had every intention of staying on the front porch until he either got the ring back or her parents disowned their meth addicted daughter.

A minute later, Raye Dawn opened the door and threw it at the man whose tattoo matched hers, whose baby she would find out she was carrying. The man with whom she said, "I do."

Since most men don't get the ring back, Lance felt a smug sense of satisfaction in the midst of turmoil. Lance knew the only reason he got it back was because he had a bargaining chip. The only thing more important to Raye Dawn than her ring was her reputation.

The divorce was granted. Although in a small town like Meeker it's impossible to avoid someone forever. One day Lance saw Raye Dawn riding a lawn mower in the yard he once tended to. Peeking out underneath her t-shirt was a distinct bump. He knew she was pregnant and could do the math. Raye Dawn told Lance the baby's father lived in Oklahoma City. Her excuse was not good enough. Lance offered to pay for an in-vitro paternity test. He desperately needed to know if he should be preparing for fatherhood or if he should resign himself to the fact that another man had fathered her baby while they were still married.

At that point Lance could hardly take care of himself, let alone a baby. He had started drinking heavily after Raye Dawn left. One afternoon as he was driving through Meeker, Lance saw Raye Dawn again. He was distracted and rear ended a truck and totaled his parents van. He didn't get a ticket, but the town got an earful. Lance's entire family showed up and began arguing in the center of town. Tensions and emotions were compounded because Kathie buried the grandmother who helped raise her that morning.

Lance hit rock bottom in the middle of Meeker, and everyone was there to witness it. It was that day Lance realized he had a problem.

The next morning, Lance checked himself into detox. He stayed there less than a week. When he got out, he began going to Alcoholics Anonymous meetings.

The tattoo on his foot was a symbol of his failed marriage. Every time he looked at the four-leaf clover, it reminded him of the woman who had brought nothing but bad luck to his life. Lance replaced it with a dark green tribal sun hoping nature's glory might heal his wounds.

Lance was rehabilitating his life. He got a job at Indaco metals, moved back in with his parents, and started talking to Ashley. His best friend's little sister.

Lance knew he never had a chance with the straight-laced, Ashley Lytle unless he was straight too. She had never smoked a cigarette in her life and didn't drink either.

That is, unless she was picking up a Big Gulp drink at the Quick Stop where Lance stopped to talk to her. He had put a little meat on his bones and had not taken a drink in a couple of months.

When he saw Ashley that day, he looked at her through a clear lens, no beer goggles. He remembered the short brunette as a little girl with braces.

He was a free man; one divorce under his belt. Ashley was still a teenager; she graduated from high school six years behind Lance. She was a good girl and Lance wanted someone by his side. So he asked her to go on a date.

Ashley told him he had to get permission from her mom. He did, primarily because he knew Ashley never thought he would go through with it. "I had to get the nerve to call Teri. She was hesitant at first but said she would leave it up to Ashley."

Ashley said yes to the date and later said yes at the altar. She was 19 with a decent job. Lance fell in love again, "She was behind me 100%. She was in love with me and I was in love with her. I had known her for more than eight years and always kind of had a thing."

During Lance's courtship with his new love, Kelsey decided it was time to join the world. Raye Dawn went into labor two days after Christmas in 2002. No one in Raye Dawn's family bothered to call the Briggs to let them know Kelsey was on her way. Raye Dawn had worked hard to convince everyone Lance was not the father.

Lance's sister, Jeanna, got a call from a friend announcing Raye Dawn was in labor. He thought Lance had a right to know he was about to be a father. When Lance heard Raye Dawn was in labor he subtracted nine months from the date and remembered that afternoon on the dirt road. At that moment, Lance knew the baby could be his.

A few hours later, another friend called to tell the Briggs it was a girl. Kathie and Royce knew it was a possibility they had become grandparents again that night but wouldn't be welcome at the hospital with pink balloons. The next morning Kathie called the hospital to congratulate Raye Dawn. When the new mother answered, Kathie couldn't bring herself to say hello so she hung up.

To clear up the genetics question, Ashley and Lance decided to go to court to get a paternity test.

Lance remembers how cold it was the day he went to the Child Support Enforcement office in downtown Shawnee. The nurse followed Lance into a tiny room. She pulled out a long cotton swab and rubbed the inside of Lance's mouth. Raye Dawn walked in holding a car seat covered with a baby blanket. That was the first time Lance saw Kelsey. When she pulled off the blanket Lance remembers thinking, "She ain't my child!" Kelsey had a full head of dark hair. She couldn't be his. Now he wishes he remembered the moment a little better. He watched as the nurse swabbed Kelsey's tiny mouth.

For months, the two families remained in limbo, waiting and wondering who Kelsey's father really was.

On Lance's birthday, April 8, 2003, the envelope arrived in the mail. "It was written in legal and medical terms, but I remember the 99.99%," says Lance. It was the perfect birthday gift.

Kathie and Royce were proud grandparents and immediately embraced Kelsey as another member of the family. They did not want Kelsey to feel like she was any different than the other grandkids. So they announced their new arrival in the weekly Meeker newspaper, just as they did with all of their grandchildren.

They knew eventually, Briggs, would be added to the end of Kelsey's name. Kathie was careful just to call their new granddaughter, Kelsey, in their birth announcement. The birth announcement was just the beginning of the battle over Kelsey and the turmoil between the two families. The paper took its own initiative and printed "Baby Girl Briggs" atop the birth announcement. When Kathie picked up the paper, eager to look inside, she knew there would be trouble when she spotted that headline.

Even though Kelsey was four-months-old at this point, the Smith family quickly submitted its own birth announcement the next week. This one was titled, "Baby Girl Smith", accompanied by a picture Kathie had taken.

Before most of the Briggs family had the chance to meet Kelsey, the women threw a baby shower for the proud father. Lance asked if Kelsey could come, but Raye Dawn refused.

As Kelsey got older, her stubborn, devilish personality was a mirror image of her dad's. No one ever doubted again who Kelsey's father really was.

Ashley and Lance decided since Kelsey was his, they would get married and help raise her together. Ashley knew she would never be Kelsey's only mom. She never wanted to replace Raye Dawn but wanted Kelsey to feel comfortable at their home.

Lance met his baby girl for the first time, officially, at Kathie's house. In awe of his baby, Lance counted each of her ten tiny fingers. Then he took off her shoes and socks to count her ten tiny toes. Lance and Kelsey locked eyes and just stared at each other. It was love at first sight.

Lance had to share four hours with the entire immediate family. Raye Dawn would not agree to any more time. Everyone was excited to hold Kelsey for the first time. Raye Dawn dropped Kelsey off before Lance got there. When Kelsey's mom came back to pick her up, Lance and Raye Dawn's eyes locked. Kathie says she could tell they were thinking, "Look what we did..."

When Raye Dawn carried Kelsey outside, Lance followed. Ashley watched through the glass door as Lance and Raye Dawn talked and laughed outside. Ashley couldn't help but wonder if Kelsey would bring them back together.

Outside, the tone quickly changed when Lance asked Raye Dawn, "If I wouldn't have gotten this test done, you never would have known whose child this was. Would you have never told her who the dad was?"

Lance remembers her saying, "Kelsey does not need a dad. Maybe someday I would have told her, but Kelsey doesn't need a dad, and doesn't need you."

Raye Dawn had convinced another family Kelsey was their granddaughter. Once she started showing, Raye Dawn told people Kelsey's dad was her boyfriend in Oklahoma City. After she was born, Raye Dawn took Kelsey over to his parents' house on the weekends. The Briggs didn't know anything about Kelsey's "first" set of grandparents until Kelsey's funeral.

Lance loved Kelsey but the reality of being tied to Raye Dawn for the rest of his life was sobering. He says her facial expressions were degrading. Lance felt Raye Dawn viewed the Briggs as being below her and was disgusted to have to drop her little princess off with them.

The glare returned every other weekend and every other holiday while Lance pushed to see her more often. Eventually, the only sound was Kelsey's goodbyes as the two families handed over the child.

Along with the paternity results came the request for money. Raye Dawn wasted little time asking to be reimbursed for the lies she told. Lance was already four months behind in child support and had to get current before he could reasonably ask for more time with his baby.

Lance says, "It wasn't my fault she lied. I saw all of my child support as nothing but beer money. Very little of it went to Kelsey. I'm paying mom support. I was just supporting her habits." Lance paid it anyway. He would do anything to spend more time with Kelsey.

Lance was trying to build a stable life for his little girl. He decided it might not look good to the judge if he was just living with Ashley. He believed a judge would know better than to put a child in that situation. The young couple wanted the court to know they were willing to do anything to ensure Kelsey had a happy and secure home. They sought out parenting classes and attended them together. Lance also went to a class for divorced parents so he would be better prepared for the years to come.

Lance had never formally proposed to Ashley. Once they learned about Kelsey, they just began planning the wedding. So one night he got down on his knee and said, "I need to ask you."

Ashley had dropped some hints saying she wanted Lance to officially ask her. He did, right there in the living room. There were no tears that night either.

"I can't get nobody to cry!" laughed Lance.

Once again it was time to shop for a ring. This time Lance's fiancé bought her own. Ashley had been in a car accident and invested her pain and suffering settlement into a diamond.

They married at a church in Meeker. Lance says, "We got married for ourselves and for Kelsey on June 14, 2003. I was a changed man."

Kathie made Kelsey her own dress to match the bride's. She was Lance's little princess. It was the one and only time Kelsey would walk down the aisle with her dad, "It was great. You're starting your life over and you've changed so much and you're happy. You're with someone who is 100% completely opposite of Raye Dawn. I couldn't get her to argue or fight. I couldn't believe it was possible."

After the reception Ashley changed into her honeymoon outfit. Again, Kelsey matched. She wore denim cropped overalls trimmed with black ribbon covered with small red and yellow flowered fabric. A couple of flowers dotted the top of the bib of her overalls. Ashley wore her veil and pearl necklace as Lance took off her garter and tossed it to the bachelors in the room.

Lance's sisters, Jeanna and Shirica, watched in their rayon flowered sundresses as Ashley tossed her peach bouquet to the single ladies. Robynn, Lance's third sister, was the only one of the sisters eligible to catch the tradition.

Ashley and Lance left in a maroon car. Shoe polish formed two hearts on the windshield. Tucked in her car seat was the most precious of wedding gifts. The newlyweds took Kelsey along on their honeymoon night. It was the first overnight visit for the three of them.

Ashley became Kelsey's other mom. Lance says, "Ashley never complained. She got up in the middle of the night while I slept and fed Kelsey. She just did it. She had them ears tuned in to the littlest noise. She'd hear something move and she'd be in there."

The precious few days they had with Kelsey flew by. It seemed like it was always time to give Kelsey back. Lance and Ashley made it a ritual to spend the last five minutes of Kelsey's visits hugging her and telling her they loved her. As their relationship with Kelsey grew stronger so did their love for each other. Lance and Ashley decided Kelsey needed to feel secure before they would have children together.

For 14 months the little family thrived. Their rent was only $400 a month. Both Lance and Ashley were working so they had plenty of money to save. All of their bills were paid on time. It was a stark change for the man whose last marriage ended in debt.

Living the dream Lance only imagined, now the couple had enough money to upgrade. They bought a house three doors down from their rent house. It had four simple walls with beige aluminum siding and a big oak tree in the front yard. Two small cement steps led up to the small porch where they kept a couple of chairs, hugged by a white railing.

Every other weekend they kept Kelsey for two full days. When she would come over, there was never enough time for her to wear all of her new clothes. Everything she had was brand new. They couldn't change her outfit enough.

Lance and Ashley created a little pink castle for their ⸱
painted Kelsey's room the same color as the tie Lance wou
mom's trial.

Years later, home video of Kelsey swinging on the swing set in the backyard of Lance and Ashley's home would haunt Oklahomans. The once happy little girl's face was covered with bruises. Her eyes were blood shot.

Kelsey died with clothes hanging in her closet that still had the tags on them.

Michael Porter

"Being pregnant you know, hormones kind of change a little bit, in pregnant women, don't they?" asked Tanner.

Porter replied, "Steve, she wouldn't hurt...I mean, any scenario you can come up with, she would never hurt her, never."

"Well then, you explain to me how that baby died," said Tanner.

"I don't know," said Porter.

"Tell me," pressed Tanner.

"I don't know."

"You tell me how that baby died. The only ones that know how that baby died, is you and Raye Dawn."

Porter replied, "Well, apparently, the Medical Examiner knows, Steve. We want to know what happened."

"She bled to death on the inside," said Tanner.

"No."

"Yes! We want to know how she died and why it happened. That's what we're looking at now. We know the Medical Examiner told us that."

"No."

Tanner explained, "Denying it isn't going to change it, Mike. It's not going to change what happened. I don't have any reason to lie to you. Saying no, it's not going to change what happened. It just isn't. You can deny it all you want, you can tell me you wouldn't do this, you can believe that Raye Dawn wouldn't do it. But, by God, one of you all did it."

"No," insisted Porter.

Raye's screams in the room down the hall, pierced the walls of Porter's interrogation room. But Porter did not acknowledge his wife's cries.

Tanner says, "I don't know what goes on in your house. I don't know what all you have in your house."

"We don't hurt children, Steve," said Porter.

"I know you don't hurt them on purpose. You don't kill them on purpose. I understand that."

"Steve this is wrong. I'm telling you, this is wrong. You're either born with the capability to hurt children or you're not."

Porter again ignored his wife's screams and continued, "We don't, we're not capable of hurting children, Steve. I mean, you as a father, that's like somebody sitting there and telling you that you could do it when you know that you can't."

Raye Dawn Smith

A female agent named Za joined Agent Kevin Garrett in hopes of identifying with Raye on a more personal level. For the first time Raye looked Za in the eye as the agent asked, "Raye, if you have a problem, listen to me. If you have a problem, with your anger, and being able to control yourself. And from what I understand you are pregnant again?"

Raye nodded.

"You don't want to be in this position again. You need to get some help," consoled Za, "Raye, you can't even look. . ."

Raye cut Za off, "Don't yell at me and everything."

"We're not yelling at you," said Za, in the same calm voice, "You can't even look at us when you're saying that. Do you know what I'm saying?"

"What are you talking about?" asked Raye.

"Every time you say, 'I don't know,' you look away. You don't. . .I mean all of these things, everything about you. . ." continued Za.

"I don't know what happened to my daughter," insisted Raye.

T·H·R·E·E

A LIFETIME OF DRAMA COULD NOT PREPARE KATHIE BRIGGS FOR THE UNTHINK-ABLE. The murder of her granddaughter.

It was a death Lance's mom predicted. Kathie told child welfare workers over and over it would happen if they weren't careful.

Her humble roots hardly prepared her for the spot she would be thrust into. She became a "spokeswoman" crusading against a failing agency designed to protect abused children.

Kathie Jo Batt grew up in Dale, Oklahoma, a town even smaller than Meeker.

Kathie got off to a quick start. She didn't give herself much time in between high school and the real world. She donned a simple dress and married her first husband Kevin before she knew what it meant to be a Mrs. She was just a baby, only 16-years-old when she said "I do".

Kevin and Kathie had three beautiful kids named Shirica, Jeanna and Lance. Being a mom came naturally for Kathie; being a wife did not. Kathie realized she needed to get out of an abusive marriage. Like Kelsey, Lance was born after his parents were divorced. However, DNA tests were not common and it was two years before Kevin acknowledged his son.

Ultimately, Kevin removed himself from their lives. On December 26, Kathie had to tell her three children their Daddy was gone. Kevin took his life on Christmas night. At the time, Kathie thought it would be the hardest thing she would ever have to tell her children.

Lance and his sisters will never forget the moment they lived past 29 years, 3 months and 8 days. It was the age of their father when he left them behind.

When his dad died, Lance was only 7.

Dwelling on the past and an uncertain future wasn't going to work. Soon after Kathie moved on to marriage number two, she welcomed a healthy baby girl. She named her Robynn Suzanne, after the husband she would soon divorce.

What was this young mother of four, to do? Her heart ached for a man to love her and her kids. She desperately wanted a place to feel safe and secure, a place to call home.

The young mother was completely overwhelmed. She was 22-years-old with four children. Her oldest was just five. During a home visit with her social worker, Kathie expressed her need for help. The social worker suggested Kathie let the children stay with family members while she got on her feet. It seemed like the perfect solution at the time.

The children were placed with family as guardians while legally they were in the custody of the Department of Human Services, or DHS. DHS is the state agency charged with protecting Oklahoma children whose parents either can't or won't take care of them.

Kathie felt she was in the first category. The single mother could not adequately provide for her kids and felt she had nowhere else to turn. She chose to bring life into the world and she needed to do what was best for them. So DHS granted Kathie's sister, Debbie Batt, custody of the little ones. Kathie saw them regularly without any restrictions.

It was a decision Kathie would be highly criticized for. People accused her of threatening to kill every one of her children if someone didn't take them. Kathie says she never said such a thing. The story was conjured up by Raye Dawn's defense team in hopes of ruining Kathie's credibility, 30 years after the fact.

To the young mother, DHS custody equaled safety. DHS never required a treatment plan for Kathie, but her sister recommended sessions with a psychologist to help her deal with her failed marriages. Soon, the children were reunited with their mother. The judge said he hoped to have more success stories like Kathie's.

Success seemed out of Kathie's grasp until she met Royce Briggs. Kathie married the final time to the love of her life. Royce and Kathie have been married 26 years.

Their vows brought instant fatherhood for Royce. It wasn't long before the children were calling him "Dad" and a real family was created.

He's a quiet, calm man of few words who has a hard time finding any words when it comes to his granddaughter, Kelsey. He can't talk about Kelsey without tearing up. When he wasn't singing to Kelsey, "You Are My Sunshine," he would grab a book, cuddle up and read to her every day.

After the Briggs learned Kelsey was Lance's baby, the relationship started quite cordially. Almost every day on her lunch break Raye Dawn would call Kathie. They'd talk about Kelsey, Lance, and his new wife, Ashley. Kathie was excited to make the designer diaper bag Raye Dawn had her heart set on. It wasn't uncommon for Kathie's phone to ring, "Would you like to have Kelsey all day tomorrow?" Raye Dawn would ask. Kathie always said yes. Kathie was Raye Dawn's nurse of choice whenever Kelsey got sick.

A decision Lance made right out of high school was about to drastically alter the status quo. Lance enlisted in the Army a year or so after high school but went on inactive status when he and Raye Dawn moved in together.

Lance and Ashley had been at Lake Texoma with the whole Briggs family for a couple of days. They came back a few days early but still had days of mail backed up. Inside the mailbox was a big manila envelope. The return address had an official seal and said "U.S. Army".

Lance slowly peeled back the edges of the envelope, wondering what it could be. He hadn't had anything to do with the military in years. He served his time in the Army after high school but had never been formally discharged.

He was shocked when in the most professional military ease it ordered him to report to Fort Leonard Wood, Missouri on September 11, 2004, for active duty. He was ordered to serve one year. The letter was a two month heads up.

He read the letter three times before he could bring himself to walk into the living room and tell his wife, "I have to go to Iraq."

She couldn't believe it.

His next call was to his parents, who were still at Texoma. Kathie already knew what he was going to say. She heard on the news a few hundred inactive ready reserves would be called to duty and she had a gut feeling her son would be one of them.

That night Lance sat in bed and read the notice over and over as if he could make the words dissolve off the page. Ashley was fast asleep next to him, but Lance could not sleep. He held the letter in his hands all night wondering what it meant.

The next morning Lance started making phone calls to his higher ups to find out the details. He learned he would be training in the states for an undisclosed amount of time before they shipped him to Iraq.

As a soldier's wife, Ashley knew what she was getting herself into; her brother was active duty military and had been to Iraq and back. She was well aware of the challenges but knew it was a soldier's duty.

Lance tried to answer his call to duty a couple of years before, the day the World Trade Center towers collapsed. He was with Raye Dawn at the time; they had been up for several days. He didn't go to work and watched television all day. As the days after September 11, 2001 unfolded, Lance became outraged at the thought of an attack on American soil. So he grabbed his papers and drove to the recruiting station.

Lance marched into the office and told the officer at the desk he wanted to go to war. They wouldn't take him, citing the domestic assault charge on his record filed by Raye Dawn earlier that year.

They refused when he volunteered to go. Now they wanted him when he had a wife he loved and a baby girl.

"I could have chickened out; I could have not gone. But I knew I had to go. I wanted to stay home, but it was my duty." After all, during World War II his grandfather, Carl Briggs, served as a medic in the Army and his great grandfather, Clarence S. Bugg, served in the Navy. Lance had patriotism in his blood.

He began making the arrangements. In some ways Lance felt as though he was preparing for his funeral while he was still alive, never expecting he would be planning his daughter's instead.

He changed the oil in their cars and the filters in the furnace. He left Ashley with her own toolbox and a freshly mowed lawn. The grass would need one more mowing that year, but he didn't want to leave any loose ends for his wife to worry about.

He had no idea what Ashley would encounter while he was gone, but he wanted her to know a little bit about everything around the house. Never knowing the challenges she would endure in the months to come paled in comparison with housework.

As Lance prepared for his deployment, the Briggs became concerned about visits with Kelsey while he was gone. Lance went to court and signed his visitation with his baby girl over to his parents. This way, Kelsey would still have contact with his family.

The process server who took the documents to Raye Dawn told Kathie he'd never heard anyone cuss like that before. He said she was holding Kelsey in her arms the whole time.

Raye Dawn fought the visitation with a full hearing. Ultimately, Judge Craig Key agreed to allow the Briggs family to take Kelsey on the same visitation schedule while Lance was gone. Judge Key told the family Kelsey cannot have too many people in her life who love her.

The team, who would fight DHS for the next 10 months, drove Lance six hours to Fort Leonard Wood, Missouri where he would begin the fight for his life. His family fought back tears the entire drive home. The van was silent but for sniffles. It would be the first of many tearful afternoons.

Lance says, "I thought that might be the last time I saw them. The Army was vague. No one would tell me how long I was going to be there before I left for Iraq."

Lance stayed in the states longer than expected because he hurt his back during combat training. For five months he would come home on leave for the weekend or his devoted wife would drive to see him. They spent those weekends in Fort Leonard Wood in a motel room, holding each other, and enjoying the moments they had as husband and wife.

Back in Meeker, Kathie says the attitude between her and Raye Dawn changed.

Every other weekend, Kathie parked her mini-van on the side of the Rainbow convenience store to wait for her little bundle of fun. Raye Dawn chose the neutral spot once Lance was gone and Kathie received visitation.

Raye Dawn usually pulled up next to Kathie's van and dropped off Kelsey. One particular weekend, Raye Dawn sat Kelsey down on the convenience store curb and walked off, without saying a word to anyone.

Kathie could tell the young mother's hatred was growing.

Lance was home on leave January 14, 2005, the day they discovered the first bruises and broken bone. When Kathie picked Kelsey up for the weekend visit Raye Dawn explained Kelsey had fallen out of her crib and broken her collarbone. Kathie didn't think much of it. After all, a collarbone is one of the most commonly broken bones on a child. Kathie called to warn Lance so he would not be alarmed when he saw his baby wearing a brace.

The injury did not stop Kelsey from playing with her cousins at a Briggs family birthday party that night. When Lance and Ashley got to the party they found Kelsey playing as much as she could with a tiny brace supporting her shoulder.

Lance immediately called Raye Dawn to ask her about the injury. He wanted to know why she didn't notify him or someone in his family. Raye Dawn didn't think it was a big deal.

The Briggs spent the next two hours together. They were so busy they didn't change Kelsey's diaper. All the while, Kelsey's clothes were hiding a secret.

A secret Ashley discovered during bath time.

Lance and Ashley left the party and went to Ashley's mom's house where they gave Kelsey a bath. When they pulled off her clothes, Ashley started screaming. She had never seen anything like it. Kelsey had bruises and small scrapes covering her entire body, more so, on her little bottom.

Ashley quickly grabbed a camera and snapped a moment in time that would become a key piece of evidence in the murder investigation to come.

Ashley took pictures of little Kelsey face down. Water glistened on her innocent battered skin. She was covered in bruises. Not just a few small bruises you might blame on a two-year-old who bumps into things. Different colored bruises dotted her rear.

They counted twenty-nine bruises to be exact.

Their first reaction was sheer panic. They quickly gathered their wits and called the Shawnee Police Department which advised the family to take her to a hospital. It became Kelsey's second trip to the emergency room in a week. The same E.R. doctor, who put her in the sling for the broken collarbone, removed Kelsey's clothes to see the bruises.

The doctor later testified the bruises were not there a few days earlier. In his opinion the bruises were not consistent with a fall out of a crib because they were all over her body and not just in one place.

The doctor carefully measured and recorded each of the 29 bruises and abrasions that covered the two-year-old's body.

Lance knew there was no way the bruises came from the fall. He hoped if DHS got involved his parents would get custody of Kelsey. The investigating agency, Meeker Police, decided otherwise.

Oklahoma state law says if a doctor suspects abuse he must call the police and DHS. The doctor made the call and Meeker's Assistant Police Chief, Matt Byers, arrived at the hospital just after midnight and began doing interviews.

Kelsey seemed unfazed by the turmoil around her. She sat in her hospital bed playing with the toys Ashley packed for her. A few books and snacks kept her busy for hours.

The assistant chief asked Lance if he felt Raye Dawn was capable of hitting Kelsey in a violent manner. Lance explained if Raye Dawn is drinking and gets mad she can go overboard. He told the officer Raye Dawn had been dating a man named Michael Porter for two or three months and that she stays at his house often, but they had not noticed any bruises or injuries before this point.

Kathie says Byers told them Raye Dawn had not been home for the past few nights. A suggestive observation she later realized was quite odd, coming from a so-called unbiased police officer. Kathie wondered how he knew Raye Dawn wasn't home. People around town suspected Byers and Raye Dawn had dated at one time.

The officers would soon ask Kathie if she was ready to raise a grandchild.

Kathie quizzed Raye Dawn about the injuries and she fired back, "You're trying to say I hurt my baby?" A line Raye Dawn repeated over and over in the following months.

The emergency room doctor advised Kathie not to give Kelsey back that night.

To let tempers cool down, Raye Dawn agreed to let Kelsey stay at Kathie's for an extra night until police could finish their investigation. Raye Dawn told the officers she did not want DHS involved.

Once Sgt. Carl Leabo interviewed Raye Dawn and her mother Gayla, Kathie says his attitude changed drastically. Kathie still wonders if it's because Gayla and Leabo went to high school together.

The officers called Raye Dawn to set up a time to come by and take a look at her apartment. Raye Dawn lived in the Meeker Village apartments.

It was the only place where people in Meeker could pay their rent based on how much money they made. She and Kelsey stayed in one of the second floor units.

Byers and Leabo listed Michael Lee Porter and Raye Dawn Smith as the two suspects on the official police report. The official document indicated police suspected one of them committed aggravated assault on January 15, 2005.

Porter was so new to Raye Dawn's life, the Briggs did not know much about him. Lance knew of him. For two years in high school, Lance worked for the Porter's family business, Midwest Industries. Lance worked on the factory side. Porter spent most of the time in the office. Lance says Porter didn't do any major work. He was the boss's son who put in the time to get a check.

Lance says he knows Porter was making money on the side selling marijuana because he bought pot from him a couple of times. Lance didn't think much of it. In his experience a lot of rich kids sold drugs.

Michael Porter grew up and went to school in Shawnee, Oklahoma. He was a star basketball player in high school. Many people were amazed at his dedication to his team when he played the night of his father's funeral.

He took on a lot of responsibility as a teenager when he got a girl pregnant. He eventually acquired custody of his daughter Whitney and raised her. Porter became a father for a second time to Michael Gage in 2003. He never married the mother of either child.

After the death of his mother, Porter took over the family company, serving as the President and running the day to day business operations.

The Porter's company was among 26 magnet manufacturing companies in the country. The industry is dying; it's now only one of six. A small sign out front is the only way outsiders would know what they do, "The Magic of Magnets, an Oklahoma business, magnets for the school, home, industries, and hobby."

Before Michael Porter's murder trial, Midwest Industries had those little pink heart stickers with Kelsey's picture on them. When he went to prison, only the sticky residue outlining the heart remained.

The officers didn't find any need to do an extensive investigation into Porter's past. During Raye Dawn's interview she told them she did not notice any bruising on Kelsey's legs and believed the bruises on her face came from the fall. She told the officers she did not notice any of the bruising to her lower back or buttocks, but admitted Kelsey had been with her for the past week. She denied ever staying at Porter's house, and claimed she and Kelsey were alone in her apartment.

Byers reported Raye Dawn "appeared to be truthful in her answers and very open towards the interviews. She seemed genuinely concerned with the health and welfare of her child."

He took diligent notes in the police report about the cleanliness of Raye Dawn's house saying it was well maintained, no items lying around and very clean, except for a random hairbrush on the floor in the nursery.

Byers looked at the nursery and decided Kelsey clearly fell out of her crib, hitting a plastic slide that was conveniently located next to the crib, breaking her collarbone. The 29 bruises and abrasions? In the middle of the "very clean house", the officers say, "We feel that the marks observed around Kelsey's buttocks came from falling on the hairbrush in her bedroom while running around without clothes."

Byers noted the child was well loved and was the victim of a custody battle. It was also the officer's opinion, "Based on the interview with Smith, there is no need for the department to continue this investigation at this time. Leabo and myself both feel that Smith has not placed her child in any danger and is not abusing Kelsey, physically or otherwise. Leabo and myself do feel that the child is being passed around too much and this may be affecting the child's recognition of the important people in her life. We feel that a better visitation schedule could be utilized to help the child identify with family members more effectively.

"Overall we feel Kelsey is well cared for by all family members, has an abundance of love within her surroundings and is growing normally for a child her age."

At that point, Lance and his family suspected it was not appropriate for officers of the law to provide their expert opinions on issues that they were not qualified to make. OSBI agents would later call it the most mishandled child abuse investigation they've ever seen.

The state agency in charge of making those decisions had a much different account of the incident. DHS was called to investigate the same case the Meeker police officers were working on. Ultimately, DHS caseworkers decide if it's child abuse and identify the abuser.

Kristal Johnson, a DHS intake worker, met Kelsey Smith-Briggs in January of 2005. It was Kristal's job to document each interview she did with the parties involved. Kristal would later write in her report that the officers told the agency the child would be safe staying at the Briggs house. But at some point the next day, she says they, "changed their mind," and would be returning Kelsey to Raye Dawn.

Kristal began interviewing everyone involved in Kelsey's life. Raye Dawn told her Kelsey fell out of her crib and broke her collarbone. When Kristal showed Raye Dawn the picture of the bruises all over Kelsey's body, Kelsey's mother repeated the same story she told the officers. She had never seen them before.

She tried to blame Lance saying she often picks up Kelsey with bruises. She referenced one bruise on Christmas Eve, saying Kelsey's ear was black and purple. Raye Dawn admitted she never reported it to child welfare or the police and did not take Kelsey to a doctor.

Kelsey's daycare provider, Julie Sebastian, also tried to blame Lance saying she noticed "finger print" bruises on Kelsey when she would come home from visitation with Lance; however, she too, never reported these bruises to DHS. When lawyers questioned Sebastian about the suspected abuse in a later court hearing, she explained she did not know the visitation schedule between Lance and Kelsey; therefore, she had no way of knowing who had Kelsey the weekends prior to noticing these so-called bruises.

Kristal interviewed Raye Dawn a couple of days later and her story changed. She says she gave Kelsey a bath on January 13, but didn't notice any of the marks or bruises. Kristal told her it didn't make any sense because the bruises were in various stages of healing and had to have been there when she bathed Kelsey.

After interviewing all of the same people Meeker police interviewed, Kristal determined Raye Dawn was the perpetrator saying, "Her stories about the incident are conflicting."

This was the one and only time abuse was confirmed against Raye Dawn Smith.

It took DHS from January 14, 2005, until February 10, 2005, to file the abuse report with the Lincoln County District Attorney's office. Even though Kristal Johnson determined Raye Dawn was the abuser, DHS did not file what's called a deprived petition, which would have started the process to terminate her parental rights. The deprived petition is a common step in cases of severe child abuse.

Lance called his commanding officer and asked for an extra day of leave so he and his mom could meet with Lincoln County Associate District Judge Craig Key in his chambers. Kathie says Key took one look at the pictures of Kelsey's rear and signed the papers, giving Kathie guardianship.

The judge agreed Kelsey was not safe with her mom, so Kelsey went to live with her grandparents, Kathie and Royce.

Lance headed to Fort Leonard Wood believing his daughter was safe. She was living with his parents and he hired a lawyer to help with the case. He put his faith in the system once again. He would soon be stationed in New Jersey and would only get one more trip home before going overseas.

For a couple of weeks, Raye Dawn did not see Kelsey as they waited for a hearing. One day Raye Dawn called Kathie to ask for a visit with Kelsey. Kathie got permission from her lawyer and allowed Raye Dawn, along with several members of the Smith family, to come over for a visit. Kathie sat in the kitchen to give them their privacy in her living room.

A couple of days later Kathie's daughter, Jeanna, got a call from her mother-in-law. She said Gayla told her they had placed a listening device in Kathie's home.

Jeanna immediately called and instructed Kathie, "You and Dad need to get dressed and get to my house. Don't say a word." Kathie thought this was a bit odd but had a bad feeling about Jeanna's news. Once they were in the safety of Jeanna's living room, she told them about the listening device. They immediately went home to search for it.

Kathie's entire family wandered around the living room in silence. Their only communication was through notes and sign language. The family couldn't help but laugh at themselves, thinking this only happens in the movies.

Since they hadn't found the device, Kathie knew she couldn't speak in her living room about the upcoming hearing. To make the Smiths pay for invading her privacy, Kathie would make things up during conversations with Ashley, just to confuse whoever was listening. One day she told Ashley Lance wasn't really in the Army. Despite records proving otherwise, the Smith family used that statement against Kathie and Lance for years. The Smiths could never confirm where they heard it because it was illegal for them to install a listening device in the first place.

Three years later the Briggs found the listening device. It still had a signal and is now in the hands of the authorities.

As Kelsey's collarbone began to heal, her memories did not. One day Kathie says Kelsey looked up at her and said, "Mommy mad at Mike." The two-year-old would not explain why.

Kelsey may have been trying to divulge what was going on in her life but couldn't seem to get the whole story out. After all, she was only two.

Kathie shuddered when Kelsey accidentally found the pictures of her bruised bottom. Kelsey looked at the bruises and said, "They mean to me." Statements Kathie passed along to DHS in hopes, if they didn't believe her, maybe they would believe Kelsey. If nothing was going on, why would a two-year-old say those things? Caseworkers would later claim Kelsey did not have the verbal skills to tell them what was going on. Kathie suspected the caseworkers did not have the skills to listen to what Kelsey did say.

Raye Dawn had supervised visits with Kelsey for a month. Once caseworkers allowed unsupervised visits, Kathie requested that Porter not be around. Kathie couldn't help but listen to her gut. The injuries began only after Porter came into the picture. Kathie believed Raye Dawn routinely violated the court order banning Porter from the visits. Beyond the repeated injuries, Kathie could never prove Raye Dawn was allowing Porter around Kelsey.

As instructed by her lawyer, Kathie reported every doctor's visit to DHS. On March 22, 2005, she took Kelsey to an allergist in Oklahoma City. Kelsey had been taking amoxicillin for two weeks and still had a runny nose and matted eyes. At that visit she weighed a healthy 24 pounds, 12 ounces. Kelsey's weight remained consistent while she lived with her grandparents.

As Raye Dawn worked her DHS treatment plan to be a better mom, she earned more visits with Kelsey. The court decided Raye Dawn should have Kelsey on Friday, Saturday, Sunday, and Monday until noon. Kathie had Kelsey for the next 48 hours. Not near enough time, but it was the court ordered arrangement.

On Wednesday at noon, the hand off would take place again. Raye Dawn had Kelsey for the next 24 hours and brought her back to Kathie on Thursday at noon. Kathie had legal guardianship, but Raye Dawn had more hours with Kelsey each week.

When Kathie picked Kelsey up on March 25, 2005, at the Rainbow, she noticed a large purplish knot on the right side of her nose and a bruise on her knee. As the day progressed Kelsey's nose began swelling more. The little girl would hold her nose and complain that it hurt.

Later that evening Kathie grew more concerned and felt she should have the nose x-rayed. She and Kelsey met Ashley at the emergency room.

After reviewing Kelsey's medical history, the doctor called the DHS hotline to report the incident. The next day, Kathie followed up and took Kelsey to the DHS office to report the injury so caseworkers could document it. Kelsey was asleep in Kathie's arms and wouldn't wake up when Kristal tried to ask her what happened.

Once again, it was up to Kristal to determine what caused the injury. Kristal interviewed the growing number of people who had contact with Kelsey. Twice, Kathie says Kristal told her Raye Dawn's visits should still be supervised. But Kristal did not take any steps to make that happen.

Kristal asked Raye Dawn if she knew what caused the bruises. She says Raye Dawn told her Kelsey fell face first on the kitchen floor of her apartment. Kelsey's mother brushed off the injury saying her two-year-old did not even cry.

Raye Dawn did not seem concerned about the bruises but was worried Kelsey's hair was falling out. Kelsey's mom decided to take her to Dr. Kelli Koons, the pediatrician her lawyer recommended. It was not revealed until much later that Dr. Koons and Raye Dawn's attorney were brother and sister. A fact that left many concerned as Kelsey's injuries continued.

On April 5, 2005, Raye Dawn returned Kelsey with another bruise. Kelsey's mom explained her daughter had fallen out of something but never could explain what that something was. Kelsey told Kathie, "Mom spanked", then said her mommy had been sleeping.

One of Kristal's first calls was back to Raye Dawn. This time Kristal says Raye Dawn explained away the bruises saying she and Porter saw Kelsey push on a screen door and fall onto a concrete porch.

During Lance's last trip home before heading to Iraq, his priority was to spend quality time with Kelsey and Ashley. They had family pictures taken for Lance's 28th birthday and took Kelsey to the zoo. This was the only birthday he would share with his little girl. The year before, Raye Dawn would not allow Kelsey to go to dinner with him.

Since Lance was home on leave that week, Kristal called him to get his perspective on the injuries. Lance told her he was suspicious Raye Dawn was hurting Kelsey. He had a hard time understanding why Kelsey always came home with bruises after visits with her mom and didn't seem to bruise easily at all with his mom. Lance suggested someone keep an eye on Kelsey while she was with her mother.

Kristal needed to take pictures of the most recent bruises. Lance and Kelsey were supposed to meet with Lance's former co-workers. Kristal decided she would meet Kelsey at Kathie's house, so Lance could keep his plans. After a busy morning, Kelsey was napping when the DHS intake worker showed up. Kristal documented the bruises without waking Kelsey. She found three penny sized bruises on Kelsey's outer thigh, one on her inner thigh and green bruises on her rib cage.

Ten days later, the DHS worker took another report. This time Kelsey had a "twisted" ankle.

On April 14, 2005, Raye Dawn's sister-in-law, Miste Smith, took Kelsey to the zoo. While they were there Miste says Kelsey fell off her platform flip flop shoe, twisting her ankle. That was around 12:30 p.m., but Miste says the group stayed at the zoo for a couple more hours. All the while, Kelsey kept complaining her foot hurt. Miste took Kelsey to Raye Dawn's work to explain what happened. They decided to go to the emergency room so DHS and Kathie wouldn't accuse Raye Dawn of hurting Kelsey.

The doctor took x-rays and diagnosed Kelsey with a sprained ankle. The x-rays only revealed the lower portion of her leg.

Raye Dawn dropped her hobbling daughter off with Kathie, along with a note from the doctor, explaining how to treat a sprained ankle. She also asked Kathie if one of the other grandchildren had bitten Kelsey on her inner arm. Kathie didn't think so. Plus, Kelsey had been with Raye Dawn for three days and the bite mark was fresh. So Kathie just asked Kelsey. Kelsey referred to herself in the third person and quickly replied, "Kelsey did it!" Once again, the little girl gave a clear answer.

Despite the court order prohibiting Porter from being around Kelsey, on April 18, 2005 Porter and Raye Dawn took Kelsey to the courthouse in the middle of the afternoon to say, "I do."

Later that day, Raye Dawn returned Kelsey to Kathie. The next morning, Kathie took Kelsey to Walmart. Kelsey wanted to walk but took four steps and said, "Can't." Knowing sprains can take time to heal Kathie was not surprised and carried her.

Throughout the next couple of days, Kelsey would take a few steps from one piece of furniture to another. It had been less than a week since she had been diagnosed with the sprained ankle, so the hobbling did not seem unusual.

Less than an hour before Raye Dawn's next visit, Kathie and Kelsey were at the elementary school waiting for the other grandchildren. Kelsey took a few steps around her chair. While they were there, Kathie asked the school nurse how long it should take a sprain to heal and how long before Kelsey would be back to normal.

Kelsey was with her mother for the next four days. Instead of returning Kelsey to Kathie, Raye Dawn took her to DHS. Raye Dawn explained both of Kelsey's legs were hot to touch and swollen when she picked her up from Kathie. The DHS worker, Yolanda Hunter, ordered Raye Dawn to take Kelsey to the doctor.

A few hours later, Yolanda called Kathie to tell her Kelsey had two broken legs. Dr. Koons and her associate, Dr. Barrett, surmised that Kelsey broke her first leg at the zoo and the second fracture was from overcompensation.

Kathie called the doctor to question the diagnosis. It was later that Kathie learned Raye Dawn had claimed Kelsey's legs had been swollen when she picked her up. If that was true, it did not explain how a mother could let her child suffer for four days before seeking medical attention.

The doctors wrapped Kelsey's tiny legs in one pink cast and a green one. Raye Dawn was the first to sign the casts. She took a black marker and wrote, "Mommy Loves You."

Immediately following the doctor visit Kelsey was returned to Kathie. Raye Dawn sat her in the recliner as Kelsey said good-bye. Kathie couldn't help but notice Kelsey never cried when her mother left. Even with two broken legs, Kelsey didn't cry for her mother. Kathie thought it was very odd for a two-year-old.

That night Kathie covered the living room floor with blankets suspecting Kelsey would need lots of room to roll around. Kelsey was miserable as she tried to sleep with both legs confined in heavy plaster. They both moved from one spot to another trying to get comfortable enough for a little rest.

———

Meanwhile, Raye Dawn called Yolanda Hunter, already doing damage control. Yolanda says, "Raye Dawn called in and stated that she felt really stupid because the child was injured and she did not take her in to the doctor sooner. Smith stated that Kathie told her that Kelsey had fallen into a hole or something like that." Again, Raye Dawn tried to place the blame on someone. Kathie says she never told anyone Kelsey fell in a hole.

The casts could not protect Kelsey from wounds on the parts of her body not covered in plaster. Raye Dawn had yet another excuse when Kathie picked up her already broken granddaughter, this time with a big, red, swollen bruise, some called a pump knot, on her nose. Another injury to add to the laundry list of wounds Kristal Johnson was charged with investigating.

This time Porter was in on the excuses. They were husband and wife now. The couple told DHS Kelsey wanted to sleep with her step-sister Whitney.

Porter says when he walked in to wake up the girls, Whitney's elbow was draped over Kelsey's face. He checked on Kelsey and noticed a bruise on her nose. Raye Dawn told them, Whitney remembers Kelsey waking up crying, asking for milk. She says Whitney just patted Kelsey on the back and she went back to sleep.

Whitney, the alleged perpetrator, told DHS she does not remember any of it and didn't hear Kelsey cry. The worker says Whitney got nervous when she realized her dad would be told about her conversation with DHS.

Kelsey had injuries from head to toe; too many to explain away. A voice inside Kathie's head would not allow her to absorb the excuses made by caseworkers in charge of protecting Kelsey. Kathie was outraged when Kristal Johnson's supervisor, David Burgess, sat in her living room and told the family the judge should give Kelsey back to Raye Dawn full time. That way he said, "If she got hurt again, we would know where it came from." Kathie compared it to a game of Russian Roulette, a deadly game of chance. A gamble where only Kelsey would lose.

Raye Dawn's cousin approached the Briggs family, concerned when she saw the casts. At the Briggs' request, she sought out one of the state's most regarded child abuse doctors, Andy Sullivan, with the University of Oklahoma Children's Hospital. Oklahomans know Sullivan as the heroic doctor who saved a woman's life during the Murrah bombing. Her leg was trapped under a pile of debris when Dr. Sullivan amputated it without anesthesia.

Kathie and Raye Dawn planned to take Kelsey to the appointment together to have her legs checked for developmental problems.

As chance would have it, Raye Dawn's great grandmother died and the funeral was the day of the appointment. Raye Dawn wanted the appointment changed. The next available opening was several days away so Kathie asked her aunt, Janis Cotton, to accompany her.

Raye Dawn called, concerned the doctor might suspect abuse and Kelsey would be taken into state custody in another county. Kathie brushed off her worries saying the Shawnee doctors already ruled that out. Later she realized it was an odd statement unless Raye Dawn knew the injuries were not accidents.

Four doctors with a combined, 90 years experience, reviewed the x-rays of Kelsey's tiny bones.

In the examination room, Dr. Sullivan asked some basic questions about Kelsey's medical history. While Dr. Sullivan was gone, Janis asked Kelsey a question of her own. She wanted to know how Kelsey hurt her legs. She says Kelsey blamed Daddy Mike, saying he pushed her off of the bed. Kelsey said, "Mommy got mad and then they ate pizza."

Kathie wasn't sure whether to be furious or simply break down in tears as Dr. Sullivan told her it was his opinion someone broke Kelsey's legs. The spiral fractures were non-accidental. In his 30 years practicing pediatric orthopedics, spiral fractures like Kelsey's were always caused from child abuse.

When Dr. Sullivan removed Kelsey's casts, he noticed the skin underneath was rubbed raw. He debated about putting new casts on and concluded the bones had already started to heal. Sullivan instructed Kathie to let Kelsey stand if she wanted to and not to be concerned if she didn't right away.

Child abuse is considered a felonious criminal act, but it was never reported. No one called Oklahoma City police. It was Kathie who called DHS. She was told they may have to take Kelsey into DHS custody while they investigated. Kathie was not surprised and suspected it could happen, knowing Raye Dawn had blamed her.

Kathie called Raye Dawn to give her the doctor's report. She begged Kelsey's mother to put a stop to all of this. The thought of Kelsey being placed with strangers had to be enough to make Raye Dawn do something. To finally tell the truth. Raye Dawn did not respond.

May 3, 2005 marked two separate events in the Briggs family. Lance left the country en route to Iraq. At the same time, his daughter was being removed from the safety of his parents' home.

Kristal Johnson called Kathie that afternoon to arrange for Kelsey to be taken into state custody. Kathie was going on very little sleep. Tears invaded her dreams. Kelsey would be left in strangers' arms, with two broken legs, and no one to protect her. She understood why DHS had to take her, but she knew Kelsey was not being hurt at her home.

While Kathie was on the phone with Kristal, her phone beeped, indicating someone was on the other line. Based on the time of the call, Kathie suspected it could be Lance and asked Kristal if she could take it. Lance had just landed in Germany to refuel before heading to Kuwait.

Kathie collected her emotions as she spoke with her son. She could not tell him Kelsey was being placed in foster care, not yet. He was an ocean away and there was nothing he could do. All Kathie could do was tell him she loved him.

Kathie and her oldest daughter spent the last few minutes they had with Kelsey at home. On their way to the DHS office, Shirica watched as Kelsey slept in her car seat. Kelsey was oblivious to the imminent upheaval of her short life. Shirica snapped a picture of Kelsey's precious face with the camera on her phone. A snapshot that captured a moment they wished never would have come.

Shirica carried the weight her mother could not bear that day. Kelsey did not wake up as Shirica carried her into the office. Shirica left Kelsey's favorite doll in her lap and kissed her forehead before she left. No good byes. Kelsey slept in the back seat of the DHS car as the worker drove her to the foster home.

Shirica had no idea this would be the last time she would hold the precious child in her arms.

The thought of Kelsey waking up in a strange bed haunted her dreams. She could only hope the doll with the long brown hair would provide some semblance of familiarity.

Later that night Ashley called Kathie in hysterics saying she thought she saw Kelsey in K-Mart with Raye Dawn's mom, Gayla. Kathie tried to convince her she couldn't have seen the two together because Kelsey was in foster care.

After another tearful, sleepless night they learned Kelsey had been placed with her maternal grandmother. Gayla was in the department store using state vouchers to buy clothes for her granddaughter.

Gayla took Kelsey back to the Shawnee doctors who put Kelsey's casts back on. The Smiths would later accuse Kathie of torturing Kelsey by having her casts removed, exposing the fresh breaks unnecessarily.

When the group went back to court, for yet another hearing, the judge ordered supervised visitation for Raye Dawn, Royce and Kathie. The visits were limited to four hours a week at the DHS office. DHS violated the judge's order and allowed Mike Porter to visit with Raye Dawn.

The visits were in a room with a couch, table, television and a few toys. Workers supervised each visit through a two-way mirror. The baby monitor inside the room gave workers the ability to record anything that was said.

Raye Dawn and Porter's visits were back to back with Kathie and Royce's. At the end of one visit, Kelsey would be taken to another room to spend time with the other side of her family.

On one visit Kathie was sitting with Kelsey on the floor. Kelsey saw Porter walk past the tall skinny window next to the door. She panicked, jumping in Kathie's arms crying, "I not want to see him", over and over again. Kathie immediately called and asked the worker supervising the visit if she saw Kelsey's fears. The worker's supervisor insisted Kelsey visit with Porter anyway.

On another visit Kathie sat on the floor with Kelsey. They were playing with a box of pencils. As they divided the sharpened pencils from the unsharpened ones, Kelsey looked at her grandma and said, "Daddy Mike hurt my legs."

Kathie knew the worker was listening and did not want to be accused of coaching her. So Kathie asked Kelsey if she cried. Kelsey said, "Yes." She then asked her if Mike said he was sorry. After the visit, Kathie asked the supervising worker if she heard the conversation. The worker said she did not hear it because she was on the phone.

Whether it was a hole, those flip flops, or angry adult hands, only Kelsey knew the truth. Ashley told DHS Kelsey pointed to Porter saying he hurt her by throwing her off the bed.

One day at the DHS office, Yolanda pushed Kelsey to say more but the two-year-old would hardly talk. She tried to warm her up by asking about a stuffed animal she was playing with. Kelsey wouldn't answer any more questions about the animal, her legs, or who hurt her legs.

Yolanda asked Kelsey if she knew what "hurt" meant. Kelsey pointed to her casts.

When Yolanda asked Kelsey who hurt her legs, the little girl puckered her lips and got a sad face.

Yolanda asked if it was a secret. Kelsey said, "Yes."

Yolanda pushed further and asked Kelsey who hurt her legs. Kelsey leaned over, tucked her head between her casts and quit talking.

A secret that was buried with Kelsey.

Michael Porter

Agent Tanner explained, *"All I know is that this baby had a broken clavicle, two broken legs, and now has some severe and significant internal injuries that caused her death. That's all I know. Rationally thinking, somebody had to do those injuries to that baby."*

"But that's not giving us the benefit of the doubt," replied Porter.

"That's not giving you any of the benefit of the doubt. Has she ever lost control with Kelsey in the past?" asked Tanner.

"No."

Tanner pressed further, *"Can you look me in the eye and tell me that?"*

Porter looked up, *"No, she hasn't."*

"She has never lost control with Kelsey?"

"No."

"Have you ever lost control with Kelsey?"

"Never."

Porter calmly asked to see his wife, *"I want to see my wife. I want to see my wife."*

"What are you going to tell her?" asked Tanner.

"I just have to hold her. This is wrong."

"So you didn't do it right?"

Porter cried, *"You're damn right. I did everything I could to save her. And Raye Dawn didn't do it."*

"And you know that how?"

"And I'm not going to turn against her because she didn't do it."

"So we'll probably never find out which one of you all did it. Maybe you both did. You know, there's three possibilities: you did it, Raye dawn did it, or you both did it, or you know she did it and now you're covering for her or she knows you did it and she's covering for you."

"Never."

"Somebody beat that baby to death, Mike."

"No, no."

"I'm telling you. What do you think people are going to believe? You that's denying it or this medical expert that's been doing this all of their lives?" asked Tanner.

"She wouldn't do it, Steve," argued Porter.

Tanner continued, *"You've known her for a year. This baby has had a broken clavicle, two broken legs. She's had other types of bruising that you're probably not even aware of."*

"No."

"*This baby has been through hell, Mike. Somebody broke that baby's legs. Somebody broke that baby's clavicle. Somebody beat her to death two days ago, Mike,*" said Tanner.

"*No, No. She's not capable of it.*"

"*How do you know? You've known her for a year.*"

"*Because she's sitting over there telling them the same thing about me, and you just know it,*" said Porter.

Tanner continued, "*Who typically causes these types of things to children? Step-parents.*"

Porter emitted a combination of a laugh and a scowl as he said, "*So you go over there and tell them that I did it. This is wrong Steve. I would never hurt her.*"

Raye Dawn screamed in the background and Porter continued trying to catch his breath and holding his heart, "*I want to see my wife.*"

Raye Dawn Smith

The agents asked Raye about Kelsey's broken legs. Raye explained, "*She was wearing some little purple platform flip flops and that's the only thing that she might have twisted on them, you know, which that's what I told everybody. I wear them.*"

"*And you fall down a lot when you wear flip-flops?*" chided Garrett.

"*Yeah, the platform ones. And we never wore them again,*" responded Raye. "*I don't know and I don't like to think about it because I have my own, I have my own observation of what was going on there.*"

"*Well what do you think?*" asked Garrett.

"*I don't know if my mom told you this too, but we always said that they were trying to set me up. They wanted me out of the picture,*" justified Raye.

"*Kathie?*" asked Garrett.

"*And Ashley. Because she called Kelsey her daughter,*" explained Raye

But Raye insisted that she tried to get along with, "*those people.*" She took Kelsey to their birthday parties and everything, "*So the day Kathie was going to take her to OU it was my great-grandmother's funeral, so I can't go. She takes her to the doctor and they have her casts taken off. They were on one week and they have her casts taken off. And the OU doctor said that they were better. Well, Kelsey would not walk. So when she took her to the doctor, it was abuse. So there was this pattern here, and my mom thinks there was a set-up. Probably for me. But DHS takes her from Kathie, thank God.*"

"So you're thinking that somewhere down the road, that Kathie has been abusing your daughter?" asked Garrett.

Raye continued, "I think somebody over there was because I never knew where Kelsey was. They shipped her around a lot. Every time, you know, like my little sister would see her at Walmart or something, Kathie didn't have her, which I said, 'Well, where is my daughter?' But when I'd call, she was always asleep. She went from eating two or three bowls of goulash, to she really didn't want any, you know, and that just wasn't her. She was depressed and nobody, nobody would listen to her."

In the years that followed, Raye often exhibited the behaviors of a sociopath. Raye began painting herself as the victim, just two days after Kelsey's death.

Agents continued to press her, saying there had to be something else, and only she knew what that was. "Don't you want us to help you?" asked Garrett.

"I don't know. I don't know what to say. I am. . .I am appalled that you all are even. . ." Raye's voice drifted off.

"You're appalled that we're trying to find out what happened to your child?" pressed Za.

"No, accusing me that I hurt my daughter," countered Raye.

"It comes back to you. And we're going to. . .you know at this point, you're the first person that we've told about what happened to Kelsey. You're the first person," said Za.

"My God. This did not happen to my baby," cried Raye.

"Your mom doesn't know, Mike doesn't know. Nobody at this point knows why Kelsey died," said Za, in a calm, quiet tone.

Raye stood, took a step to the corner of the room and kneeled down sobbing, "What happened to my baby?"

"I'm telling you, they deserve an explanation," said Za.

"I deserve an explanation!" exclaimed Raye.

Za grabbed her hand and ushered her back into the chair, "Raye come back and sit down. Come back and sit down."

"I don't want to sit," whined Raye.

"Raye, I know this is the hardest thing that you've ever had to deal with in your life," Raye shook her head no, as Za continued, "I can't imagine what you're going through. I cannot. I truly cannot."

"I've cried and I've cried and I've cried," said Raye.

"It's time for you to cry for some help," said Za.

Raye told agents about the time she spent rocking her dead baby, "I always told her I was sorry."

Za pressed, "Well, you always told her you were sorry. What were you sorry about?"

"That I tried to protect her and make her so much better, and I feel as if I failed."

Za said, "You know what Raye, you didn't fail."

"I did everything to protect my baby," insisted Raye.

"You didn't fail. I think all of those people that you went to for help in this whole situation, my opinion is they failed. They failed. Because I think that all those times you were taking her, it's like I said before, you were crying for help. I really believe that you had a problem and this has been going on for awhile. And I think that what happened that day was not something that you had planned," said Za.

Two hours into questioning Raye still refused to respond. Za said, "I think you feel like you did everything that you could to try to protect her."

Raye said, "My worst nightmare came true."

"I think it is your worst nightmare. I think you were trying to get help, that you know that you had a problem, and that probably no one listened and that it finally came to this conclusion."

Garrett added, "And the system failed. It failed you. And we're sorry for that."

"It failed me because I tried to help her and nobody would listen to me," cried Raye.

Garrett speculated Raye could have been stressed out because she was under a microscope by state child welfare workers, "It's people wanting in your business. Do you really like people in your business?"

"I just wanted to protect Kelsey."

"What were you trying to protect Kelsey from? You keep saying that you were trying to protect Kelsey. What were you protecting her from?" asked Za.

Raye avoided answering that question, but rather answered an earlier one, "About the CHBS, I told them I didn't care if she came."

Za tried to redirect the conversation, "But I'm talking about what you were protecting her from. Because even if you take out the broken clavicle, she had a sprained ankle, which we really don't know how that happened. I know she was with your cousins, okay. She had not one but two broken legs. She had bruises. You know, something's happened. Something's wrong."

"Right," was all Raye said.

Za pressed further, "Who did you think that you were trying to protect her from? From what? From who?"

"From everything. I wanted to protect my daughter from everything," said Raye.

F·O·U·R

ON MAY 3, 2005 THE ARMY FLEW 300 SOLDIERS, ONE OF THEM SPC LANCE BRIGGS, OVER THE OCEAN TO CAMP ARIFJAN IN KUWAIT. As Lance walked off of the plane and stood on the tarmac in the dark, it was 90 degrees at night. All he could see was sand, just sand.

He remembers thinking, "If I didn't know I was on earth, I would have thought I was on another planet when I got off that plane. I don't know how they live over there." Since Lance thought he would be there for a year, he had to get used to it.

"This is day one," he shook his head and began unloading his life off the plane.

He slept in Kuwait but traveled through Iraq almost every day. He worked for the 1864th Transportation Unit out of Las Vegas, driving 40 foot tractor trailers, hauling supplies and equipment to the various U.S. bases in Iraq.

Lance had never been out of the country, let alone dropped in the middle of a desert. He drove a big tan armored tractor trailer from base to base. "When you get there, you get there." Outside of Iraq they could drive during the day, but the most dangerous parts of the trips had to be traveled at night.

The Army does not design for comfort, neither do Iraqi road engineers, "They've got a lot of highways but so many have been bombed. They are all under construction."

Lance had seen some of Oklahoma's dust storms. In Iraq he says there is no grass, so a slight breeze stirs a sand storm, blowing in your face and ears.

His body was covered in armor, heavy, uncomfortable, restrictive gear designed to save his life should an Iraqi open fire on his vehicle. No Kevlar helmets could protect his unit from the improvised explosive devices, or IED's, hidden throughout the terrain.

His weapon never left his side. They lived out of a bag, with only enough clothes to complete the mission. Once they left the base in Kuwait they would typically drive to the gulf to pick up a load and deliver it somewhere in Iraq. Just like Lance's weapon, the truck was never empty. If they were hauling something to a base, something had to be brought back.

Between missions he'd call home more often, catch up on some sleep and laundry and get the truck ready for the next mission.

Preventative maintenance checks and services, or PMCS, were vital to staying alive in enemy territory. The soldiers knew if the truck broke down, it put the entire convoy in a deadly situation. They always kept a spare tire and the tools to change it.

Enemy lines in Baghdad shot at his truck once.

"The adrenaline flows; you almost don't even feel scared; it's adrenaline. Energy rush. Your body goes crazy, your senses are blown, you're just completely aware of everything. But when the adrenaline wears out, it drains you, and you become exhausted, both physically and mentally.

"I started thinking I could die any second. You just don't know. You've got kids coming up around you. You don't know if they are going to try to kill you. You don't trust nobody."

Lance didn't even trust his own. The camaraderie that gets many soldiers through their deployments was nonexistent for Lance, "I didn't like the guys I was with. I got stuck in with a unit. They all knew each other-had trained with each other for years."

Half of the soldiers he worked with were from Reno; the other half from Las Vegas. Within fifty states, their world could not have been more different than the world where Lance Briggs grew up in Meeker. "I showed the guys a picture of my two bedroom house. They told stories of their $800,000 homes and I was an outsider. They didn't take me in."

Lance says he hated the men he had to rely on to stay alive. "I thought it was going to be cool and they would take me in and we'd do things together, but I hated that unit. Although I didn't have much of an option, I had to deal with it, but I thought I had the worst luck."

One soldier who befriended Lance was SPC Anthony Cometa. Cometa died June 16, 2005, one day after his 21st birthday. He was thrown from his perch in the machine-gun turret when his Humvee flipped. Lance and his fellow soldiers honored Anthony with a ceremony. Lance had no idea this would help him prepare for his daughter's funeral to come.

Lance spent most of his free time on his own. He used the phone in the tent and called home as often as he could.

A few times when Lance called home he talked to Kelsey, or tried to. She was barely two years old.

A month after Lance left for Iraq, Kathie and Royce along with their attorney, Jim Hodgens, walked into the Lincoln County Courthouse. They were armed with enough evidence to clear Kathie's name and intended to bring Kelsey back to safety. Kathie knew the judge would either keep Kelsey with Gayla or allow Kelsey to go back to the Briggs side of the family.

Kelsey was not going home with them that day, or the next. No verdict had been reached. Not one minute of testimony spoken, but Porter and Raye Dawn already had Kelsey's room ready. There would be no more supervised visits at DHS. There would be no more fake smiles for the case workers. There would be no more Kathie Briggs.

Judge Craig Key called Raye Dawn's lawyer a few days earlier. Key told Greg Wilson not to worry; he already made the decision that Raye Dawn and Porter would get Kelsey back.

The Honorable Judge Craig Key sat in his chambers that morning awaiting the 9:00 a.m. gavel. The hearing would have to be over by Friday; he had a plane to Vegas to catch. He had already heard the information he needed to know. That was the way he operated. He would get the real story through his contacts in the community. This case was no different. He made the same calls he made about most cases. He found out a little about each family and quickly decided the Smith family, in his opinion, was the more reputable of the two. He had represented Raye Dawn's sister Janet Gragg while he was in private practice, and they had tons of people in the community writing letters supporting their cause. Sure, Kelsey had been abused, but there was no way that good looking blonde could have hurt her daughter.

Kathie learned that Raye Dawn's grandmother was contacting former family members trying to dig up dirt. She had no idea the family had summoned a letter writing campaign. Kathie could not understand why Raye Dawn's family and friends would want to influence a judge in a child abuse case when they did not know the facts.

Judge Key remembers Raye Dawn looking so tiny, armed with an arsenal of a family who would stand beside her until she walked away with her daughter. Some may have viewed her as cold or callous but Key says he could tell she had come to fight for her daughter.

Key should have taken better notes on June 15, 2005; he would later write a book, filled with inaccuracies, defending the decision he made the next morning.

The atmosphere in the courthouse that day was tense. It was a building full of people who did not want to see each other. Each side dodged eye contact with the other.

As Shirica walked past the Smith family, she saw Michael Porter for the first time. He was sitting on a bench outside the courtroom. She wanted to break the ice so she walked up, shook his hand, and introduced herself as Kelsey's Aunt Shirica. He extended a warm hand shake. Shirica remembers thinking he seemed genuinely kind.

The two families tried to keep at least a hallway between them, but comments can echo down an empty hallway. Someone in Kathie's family heard Michael Porter say, "I can smell the stench at the end of the hall." Apparently the Smith family morphed him into a Briggs hater.

Kathie also heard her two-year-old granddaughter's voice as she walked to the bathroom before the hearing. From Gayla's lap, Kathie heard Kelsey say, "That's my grandma, that's my grandma." Kathie knew she had to keep walking. If she stopped, she knew there could be a confrontation and did not want to put Kelsey through that.

Once they filed into the courtroom, Kathie, Royce and Jim Hodgens sat to the judge's left. Michael Porter and his lawyer would defend first degree murder charges from those very chairs. Raye Dawn and her lawyer, Greg Wilson along with Assistant District Attorney Greg Pollard, sat to the judge's right, at the table for the prosecutors. Filling the jury box was Brandon Watkins, Kelsey's court appointed attorney, Carla Lynch, the Court Appointed Special Advocate or CASA, and Lynch's supervisor, Sheila Walker. CASA volunteers are assigned to represent the child's best interest in court. The rest of the witnesses sat outside until they were called to testify.

Twelve witnesses would be asked to identify Raye Dawn as Kelsey's mother, point her out in the courtroom, and describe her as wearing a black and white checkered shirt with black slacks.

Raye Dawn would testify on her own behalf that day. She had become an expert at lying under oath. Before Kelsey was born, during Raye Dawn and Lance's divorce proceedings, the judge asked if she was pregnant. Raye Dawn said, "No." One word. It was easy.

When the arms of the clock hit the 90 degree angle signifying 9:00 a.m., Judge Craig Key walked out of his chambers. Key wanted to get the show on the road. He didn't want this case to run long. He knew the Briggs family was planning to put up a fight, but he didn't have time for an extensive list of witnesses. The major players alone would take most of the day, if not part of the following day.

First up, prosecutors called Kellie Mullen to the stand. Kellie explained to the judge she was Kelsey's DHS intake worker. She described Kelsey's health when she left Raye Dawn after her legs were broken. She had some concerns Kelsey's hair was falling out and had dark circles under her eyes while she was living with the Briggs.

Mullen told the judge she did not believe her condition was ruled to be an abusive situation, just an indication she was not adjusting well to the change.

Kathie's attorney had specific questions about the notes Mullen took regarding Kelsey's two broken legs.

Jim Hodgens asked, "Ashley reports her brother asked Kelsey what happened to her legs and she reports Kelsey told him that Mike hurt her by throwing her or pushing her off the bed? Did you all follow up on that at all?"

Mullen answered, "We spoke with Mike about it and he denied that it had occurred. Kelsey, when she was interviewed, would not give any specifics to us regarding that."

Hodgens countered, "Didn't Kelsey indicate when Yolanda Hunter interviewed her that someone hurt her? But she won't tell you who it is?"

"Correct."

"And that's typical behavior for a child that may be injured by somebody who is close to them?"

"It's a possibility."

Mullen told the court she and the other case workers did not feel the need to interview Ashley's brother about what he heard Kelsey say.

53

Hodgens pointed out that Kelsey broke her collarbone while in Raye Dawn's care. And while DHS did not confirm abuse against Raye Dawn for the broken collarbone, they believed she was responsible for the bruises on Kelsey's rear. Hodgens pointed out that the other problems, the bruise to the tip of her nose and the knot on her nose on April 27th, all happened while Kelsey was in Raye Dawn's care.

As for the initial diagnosis that Kelsey had sprained her ankle, Hodgens pointed out that the x-ray was not high enough up on the leg for the doctor to see whether there was a break on the date the x-ray was taken.

Hodgens asked, "You don't have any direct or inferential evidence whatsoever that would indicate that the Briggs were responsible for any of these injuries that the child has received; isn't that correct?"

"Correct."

Wilson had a plan for that argument. Raye Dawn's lawyer pointed out that the Briggs were not ruled out as perpetrators either. DHS made the decision to remove Kelsey from Kathie's home because she violated the court order by giving Raye Dawn an extra visit. Mullen told the judge Raye Dawn never violated the court order. The worker apparently forgot Porter was banned from seeing Kelsey, but Raye Dawn allowed it.

Next up, Kristal Johnson. Johnson was a young DHS caseworker with short, dark, curly hair. Her round face resembled her round body.

Lawyers asked Kristal to identify Kelsey's grandmother on her dad's side. With her meek, southern drawl Kristal always referred to Kathie as Ms. Kathie Briggs. If lawyers would have had any idea Kristal Johnson would spend hours recounting the details of Kelsey's life during the court proceedings to come, they would have spent more time training her. Kristal often had a hard time recalling the times, dates, and allegations that would comprise the highest profile child abuse case in Oklahoma history.

Lawyers questioned Johnson about the list of witnesses she and the other caseworkers interviewed to form their decisions. Johnson told the judge she had not finished her investigation into Kelsey's broken legs.

Hodgens knew it was to his clients' advantage that Kristal was one of the DHS witnesses. She was easy to manipulate. He asked her, "Do you have any evidence, direct or circumstantial that Mr. and Mrs. Briggs is responsible for any of the injuries that this child had beginning in January up through April whenever the legs were reported?"

"No," replied Kristal.

"All of these injuries occurred at, or were reported, immediately after the mother had the child; isn't that correct?"

"Yes."

As of June 15, 2005, DHS had not determined who broke Kelsey's legs. The state agency in charge of protecting children had not finished its job.

Before lawyers called the next witness, there was much discussion about Matt Byers' testimony. Byers had testified in previous hearings and some of the parties felt his testimony would be redundant; however, Key ruled he should be called. No one questioned why he was never called. The hearing would wrap up before the Meeker police officer could describe his somewhat opinionated investigation into Kelsey's broken collarbone.

The CASA volunteer told the judge she was trained in the Girl Scouts to recognize child abuse. Carla Lynch had been in that line of work for only six weeks, yet managed to form some opinions of her own about Kelsey's case.

Lynch told the judge she had been on the case just two weeks and only spent time with Kelsey on three occasions. During that time, she quickly realized the two-year-old had more energy than the Hoover dam.

Lynch had time to interview Matt Byers, Gayla Smith, Kristal Johnson, Yolanda Hunter, Lisa Mendenhall who worked with Raye Dawn, and Julie, the owner of Kelsey's daycare.

Lynch admitted she interviewed her own sister Lisa Mendenhall only because Mendenhall worked with Raye Dawn for five years.

Based on those interviews, it was Lynch's professional opinion that Kelsey be placed back with her mother, Raye Dawn because she could not find any evidence that Raye Dawn caused any of the abuse.

Lynch says she looked at everyone involved in Kelsey's life. She never interviewed anyone on the Briggs side of the family because she claims she could not locate Lance. Lynch explained, "I looked at everyone. I looked at Lance, who I could not find, have not had any contact with him since he was still in Lincoln County in April; and I also looked at Raye Dawn to see exactly who had custody, where the child was, and I could not substantiate it either."

Lawyers asked, "What did you do to try to locate Lance Briggs?"

"I have asked for a subpoena from the DA's office to get records to try to find him. I've gone through DHS's records. They have no accounting of an address or phone number. It's like, he's just disappeared."

Hodgens questioned Lynch further about Kelsey's "missing" father, "Have you asked his mother where he is?"

"No," replied Lynch.

"Have you asked his wife Ashley?"

"No."

"Did you go to Raye Dawn's home?" asked Hodgens.

"No sir, I did not."

"Have you interviewed Mike Porter?"

"No, sir. But I did not find anything on Mike Porter."

Hodgens explained to Lynch that Dr. Sullivan had concerns about her going back to her mother for any unsupervised care because of the nature of the healing fractures. He asked if she took that into consideration in forming her opinion that Kelsey should go home with Raye Dawn.

Lynch replied, "I took him like a doctor. You know, he has some concerns."

"Your opinion about what should happen to this child is primarily based on what your sister, Lisa Mendenhall told you?"

"No, sir," answered Lynch.

"Has your sister ever been in the home?" pressed Hodgens.

"No."

"Did your sister know Kelsey had a broken clavicle back in January?"

"Yes."

"Was your sister aware Kelsey had bruises on her face that were not consistent with the story that was given about the broken collarbone?"

"No," said Lynch.

"Does that change your opinion any after you've heard the testimony here today about how many other times the child has been injured with the mother?"

"No, sir."

"Did you interview Mr. and Mrs. Briggs?"

"No."

"You pretty much made up your mind that the child should go back with the mother regardless of the evidence or facts that may be presented here today. Isn't that correct?"

Lynch explained, "After I reviewed the DHS case file, after I have reviewed a number of documents, that is what my report to the court is based on."

"And nothing that could be said today in court with people actually here testifying is going to change your mind, isn't that right?"

"That is correct."

Kelsey's attorney, Brandon Watkins, pointed out that Lynch's report referred to Kelsey as "juveniles" plural. Lynch told him since this was her first report she had to re-write it a couple of times but she tries to be as accurate as possible.

Next up, Yolanda Hunter. Yolanda was in charge of prescribing DHS services to Raye Dawn after caseworkers confirmed abuse against her. Yolanda told Judge Key she had been involved in child welfare since 2001.

Raye Dawn successfully completed parenting classes, domestic violence classes, anger management, and a DUI assessment.

Yolanda told the judge she did not agree Kelsey should be immediately returned to her mom's home. Yolanda explained her intention was to gradually phase Kelsey back into Raye Dawn's home, using CHBS, a program where caseworkers make regular visits to the home.

Hodgens asked if it concerned Yolanda that Kelsey's most severe injuries occurred while Raye Dawn was going through all of the classes. Yolanda said that's why she believed Kelsey should stay with Gayla for the time being.

When the conversation turned to Michael Porter, Yolanda had to defend her actions.

"What about Mr. Porter? Is he allowed to see the child?"

"In supervised visitation," said Yolanda.

"Were you aware that the court order, the last court order in this case says he doesn't get to see the child?" asked Hodgens.

Yolanda said, "When they are brought to the office, we have them come in under supervision and he was able to see the child."

Hodgens pressed further, "So in some circumstances you're not going to follow the court's order. You're going to do what you want to do? So why are we doing that?"

Yolanda explained, "Because I work with the parents, and if this child is to be reunified with this mother I would have to take a look at the father since she is currently married to him."

"But the order doesn't allow that. Do you understand?"

"Yes."

"But you're going to do it anyway?"

"Under supervision," said Yolanda.

Before Yolanda left the courtroom, Judge Key asked the question that sparked a chain of events the Briggs believe led to Kelsey's death. Key asked, "Yolanda, if there was an adjudication are there any additional requirements that you would have of Ms. Porter, Raye Dawn Smith Porter?"

"No you're honor, there's not," replied Hunter. Even if Judge Key decided Kelsey was being abused, it was Hunter's opinion Raye Dawn had completed all of the parenting classes and treatments necessary to get her child back.

Two years before Gayla Smith's testimony would solidify her daughter's spot in prison, the mother took the stand in the custody matter. Gayla proudly explained to Judge Key why Raye Dawn should get her baby back.

Hodgens asked, "Have you ever heard your daughter say that if Lance and his new wife got custody of the child, that your daughter would kill Ashley?"

Gayla replied abruptly, "No. I've never heard her say that."

"Was there ever a time period when your daughter had a breathalyzer machine or a restricted device on her car where she could not drive because of a DUI charge?"

"I don't think it was a DUI charge."

"Well did she have some type of restrictive..."

"She sure did," retorted the mother.

"Where she had to blow into it to get the car to start?"

Gayla explained, "Yea, she had that right after her daddy passed away because she cared for her daddy for a year and a half with the baby."

"Well, I didn't ask you about that," chided Hodgens.

"I know you didn't."

"Did she ever ask you to blow into the device for her because she couldn't get it to work?"

"No," said Gayla.

"In your opinion does your daughter have a drinking problem?"

"No."

"Has she in the past had a drinking problem?" asked Hodgens.

"Not that I know of."

Another witness gave another glowing report for Raye Dawn. The man who would later admit his wife got very angry when she was drunk, told Key he had no concerns about Raye Dawn as a mother. Michael Porter described her as a fit parent for Kelsey and his children. Porter claimed to have no idea how Kelsey was getting hurt with Raye Dawn, "I know that I haven't been present. I know what she's told me which I believe."

Despite the fact Porter said he and Raye Dawn spoke on the phone at least ten times a day, he was unaware the court had restricted him from spending time with Kelsey. Porter claimed Raye Dawn never told him. Regardless, Porter explained to the judge he had never spent time alone with Kelsey.

Key believed him. The judge respected that Porter voluntarily took parenting classes and seemed to be a man who was committed to his own children.

The only person left to defend Raye Dawn was Raye Dawn herself. Kathie watched as her former daughter-in-law walked up to the witness stand. Kelsey's mom was very confident that day, very sure of her-self.

Kathie says Raye Dawn did not seem scared or nervous at all. Raye Dawn denied ever hitting Kelsey and again explained she never noticed the bruises on Kelsey's rear. Kelsey's mother said she wished she could tell everyone where they came from because then she wouldn't have had to go through all of this.

Raye Dawn told Judge Key about her violent marriage to Lance saying he hit her, reared back and punched her in the face. When she tried to fight back, the now meek woman playing the role of the battered wife, told the judge it only made Lance stronger.

Raye Dawn said she had no concerns about Porter being around Kelsey. If she did, she would not have married him.

Her performance continued as she explained she was not concerned Dr. Sullivan ruled Kelsey's legs to be abuse, because she knew the bruises and broken bones were out of her control and simply accidents. In the last few moments of her testimony, Raye Dawn alluded to the idea someone was brainwashing the two-year-old.

Hodgens asked, "You don't believe the Briggs had anything to do with those injuries, do you?"

"I don't really know who did this, if anyone."

"But they always showed up after you had contact with the child?"

"She had accidents, yes."

"Has Kelsey told you that Daddy Mike caused these injuries?"

"No."

"And if she has told other people that, is this child generally truthful when she talks to you about things?"

"Yes. And also if you tell her something over and over, she's eventually going to repeat it."

"But generally she's truthful in her statements. Isn't that right?"

"As much as a two-year-old can be on her own."

Kathie knew Raye Dawn's answers were quite rehearsed. She had testified a few months back at another one of the hearings and said some of the same things. Kathie says it was the second time Raye Dawn told the judge a two-year-old repeats what she is told.

Kathie thought the hearing was an open and shut case until lawyers called her witnesses and began picking up the pace. The questioning got shorter as the day wore on. Debbie Hammons, a relative of both the Smith and the Briggs family, as well as Gayla's best friend, was full of information that was not conveyed on the witness stand.

Debbie testified Gayla told her that if Ashley got custody of Kelsey, Raye Dawn would kill her. Hammons says Gayla continued, "If she doesn't I might."

Raye Dawn's lawyer asked, "You're telling the court that Kathie has told you that Raye Dawn ought to get Kelsey?"

Hammons replied, "When she gets straightened up, yes. She does not want to raise her no more than I want to raise a child. I think Raye Dawn is a good mother. I do think Raye Dawn has a drinking problem. I told Gayla a year ago that Raye Dawn needed some counseling."

"Do you think Raye Dawn abused Kelsey?" Wilson continued.

"I don't think her herself did, no," said Hammons.

"Do you think she let it happen?" pressed Wilson.

"I think Mike did."

Key interrupted, "I don't want to hear your opinion as to who you think did it, all right?"

The next witness substantiated the opinion Key did not want to hear. Janis Cotton, Kathie's aunt, testified she went with Kathie to Oklahoma City to meet with Dr. Sullivan. Wilson accused Kathie of wanting Raye Dawn to go with her so if the doctors in Oklahoma City suspected abuse, she would be arrested on the spot. Janis told the court that was not the case.

Hodgens asked Janis about one of the only times Kelsey gave anyone insight as to what was going on in the shadows, "What does Kelsey tell you about what happened to her?"

Janis says she asked Kelsey, "How in the world did you get that other boo boo honey?" And she said, "Daddy Mike kicked me off the bed and my mommy yelled at him and then we had pizza and French fries."

Kathie's daughter, Shirica, told Key she heard Raye Dawn tell Kathie she did not want to go to OKC to the doctor's office because she was concerned that DHS in Oklahoma City would take Kelsey into custody if they suspected any abuse.

The last witness of the day had a lot to defend. She had been accused of withholding her son's contact information from DHS, even accused of breaking Kelsey's legs, herself. Kathie Briggs walked up to the witness stand, held up her right hand, and promised to tell Judge Key the truth, so help her God.

Kathie explained she had three to four different people examine Kelsey every time she would leave to go stay with her mother, and again when she would come back. At first, Kristal Johnson told Kathie to call her every time she saw a mark on Kelsey. Soon, the caseworker got frustrated and told Kathie not to call unless she thought it was abuse. Following Kristal's wishes Kathie did not call her when Kelsey's nose was swollen. Instead she took her to the emergency room, but that too angered Kristal. The DHS worker scolded Kathie because she didn't call to tell her that she took Kelsey to the E.R.

The lawyers asked Kathie to explain how she realized Kelsey's legs were hurt worse than she had originally thought. She told the court about the day she took Kelsey to Walmart, "She took four steps. She didn't want to get in the cart. She wanted to walk. She took four steps and just said, 'can't.'"

Kathie told the court she asked the school nurse about Kelsey's growth plates. It was the nurse who told Kathie to get a second opinion. She in no way sought out doctors who would diagnose Kelsey's broken legs as child abuse. It was actually Gayla's cousin, who worked for a foot doctor, who made the appointment in Oklahoma City. Kathie told Judge Key she was surprised when Raye Dawn asked, "What if we take her to Oklahoma City and they suspect child abuse and then we're in Oklahoma County? They would take her."

Kathie told the court she was shocked when Dr. Sullivan walked into the room, "He just pretty much point-blank said that it was not accidental; it was abuse."

Kathie explained why Dr. Sullivan took off the casts. She says he contemplated putting Kelsey's casts back on up to the knees, but noticed her skin was rubbed raw on her foot and he did not want to irritate it further.

Up until this point, Kathie had been painted by Raye Dawn's lawyer as being a vindictive grandmother striving for custody of Kelsey. Kathie quietly told the court she actually had spoken with Raye Dawn about Kelsey going home earlier that week, "I really expected on June 6th that Kelsey would be going home. And then when the doctor said he felt like her legs had been abused, that totally just changed the picture. I would like to remain as the guardian until there are further classes taken either with Raye Dawn or Mike or until we can get to the bottom of what actually happened to her."

Hodgens wrapped up his questions by asking, "You didn't do this did you?"

"No, I did not," replied Kathie.

"Did your husband do it?"

"No."

"Anybody in your household?"

"No."

"Do you think that the child should be returned to the mother now?"

"Not at this time."

Greg Wilson had every intention of dismantling Kathie on the witness stand and she was prepared for it. Wilson could not be prepared for the thought that everyone surrounding the case was lying to defend Raye Dawn. Kathie was not nervous because she knew everything she was going to say was the truth. Her explanations made sense in a case where logic had been thrown out a long time ago.

Wilson questioned Kathie about hiding Lance's whereabouts from DHS. She said, "I have told everybody where he was. The only time they asked me for an address, I did not have one. And when they asked for a phone number, I did not have one. They've had his cell phone number up until the day he left on May 3."

As for those supervised DHS visits, where the caseworkers were too busy documenting issues between Kathie and Kelsey to ask for Lance's phone number, Wilson asked, "You've heard testimony that when you've had supervised visits at DHS, the child will pinch you and bite you and scratch you and scream. And that's all true, isn't it?"

"No that's not true," answered Kathie.

"So the CASA worker lied about that?" asked Wilson.

Kathie replied, "She screamed one time when she was standing up with a pair of child safety scissors, and I tried to take them from her. She screamed because she didn't want me to take them."

"She doesn't pinch you?"

"She scratched me when Yolanda Hunter tried to take her from me when she was going to a doctor's visit."

"She doesn't bite you?"

"No, she did not bite me."

Wilson asked why Kathie gave Raye Dawn extra visits since she was documenting bruises following every visit. Kathie explained it was not an extra visit; it was a make up visit from a weekend Raye Dawn missed.

"You're telling the court that when the child came up with two broken legs, and is in a body cast, or leg casts on both legs, that you never wondered if there might be some abuse on that?" asked Wilson.

"I talked to Dr. Koons that day, and she told me she had ruled out abuse."

"Even though she's my sister and all that?" chided Wilson.

"I did not know that at the time. I couldn't imagine anybody breaking a child's legs. I never suspected abuse on her legs until Dr. Sullivan said that. He just told me someone yanked on her."

When Wilson realized he was not getting anywhere with Kathie's testimony he asked point blank, "In your opinion, what is it going to take for you to tell Judge Key, now it's okay for Kelsey to go home with Raye Dawn?"

"No injuries."

Judge Key interrupted Kathie saying, "Hold on. I think that's Judge Key's decision."

Wilson continued by asking the same questions he asked every witness, "Do you think Raye Dawn jerked on Kelsey's legs?"

"I don't know," replied Kathie.

"Do you think she might have?"

"I don't want to think that," said Kathie.

"Do you understand that DHS at this point thinks that you might have?"

Kathie corrected him, "I think they don't know who did."

"But you know that they haven't ruled you out as the one that yanked on those legs, right?"

"Exactly."

In child custody matters, the judge is allowed to ask witnesses questions as well. Judge Key exercised this option with Kathie, "Let's talk about March, a bruise here, a bruise there. At the end of March, did you think anything outside of normal wear and tear for a two year-old on these bruises?"

Kathie replied, "I thought it was odd that she had a bruise almost every time she came back, but each bruise in itself was not a big bruise. It was just that it was so consistent that it was almost every time, whether she had her 24 hours or a three-day weekend."

Kathie left the witness stand confident she illustrated the danger her granddaughter would be facing if she was placed back in Raye Dawn's house. She explained she knew Kelsey was only two but she had made a couple of comments about Daddy Mike. Kathie warned Judge Key, "None of these problems started happening until he entered her life."

Kathie's warning was the last piece of testimony Judge Key heard that afternoon. Key came back the next morning to watch the video taped depositions from Dr. Sullivan and Dr. Barrett.

No court reporter was present while Key watched those videos. The record reflects that Carla Lynch, the CASA worker, and Brandon Watkins were present. We will never know for sure whether the tapes were watched or more importantly, who visited Judge Key during those morning hours.

Key says he wandered out to the hallway at the front of the courthouse because he wanted to see the little girl he had heard so much about. Kelsey was in the foyer playing peacefully. That day she didn't have the bruises or the casts. She looked beautiful and most of all happy.

When no one from the Briggs family was around, Porter later admitted, the judge walked up to him and Raye Dawn and said, "I created this monster, now I'm going to fix it."

64

Royce and Kathie were the only people from the Briggs family who came to court that day. The rest of the family had taken off the day before, and couldn't use another personal day.

At nine the gavel sounded and Judge Key tucked Kelsey inside a tiny bed that sits in the house of a murderer.

Key announced, "The court is not a fan of having adjudication for deprived with an unknown perpetrator; however, after listening to seven hours or so of testimony yesterday, this Court feels there's a week in question when the child was with both paternal grandparents and Mom, and the Court cannot narrow down a time line, just as DHS had difficulty."

By adjudicating Kelsey deprived, Key admitted someone was abusing Kelsey and therefore she should be in DHS custody. Key continued, "After reviewing both depositions, the Court feels that an adjudication will occur with regards to the deprived petition against an unknown perpetrator."

Until this point, Kathie and Royce say Key seemed as if he had rehearsed what he was going to say. He did not give either lawyer an opportunity for a closing argument. Before continuing Key hesitated, almost as if he knew he was not supposed to say what he was about to, "This Court, though, does have the authority to place children. I recognize that may be in direct conflict with what DHS, not local people, DHS state office sometimes believes I have the ability to do. They're always welcome in my courtroom to argue that point.

"But this Court is going to place the minor child back in the home of the natural mother. This Court is doing that because from testimony of Yolanda Hunter, 'There are no additional requirements that will be made of this particular mother even if she was adjudicated.'"

Key refused to answer any questions or explain his ruling, even after Kelsey was killed in the home he sent her back to.

Kathie's head began spinning as she and Royce stood with their lawyer. Hodgens told the grandparents, "The next time you see her she'll probably be dead."

Kathie left quickly, avoiding the smug stares coming from the Smith family. The only person Kathie remembers seeing as she walked out of the courtroom was Whitney. She smiled at Porter's little girl and kept walking.

When they got home that afternoon, Kathie had to break the news to everyone in the family. Once the feeling of disbelief began to fade, the fear set in. The judge didn't know that Kelsey was not hurt in Kathie's home. But Kathie did. She knew it happened with Raye Dawn and Porter. She still didn't know who was doing it and never would. The only thing she knew for a fact was that it didn't happen under her roof. Which meant Kelsey was not safe.

The sleepless nights began. Kathie spent every night in front of her computer, composing emails. It consumed her life.

In those emails, Kathie told anyone who took the time to read, she was trying to save her granddaughter's life. She knew her words were drastic, but she was trying to get someone's attention. She had a gut feeling Porter or Raye Dawn would hurt Kelsey again. She thought one time they would hurt her so bad, DHS would open its eyes and take Kelsey away from Raye Dawn and Porter. Abuse had been confirmed against Raye Dawn once and it didn't stop. It didn't stop while she was taking parenting and anger management classes. She couldn't believe Kelsey's mom and step-dad would get smart all of a sudden, especially since everything had gone their way.

Although her words were prophetic, Kathie never truly believed they would kill her.

Michael Porter

Porter explained to agents, "I guess after Gayla had had her for, I don't know, a month or. . .I think she had her for a month, then the judge. . .we went back to court and the judge said, 'You know what?' He said, 'I screwed up and I'm going to place the child back with the mother, back with the natural mother."

Tanner asked, "That was in?"

Porter continued, "June. I think June. Because we've had her back for. . .it would have been I think about four months and she was getting along much better. I mean, you could see when Gayla had her, Steve, it was within a week she was back. I mean, she was gaining her weight back and she just had that light back in her eyes. And that was what was missing when she was with Kathie. That light was gone out of her eyes. I mean mentally she was very upset. You could tell."

Tanner was skeptical, "She just turned two, right?"

Porter replied, "Yea, she turned two in December. But I mean, Steve, I'm telling you, she was. . .I've got a two-year-old and he's very smart, and she was very bright for her age. We always called her an 18-year-old in a two-year-old's body. She would just look at Raye Dawn, you know when Raye would get to visit her, after Kathie took her. She would look at Raye and say, 'Mommy, what happened?' She had no clue. I mean, she knew, you know, that her mom would never hurt her. And she would just look at her and say, 'Mommy, what happened?'"

"Now from the time Raye got Kelsey placed back with her, how would you describe Kelsey?" asked Tanner.

"She was home. That was the best way, the first day she got her back, I mean, Kelsey this is how grown up she was. She looked at her and she said, 'Mommy, I am so proud of you. I'm so proud of you.' And she said, 'Mommy I'm home.' That was it. She was back. I don't know how else to say it. You could just see the relief in her face. Within a week, that gleam was back. In pictures, you can see it was back in her eyes. I mean, I know that that's probably, you think that's a subjective thing, but I mean, I can tell you I've only known Kelsey since October and I saw the difference when Raye got her back. I mean, it was just, it was like relief. 'God Mommy, why did you take so long?'"

Raye Dawn Smith

Garrett asked Raye Dawn, "Now who was the judge? Was it the Lincoln County judge?"

"Judge Craig Key. And I have talked. . .I have talked to him. I think it was yesterday."

"What did you guys talk about?" asked Garrett.

"He was just very upset and he told me how sorry he was. He said, 'We tried normalcy with these people.' He said, 'I just realize now. . .normalcy with these people was not going to happen.'"

"Talking about who?" asked Garrett.

"The Briggs. I tried to tell them from the beginning how they were and what they were going to do. And nobody and now everybody is saying, 'You tried to tell us,' you know, because I tried to tell them because Kelsey was supposed to go for a visit supposedly in two weeks, to see Lance unsupervised. He just comes back from the Army, which that upset me because you know, he just came back from war. I called Kelsey's attorney, CASA, and told them, I said, 'Kelsey can't go through this again.' She couldn't be away from me because if I would go to the bathroom and come back to her in the living room, she would say, 'Mommy, you wasn't coming back.' You know the seizures had stopped."

During the interview Raye told investigators she could usually bring Kelsey out of the seizures. At another point she claimed she had never witnessed a seizure. Neither agent seemed to notice she changed her story.

Garrett pried a little further, *"So you're worried that Lance might hurt her?"*

"I just don't know. I've never seen him with her."

"So you don't know if he would hurt her or not? But you're thinking that the mental, emotional problem would be rough on Kelsey?"

Raye nodded her head, *"That's all I was worried about. I just. . .she worried too much for a two-year-old. Sometimes you could just tell. You'd think she carried the world on her shoulders."*

But the agents said they couldn't understand how Raye could tell Kelsey was so stressed and worried.

Raye explained, *"Like Tuesday, she didn't lead on that she was worried or anything. But when I would go visit her at DHS and when she was with my mom, she'd say, 'Mommy, I can go with you,' when I was leaving. And I'd say, 'Kelsey you can't go with Mommy.' And she'd say, 'Mommy, what happened?' But when I got her back, the first day she was home she gave me a big hug and said, 'Mommy, I'm so proud of you, we're home.'*

"I love her to death. She was half of me," said Raye.

"But you know you've got Lance coming back, and that's causing some stress," said Garrett.

"I was wanting to protect her," said Raye, in a matter of fact tone.

"You have to understand we're fighting for Kelsey right now," said Za.

"How come no one would listen to me when I was fighting for her?" asked Raye.

F·I·V·E

LETTER TO BRAD HENRY, GOVERNOR OF OKLAHOMA:

Mr. Henry,

My son is fighting for his country and now we are asking someone to fight for him. Please help me to clear his name. My family and his current wife's family will be contacting every State Representative and US Representative we can. We are also talking of contacting the media nationwide if we cannot get help any other way. We feel like our family has already been falsely accused of many things and so was my son in the report that we were never allowed the opportunity to clear. Our family would love a long visit with any State DHS official to set the record straight now that the court date has passed. Basically if we can just clear Lance's name as an alleged perpetrator we can probably accept the rest. Hopefully when my son comes home we can see Kelsey once again and have our seven grandchildren all back together. It is very painful to Lance's sisters not to see their brother's only child while he is away at war. We pray for a happy ending to this someday. Most of all Lance's current wife, Ashley, has not only had to deal with her husband leaving, but no longer has contact with his child that she has cared for since she was 4 months old. Ashley's step-dad is Kim Henry's cousin. His name is Jay Sigman. He is also helping us in our crusade to clear Lance's name. Because Lance was an IRR he does not have a unit in Shawnee to offer a support group during this time. We are trying a few avenues with the Military to help, but we need everyone's help.

Sincerely,

Kathie Briggs

If the Governor or his aides read the email, Kathie says no one responded.

Meanwhile, a myriad of emails circulated among Kelsey's caseworkers and supervisors with instructions to continue to look Kelsey over for injuries.

Internal emails explained a seemingly inexplicable decision by Judge Key to send Kelsey home with her mom. One explanation was, "If anything else happened to her, at least they would know who the perpetrator was."

After Kelsey's death no one knew for sure who hit her this time, or that time, and ultimately, no one knew who dealt the final blow.

In the subject line in each email in Kelsey's case file are two words, "Importance: High."

While DHS amassed hundreds of emails with Kelsey's case number, Raye Dawn was apparently writing down all of the details of Kelsey's life in a book. No mention was ever made of this so-called book after Kelsey died.

Kelsey was back in Raye Dawn's home but still in state custody; thus, DHS was in charge of protecting her. The judge assigned Jean Bonner, a CHBS worker, to Kelsey's case. Kelsey met yet another character in the web designed to be a safety net. A safety net that did not catch her fall before her little body smashed into a million pieces.

At least a dozen case workers were assigned to Kelsey's case. Nearly each day of her short life was documented in great detail. Nearly each scratch and bruise came with an explanation attached.

Two weeks after Kelsey went home to live with Raye Dawn and Porter, Debra Winn, Lincoln County's DHS Director warned Kelsey's supervisor, David Burgess, that Kelsey's case needed to be "cleaned up".

Winn said, "We probably need collateral for Raye Dawn, a non-family member who will honestly be able to explain how much she drinks, how often, what her behavior is like and how she is as a mom when she has been drinking...especially since someone said they have seen her drunk since she and Porter started dating. I think those are questions we can also ask Miste. What happens when Raye drinks? How often? When was the last time you saw her drunk? Understand that she has a hard time with losing her dad and grandmother...this is why she has 'rages'...what are they like? Stuff like that."

The supervisor supported Kathie saying she would have no way of knowing whether Porter was at visits. Winn questioned why Raye Dawn violated the Judge's order, "Why did she let him be with her at visits when she was aware of the court order? What does she have to say about that?"

Nowhere in Kelsey's 6,000 page case file are those questions answered.

Answers were missing and so was Kathie Briggs, as scheduled supervised visitation began in July of 2005. The visits were designed for Kelsey's step-mother Ashley. Ashley and the rest of the family were surprised when Yolanda Hunter called and offered Ashley a visit. She was given permission to bring Kathie along. Kathie wanted to see Kelsey but no longer trusted DHS or the reports issued to the judge. She made the tough decision to allow Ashley this time to reconnect with Kelsey.

So Ashley went to the DHS office alone. When she arrived Kelsey was sound asleep. No one could wake her. Ashley sat and held Kelsey for the entire visit. She noticed a bruise on Kelsey's forehead accompanied by a scrape on her nose. Kelsey's step-sister, Whitney Porter, later told a school counselor her dad would slam Kelsey's head into a brick wall. Porter eventually revealed Raye Dawn gave Kelsey a big dose of Benadryl before the visit, and other visits, causing Kelsey to sleep.

DHS documented the bruise on July 12, 2005. A week later Raye Dawn had no explanation as to why it had not healed. Kristal Johnson recorded, "The skinned place on the child's nose was redder and not healing well. She had a faint bruise still remaining on her forehead from last week and a newer bruise on her right cheek. Raye Dawn says she did not know how Kelsey got the bruise on the cheek and that the nose is not healing because she can't get Kelsey to stop picking at the scab."

Against the court order, Raye Dawn and Porter took Kelsey to Branson for a vacation before they moved into their new house. By the end of July, the scrape on her nose, was better, but still not healed.

Carla Lynch, Kelsey's CASA volunteer began to ask a few more questions. July 14, 2005, Lynch says she saw Kelsey have a seizure during a court recess. Kelsey was sitting outside the courtroom with Gayla. While the adults were standing around talking, Kelsey said ouch and pulled on Gayla's hand. When Gayla bent down to check on Kelsey, Porter asked what was wrong. Lynch says Gayla told Porter, "I think she is having another seizure." Porter picked Kelsey up and put her against his shoulder, rubbing her back. Raye Dawn asked if she was okay and Porter told her Kelsey was starting to relax. A few minutes later she began playing again.

After court that day Judge Key called Lynch into his chambers ordering her to appease the Briggs family. Lynch told him she did not want to upset Kathie Briggs and had developed a fear of her. Kathie's strong opinions about the case were intimidating to Lynch. Key told Lynch to find a way. She decided to start working with Lance and Ashley instead.

Once Lynch opened communication with Ashley, she set up a home visit. Lynch says she could tell instantly Ashley had built a home of love. Ashley was concerned about Kelsey being in Raye Dawn's care, but Lynch explained there was no proof and she could not ask the judge to take Kelsey based on a gut feeling. Lynch says toys, clothes, and shoes filled Kelsey's room at Ashley's house. It was a little girl's dream room. Safe for a visit.

Lynch finally made contact with Lance on the phone. She says he talked to her for an hour and she could feel the love he had for his daughter all the way across the ocean. He wanted to spend as much time as possible with Kelsey when he got home and wanted Kelsey to be safe. He knew Ashley would make a good mother and wanted to have more children. He promised to try to work with Raye Dawn. He had a special request for Lynch. He was upset he was not receiving information about Kelsey's case. He had not heard from the D.A. or D.H.S. and was hoping Lynch could mend those fences. Lynch soon realized she may have made a big mistake in her testimony in June.

August 1, 2005, Raye Dawn called and rescheduled Ashley's scheduled visitation. The next day when Ashley arrived at the DHS office she noticed Kelsey had bitten one of her fingers. It was swollen, and she had a sore spot on the top of her hand. DHS explained Raye Dawn told them she saw Kelsey digging into the back of her hand with the fingernail of the other hand. Another injury, another excuse.

DHS spotted a bruise in the shape of a bite mark on Kelsey's upper arm. Kristal said she did not know whether Kelsey bit herself or whether her step-brother Bubby did it. This was the third bite mark noted by DHS. Yet, no one noticed a pattern.

At night the person causing bruise after bruise haunted Kelsey's sleep. Mike Porter told caseworkers he sat up rocking Kelsey for hours. He says one time Kelsey had a night terror. She screamed and cried in her sleep. Her eyes rolled back in her head. She was unaware of her surroundings and terribly afraid. Kathie had reported night terrors several months earlier, in the nights following the broken legs.

Long after Kelsey died, Raye Dawn claimed the night terrors were actually seizures. She remembers walking by Kelsey's room after she had put her to bed and seeing Porter in the bedroom holding Kelsey. Raye says when Kelsey's eyes rolled to the back of her head she grabbed her little girl from her husband saying, "Kelsey, Mommy's here. Mommy's here." When Kelsey came to she said, "Mommy, I'm so tired."

Raye Dawn did not immediately take Kelsey to the emergency room.

She claimed she wanted to call 9-1-1, but Porter told her there was nothing they could do for seizures.

Lawyers questioned her further saying she could have gotten in the truck and taken her to the emergency room. But she did not. The Smith family would later say Kelsey had at least five of what they thought were seizures between June and October of 2005. They say she would stare ahead and stiffen up. When Kelsey came out of it she was sleepy.

A few days later Raye Dawn finally took Kelsey to the doctor. Dr. Koons said she was not concerned about the seizures, but scheduled Kelsey for an EEG anyway. Kelsey already had an inconclusive bone density test and caseworkers wanted her to visit OU's child counseling center.

In the next two months Kelsey would see numerous doctors. She was losing weight, losing hair and bruising easily; but not one doctor diagnosed Kelsey with any of the rare disorders being investigated.

While Kelsey visited doctor after doctor, caseworkers recommended Raye Dawn get a mental health examination for depression. Raye Dawn told caseworkers she was the victim of domestic abuse during her relationship with Lance. She continued to use this as her defense each time she was questioned about Kelsey's abuse.

Porter admitted to drinking in college but says he does not drink anymore and does not use drugs. Porter said he had a previous partner who was physically and mentally abusive. He did not live in fear of her because he knew he was stronger. Porter claimed the abuse hurt him more mentally than physically.

Yolanda Hunter says Raye Dawn was afraid to let Kelsey play and be a "normal" child, fearing that an accidental injury would be considered abuse. Raye Dawn knew she could lose her daughter again.

Yet week after week caseworkers reported Kelsey's condition had deteriorated. They called it "self injurious" behavior. August 8, yet another caseworker visited Raye Dawn's home saying, "I was at the house Friday and Kelsey had a nose bleed. It appeared to be sinuses; her nose was raw and red, etc. Raye Dawn and her husband both said they had not had good luck with doctors but did mention a doctor appointment." Again, investigators did not notice the pattern of injuries to Kelsey's nose.

The doctor tested Kelsey for a blood disorder. The results came back negative, making it more difficult to explain the faded bruises on Kelsey's legs. The caseworkers noted Kelsey was extremely pale and seemed anxious about being away from her mom, if only for a few minutes.

They took her back to Dr. Koons still searching for a remedy to Kelsey's declining health. In the waiting room, a smiling Kelsey brought Porter magazines and the two looked at the pictures of babies together. Caseworkers say Porter and Kelsey wandered to other parts of the clinic looking for toys. When they came back, Kelsey was in Porter's arms, still smiling. They did not find any toys but Kelsey loved the elevator ride.

At that visit, Kelsey weighed 22.5 pounds, two pounds less than the previous month. For the swelling in her nostrils, the doctor prescribed a nasal spray and made a referral to OU Medical Center.

Dr. Koons noted Kelsey's hair was growing back. Koons did not seem to be concerned with Kelsey's health problems. In her opinion, children that age sometimes lose weight and injure or bite themselves. An odd diagnosis from a doctor who knew the child was in DHS custody because of abuse. Koons recommended Pediasure to help Kelsey put some meat back on her waning bones.

August 17, 2005 Raye Dawn learned Carla Lynch, Kelsey's CASA, suggested Ashley be allowed to spend time with Kelsey, alone.

Raye got angry saying it was not in Kelsey's best interest and told caseworkers she was concerned about what the judge would say. She called Lynch, "How could you do this to me and Kelsey?" Raye Dawn clearly did not want Kelsey around the Briggs, but Lynch was not giving up.

It was the last time Lynch heard from Raye Dawn while Kelsey was alive. Raye Dawn called Lynch's boss, but refused to talk with the volunteer who had turned against her.

Judge Key agreed with Lynch and allowed Kelsey to visit Ashley's house unsupervised. But first, Yolanda Hunter had to pay Ashley a home visit to make sure it would be safe for Kelsey.

Yolanda seemed to spend more time examining Ashley's home than the bruises that continued to surface on the two-year-old's skin.

That same week Yolanda showed up at Raye Dawn's house to check on the two-year-old. Yolanda reported Kelsey had a new bruise on her left cheek and was asleep again. Raye Dawn says Kelsey pulled a ceramic lamp off a table. The lamp hit Kelsey's cheek bruising it.

Raye Dawn says she had to prepare Kelsey for the Saturday visit with Ashley. Raye Dawn claimed when she told Kelsey she was going to see Ashley, Kelsey started to cry and then asked mom if she would go to "Grandma Gayla" after she was with Ashley. Raye Dawn figured Kelsey remembered this was the order of things before. She was with the Briggs family, then went to live with Gayla, before coming home.

The night before the scheduled visit, Porter and Raye Dawn totaled their new truck. Kelsey was secured in her car seat on the passenger side of the truck when a drunk driver hit the opposite side.

Raye Dawn called Yolanda Hunter who told her to take Kelsey to the emergency room. After a long wait, Raye Dawn left the ER at 2:30 a.m. before Kelsey saw a doctor. Raye Dawn claims a triage nurse allowed her to leave saying Kelsey looked fine. Hospital records do not reflect Kelsey's mother's claim.

Yolanda Hunter attributed the new bruises covering Kelsey's face to the accident. Though common sense would say the straps on the car seat would have only bruised her lower abdomen.

Judge Key cancelled the visit with Ashley saying it was in Kelsey's best interest to stay home the day after the wreck.

That day, Kelsey's CHBS worker, Jean Bonner, called to check in. Porter answered and explained Raye Dawn and Kelsey were napping. Raye Dawn would later tell the OSBI Kelsey had what appeared to be a seizure the night following the accident. Again, Kelsey's mother did not seek medical attention.

A week later, in an internal email, DHS supervisors asked if Yolanda got a copy of the police report to see who was cited for the accident and to make sure it didn't show Porter or Raye Dawn were drinking.

No copy of the report was included in Kelsey's file.

Apparently the "accident" caused so much stress on Kelsey she began biting the inside of her mouth raw. Gayla brought her into the DHS office saying Kelsey would not eat. Kelsey clung to Gayla. No words; no smiles. She even refused a treat. Caseworkers finally traded a sucker for a half smile from Kelsey.

Kelsey's smile was darkened by several bright purple bruises. When Kelsey pulled up her shirt to show her belly button, the caseworker did not see any bruises. Another worker reported the bruises were lower. The evidence on Kelsey's face was once again ignored by the agency in place to protect her.

A CT scan became Raye Dawn's next desperate grasp for something to blame besides human hands. The test for seizure activity again, came back negative.

Dr. Koons wrote a letter to Yolanda saying she was concerned about tonic seizure activity. The doctor explained Kelsey was under close doctor supervision. While they worked to schedule an EEG Koons wrote, "It would be beneficial that she remain in one home so the seizure activity can be closely observed and documented." The sister of Raye Dawn's attorney went along with the plan to keep Kelsey away from the Briggs.

Raye Dawn got her wish.

The last time anyone in the Briggs family saw Kelsey was August 27, 2005. Raye Dawn says Kelsey went with Ashley without hesitation; although Raye Dawn claims Kelsey cried a couple of times earlier because she did not want to go. Raye Dawn says she reassured Kelsey she could call home at any time.

Ashley picked Kelsey up at Braums Ice Cream shop at nine that morning. Kathie gave Ashley an hour alone with Kelsey before she came over, a little mother-daughter time.

Kelsey wore a green striped, short sleeved t-shirt and green Capri pants. Part of her hair was pulled up in a small pony tail at the top of her head.

Kathie, Shirica, and Jeanna walked in together. Kathie reached down to pick up her granddaughter and braced herself to pick up what she expected would feel like a 20 pound bag. Instead, the little girl felt like she only weighed two pounds. Kathie knew it was not a matter of Kelsey getting taller and slimming down, something was wrong. She was thin despite the fact Raye Dawn told DHS she had "eaten like a pig" at supper the night before.

As Kathie held Kelsey, Ashley's mom Teri started crying because she knew exactly what Kathie was thinking.

Kathie's concerns about Kelsey not remembering her as her grandmother paled in comparison to the situation sitting before them. Kathie got on the floor with Kelsey and played with some stickers. While they were playing, a bit of the Kelsey they remembered slipped out. She corrected the place Kathie put the sticker saying, "No grandma, not there!"

The Briggs set up a video camera in the living room to record all five hours of the visit. They didn't want Raye Dawn to accuse them of doing something to Kelsey at Ashley's house.

Ashley tried feeding Kelsey chips but the little girl's mouth had so many sores the salt burned the small wounds. Ashley tried a grilled cheese and Kelsey was able to eat a few bites.

The video camera caught moments of childhood. Kelsey and her cousin Eryn ran back and forth from the bedroom to the living room playing with plastic cheeseburgers and French fries from McDonalds.

While Ashley played with the kids inside, Kathie and Teri went out to the porch. The grandmothers had to talk about what they were witnessing but didn't want Kelsey to hear. They talked in circles. Calling DHS seemed futile, at least until Lance got home.

Kathie planned to send video to Lance and take a picture of all of the grandkids for him. Once she saw Kelsey's delicate health she called everyone and told them not to come over. Kelsey couldn't handle any more visitors and Kathie knew Lance couldn't handle seeing how bad Kelsey looked.

Lance called to talk to Kelsey. It was the last time he would hear his little girl's voice. He tried calling her at Raye Dawn's house numerous times before her death, but Raye Dawn would not answer the phone.

In hopes of seeing a glimpse of the girl they used to know, they took Kelsey out to the swing set. She loved to swing. Only today she didn't have that same excitement. This was not the Kelsey that used to laugh and beg to be pushed higher and higher. Royce was able to get a small smile from her as they looked at the moon. It was heart wrenching for the family to see her this way.

Her once happy spirit had been taken from her. The light in her eyes was out.

This is the way Oklahomans would remember Kelsey forever. Sitting in her blue swing, the little girl was barely recognizable from the smiling pictures with chubby cheeks they took a few months before. She had dark circles under her blood hemorrhaged eye. Her blues eyes were dead.

Her face was covered with bruises nowhere near an area where her car seat would have hit.

Her head rested on the side of the baby swing, her eyes gazed off into the distance. The secrets were trapped somewhere inside.

The two-year-old clung to her step-mom and stared at the video camera. Kathie recorded evidence her son's two-year-old girl was dying, despite dozens of people responsible for keeping her alive.

Kelsey was still sitting in her blue swing as Kathie walked away. From the porch Kathie turned around, looked at her granddaughter and said, "Kelsey, I need you to know I love you and I'll see you again."

Kathie wishes she would have stayed longer. Wishes she would have played longer. Wishes she would have held her granddaughter longer. She wanted to give Ashley the last hour with her. This was the person they expected to become her "mommy" again one day. It was another decision Kathie would forever regret. She never thought she would have to wait until she gets to Heaven to see Kelsey again.

Shirica left with tears streaming down her face. She did not recognize Kelsey. It was her body, but it was as if her spirit was already gone.

Ashley reached out to the only worker who seemed to be listening. She called Lynch, Kelsey's CASA, to ask if Kathie could send a DVD of the visit.

When Lynch saw the pictures Kathie had recorded she knew she had to get Kelsey out of that house. Her first call was to DHS. She was put on hold. Another fitting pause. Finally Yolanda's voice resonated on the other end of the line. Yolanda admitted to Lynch there had been a couple more incident reports filed. And no, they had not been passed along to Kelsey's CASA.

The family spent the rest of the weekend in turmoil knowing the people who should care didn't. Kathie called her aunt, upset about the Kelsey they saw that day. This time Janis went straight to the DHS office in the neighboring county in person. Surely they would do something. Wrong again.

Another day, another email. Kathie learned Raye Dawn was using these so called seizures to try to keep Kelsey away from them.

August 29, 2005

"Lincoln County has become so involved with helping the mother, that it seems they have forgotten about Kelsey. Last year when Kelsey had a large pump knot on her nose, the mother claimed Whitney elbowed Kelsey in the middle of the night. David Burgess said they would go to the school and question Whitney, but were told later they did not follow up on that until weeks later after she could have been coached by her father. Something is definitely not right and the connection between that family and DHS is incredible. If you read previous reports, Whitney's grandmother was concerned with Raye Dawn's drinking and witnessed problems with it. There were never any problems until this new stepfather Mike Porter entered the picture. It was our hope when Kelsey was reunited with her mother this would all be put behind us and she would then be in a loving environment. We never wanted to keep her from her mother for any long lengths of time."

In an internal email, never released to the public, DHS admitted Pott County and Lincoln County were not working together on Kelsey's case and supervisors were concerned they were starting to make the agency look bad.

Dr. Koons' recommendation to end visitation with Ashley called for another court hearing. Kathie was forced to make a decision. A decision Judge Key would later use as his excuse for sending Kelsey back into an abusive home.

September 6, 2005

"After much consideration we have decided that no one from our family will be in court Thursday. DHS has been fighting any kind of reunification with our family since the beginning. Why hasn't the EEG been scheduled? She is the sister of Raye Dawn's attorney. She did have two night terrors while she was in my care. Kelsey seemed heavily medicated on her five hour visit last week. She seems to have lost weight. Ashley can no longer take off work to attend such visitations so we will concede this fight and pick up again when her father comes home."

Kathie Briggs

Not being able to take off work was just an excuse for the young step-mother. The same day Kathie told DHS she and the family would not be coming to court, Ashley told Lance she was filing for divorce.

Lance never imagined his perfect wife would fall victim to the path so many military wives take. The distance was difficult, but Lance always thought, "Ashley, I completely one-hundred percent thought it was going to last."

One day in his tent, Lance read an article in the Army Times, about the divorce rate among activated soldiers.

Lance remembers, "It was like 40% of married soldiers deployed get divorced. It was high; it was unreal. I told myself that sucks for those guys. But thought I'm invincible, it would never happen to me, I've got the best wife. I got the biggest bombshell dropped on me."

Lance was making good money in Iraq. Ashley was in charge of the checkbook. Lance figured they were saving thousands of dollars a month. He planned to have $10,000 in the bank by the time he got home. He promised Ashley the honeymoon they never took and the breast implants she always wanted. It would be Lance's gift to her for being such a devoted wife while he was gone.

One day he asked her, "How much money is in my account?" She told him he had $900 in there. Lance knew she had nothing to show for the money. No explanation. So they got into a big argument over where the money went. He wanted to know. He was stuck in the middle of the desert and the woman he trusted with his life had spent everything he risked his life to earn.

It was that day Ashley told him she wanted a divorce. He remembers her saying, "I'm sick of this."

Those words were hard to understand for the man who didn't know anything about her new man. At some point after Lance left for Iraq Ashley began seeing someone else. Lance says Ashley's tone was very matter of fact and she continued whatever she was typing at work while she told him, "I'm tired of this, us, I don't want to be with you."

"My heart dropped," says Lance.

Kathie was helping Shirica move into her apartment when Lance called and told them about Ashley. The announcement was hard to stomach. They knew Ashley had already bought Christmas presents for Kelsey's little cousins. Ashley just asked Jeanna to pick up some material for the new bedspread she was sewing for the bed she shared with Lance.

Standing in the empty apartment Kathie looked at Shirica and said, "Call Ashley." So she did. A young woman they didn't know answered the phone. She was a robot, completely void of any emotion. Not the girl they had fallen in love with. She confirmed the news they heard from Lance; she wanted a divorce. When they called Ashley's mom, Teri, they learned Ashley had not told her own mother yet.

The next day, from an ocean away, Lance took Ashley off his account. Lance knew if she wanted a divorce he wasn't going to allow her to take any more of his money. He asked the bank for a list of the last month's transactions. He stared at it in awe; she averaged $150 a day, every day.

Ashley told Lance she didn't want to be in a relationship. She got married a few months later.

Two years after Ashley uttered the word divorce Lance says, "I don't hold anything against Ashley except the fact she cheated on me."

Ashley suspected her relationship with Kelsey sparked jealously in Raye Dawn. She thought Raye Dawn could have been hurting Kelsey to get back at Ashley.

Ashley justified leaving Lance by saying if she got out of the picture Kelsey would be safe. Kathie called Ashley and begged her to stay in the picture until Lance returned, so they could get information about Kelsey. In an email, Ashley told Kathie she could not pretend to care.

September 7, 2005
From: Ashley
To: Margaret Noble, Debra Winn and Carla Lynch
"I thought I should notify you of the change that is going on in mine and Lance's life. After going through this fight for Kelsey for over 9 months now, I have decided that I can no longer be a part of this. It has taken a toll on me both emotionally and physically, and taken its toll on mine and Lance's marriage. Lance and I are divorcing. So I will no longer be attending any court hearings or dealing with DHS in any way."

September 8, 2005
From: Debra Winn
To: Ashley
"I am willing to acknowledge there is something wrong. We can all see that this child is not doing as well as she was when we first came in contact with her."

Ashley's announcement further complicated the already difficult custody situation. The Briggs would be criticized for years for not attending the court hearing before Kelsey's death. The family was under the impression that once Ashley was out of the picture they had no rights. Since the hearing was to discuss Ashley's visits with Kelsey, it was their understanding attending would not change anything.

No one told the Briggs family Kelsey had developed a raw sore on her eye. Raye Dawn said she washed the two-year-old's hair with adult shampoo because someone told her it would make Kelsey's hair grow back faster.

When Jean Bonner walked up to the house for a regularly scheduled visit, she thought Kelsey had a black eye until she saw the scabbing. Raye Dawn said she did not realize Kelsey had rubbed her eyes too hard until the next morning. Raye Dawn couldn't understand why Kelsey seemed to rub her right eye more but the left eye looked worse.

DHS was watching Raye Dawn's every move but the mother did not call anyone to report the injury. According to DHS records Raye Dawn called frequently to let caseworkers know when everything was fine, injuries were a different story.

Bonner noted Raye Dawn let Kelsey wear the thick soled flip flops she was wearing when she "sprained" her ankle at the zoo. Also during the visit, Kelsey wandered into the middle of the street. Again, Raye Dawn blamed someone besides herself. This time she said Whitney, her step-daughter, should have been watching Kelsey.

Bruising aside, it took a raw eye, dangerous flip flops and playing in the street for a report to be passed along to the DHS supervisors. The subject of this one had a different tone.

From: Yolanda
To: Darrell Ryan and David Burgess
Subject: Critical incident report on Kelsey

"Okay here is another one that Kelsey has had her hair washed and her mother gave her a towel to rub her eyes with, but that is not what I am upset about. Mother washed her hair with adult shampoo because some person told her that the child's hair would grow faster. What is she thinking??? Then apparently, she gave her a towel to wipe her eye raw!!!! I spoke with CHBS and told her that we need to go over with the parents on their treatment plan on what is appropriate parenting. Also I was approved to go last night to observe Kelsey at her home. I walked up on her and Whitney outside riding the John Deere little ride, battery operated ride in the front yard and asked Kelsey what had happened to her eye. NO parents were outside but had the door open. Kelsey told me after I asked her directly what happened to her eye. She said "soap got in my eyes!" The parents came out and I visited with them about not washing her hair with adult shampoo, and they agreed to go back to the baby shampoo, not washing with the other children in the bath tub, and Mrs. Porter understood and did not get upset. Mr. Porter got upset with me and stated this was not something planned. I explained once again that this is a high profile case and she is in DHS custody and needs to be extra aware of situations and cautious. I also offered that Kelsey does not need to be removed again from them and that this would cause extra harm to this child emotionally she could not handle another removal but if they continue to use poor judgment about using adult shampoos, etc. Then that is probably going to be occurring and that they are only fueling the fire for other referrals to be turned in."

The pending divorce was enough for Lance to convince the U.S. Army to send him back to the states to try and put his life back together. He had asked to return to the states for Kelsey but was not allowed since she was living with family. This time the Army granted the leave because Lance was on medical hold again, following an injury he got on duty. No one was given an exact timetable, but Lance began speaking with DHS over email to set up a reunion with his daughter when he made it back home.

Judge Key said Lance could begin the regularly scheduled visitation as soon as he arrived back in Meeker. Lance planned to go to court for full custody once he got everything settled with the military. Raye Dawn later claimed the judge told her he never intended for Lance to have his visitations.

Kathie continued to write letters hoping Kelsey would be standing in the airport terminal, waving to Lance as he walked off the plane. Kathie pleaded with DHS for any information on Kelsey's condition. She offered to get a power of attorney on behalf of Lance.

Debra Winn told her, "I know you want to know what is going on with your granddaughter because I know you love her But the only way to get information to you is to let it come from Lance and without any contact with him no information will get to your family. We are not trying to exclude you, but we must comply with the court orders and the Title 10 statute."

August 12, 2005
From: Kathie Briggs
To: Debra Winn
"Lance will be mediflighted to Germany today. We do not know how long he will be there. They already had him on hold for his back injury when Ashley broke the shocking divorce news to him on the phone. On top of Kelsey's situation this was just enough for the Army to take pity on him and send him home."

From: Debra Winn
To: Kathie Briggs
RE: "I don't have any negative information regarding his daughter, which is good, but did want him to know that we are taking her condition...thinner, not as happy as she had been several months ago and the concerns about the seizures very seriously and that we are not to release any information to Ashley as she will not be part of the family."

Due to their heightened concern, Jean Bonner went with Raye Dawn and Porter to a hematologist who ordered more blood tests. The doctor suspected bone weakness was the contributing factor in Kelsey's problems.

Bonner says the doctor was surprised the testing for a condition called osteogenesis imperfecta was inconclusive. It would have explained the fractures and bruising.

Between visits to the doctor Kelsey had lost another pound.

As Kelsey's baby fat disappeared forever so did Raye Dawn's excuses. She had no explanation as to why Kelsey threw up all night. No one else in the family was sick. Raye Dawn rescheduled her visit with Bonner because she was going to take her in to see Dr. Koons, again.

Caseworkers could not tell Kathie that Kelsey was sick. When the grandmother emailed them to say Lance would be in the states in a week, Debra Winn sent this message to Kathie.

"I do want you to know that we notice the changes in Kelsey so I am sure it is shocking to you, since you had not seen her for awhile. Hopefully we can discover the cause of the symptoms and get her to looking like that little girl in the picture, smiling at her daddy."

The state agency in charge of protecting Kelsey questioned the Porters about their finances. Caseworkers were concerned the couple was buying a house they could not afford. When someone reported Mike Porter's business was in trouble, the caseworkers pressed Raye Dawn about the household. The questions irritated Raye Dawn because she did not like being accused of spending more money than they had.

Given the other financial questions, DHS was finally acting on a concern a family member reported months earlier. The family member told DHS, "We were not concerned about Kelsey's well being at Raye Dawn's until after we heard about Porter and Raye Dawn having hot checks at Bedlam liquor store about one week before Kelsey was returned and one week after she was returned. Alcohol was a problem before, and from everything we hear it is still a problem."

Doctors continued to search for problems with Kelsey's health. They searched for a medical explanation rather than the suspicion someone was killing the child a little everyday. On September 27, 2005, two weeks before Kelsey was murdered, Bonner went with the family to see another doctor who reported the more detailed blood work from a few weeks earlier also came back normal.

The doctor did not suggest any further testing. If she had a rarer condition those tests would not be normal. The doctor said genetic testing through Washington State University was the last resort.

On October 4, 2005, Bonner visited Kelsey in Raye Dawn and Porter's new house. Bonner reported Kelsey seemed to be adjusting to the new house easily; she had no problems sleeping in her upstairs bedroom. It was the same house Kelsey came home to when she was born. Gayla sold Porter and her daughter the house. Raye Dawn's father Ray died a few years earlier and Gayla was moving in with her new boyfriend. Raye Dawn and Porter slept in the master bedroom downstairs.

During that visit Raye Dawn made Kelsey a tuna salad sandwich. Kelsey was as stubborn as ever and would not eat it. Raye Dawn gave in and let her eat chips. Later Kelsey washed the chips down with some pudding and a hotdog (no bun) dipped in ketchup.

Kelsey told Bonner she had stayed home with Daddy Mike the night before, while mommy was gone. Her eyes lit up as she smiled and told the social worker, her "daddy" had cooked her some pancakes.

Kelsey's real daddy was still trying to determine the exact date he would land on red dirt to see his little girl. The Army couldn't make any promises, but Lance wanted to be home long before Halloween so he could go trick-or-treating with his little princess.

October 6, 2005, Yolanda Hunter visited Kelsey and reported no signs of abuse or neglect.

October 9, 2005, Jean Bonner learned Lance would be coming home. She was concerned Kelsey would not remember him.

A concern that was soon overshadowed.

Michael Porter

"But it's just. . .it's just so far fetched to think that Raye Dawn could do that," said Porter.

Tanner explained, "It is far fetched. Do you want to know why it's farfetched, Mike? Let me tell you why it's farfetched, because it's out of her character, because she loved that baby too. That's why it's farfetched. And I don't disagree with that at all. That's what I'm telling you. And maybe you missed it, but there could have been a very, very, very short period of time when she just lost control."

Porter replied, "I'm not going to point my finger at my wife right now and say, 'You did it.'"

Tanner said, "I don't blame you. I wouldn't either. She's your wife. Let me go talk to my supervisor and see if he wants to interrupt an interview or whatever and see if maybe you guys. . ."

"I want to talk to her."

"Okay. Well, let me go talk to my supervisor and I'll be right back. Do you need to go to the restroom or anything?"

"Can I go get some water? I need to get out of this room."

"Okay. Let's go walk down and get some water."

Tanner offered Porter a cracker as they left. When they got back, Porter sat down, looked up and began adjusting his pants.

Tanner continued, "As far as you talking to her, you know, I don't have a problem with it, but. . ."

Porter said, "I mean, you told us earlier we could leave. Why can't I talk to her?"

Raye Dawn Smith

Raye told agents Dr. Koons said the two-year-old's seizures were no big deal.

Za asked, "How many of these seizures did she have while she was with you from June until. . ."

"She had, maybe four," replied Raye.

"Now the first one was with Gayla, your mother?"

"I think she had four and then Tuesday was five because she had them after, because we were in our wreck in August or September. The night after the wreck she had a little seizure. But they said Kelsey didn't have any internal injuries or she would be in shock or something. She was too active to have anything wrong with her."

"What do you think happened to Kelsey? I mean why do you think that Kelsey passed away? I mean, what do you think is the cause?" asked Za.

Raye Dawn paused and spoke slowly, "A massive seizure, I guess, because the EMT told Mike that was the worst kind you can possibly have. And they said sometimes people don't have them, and they said they can have one and it will be fatal."

"Raye, listen to me," said Za, "You're going to have to at some point. . .you're going to have to tell your mom what happened. You're going to have to tell Michael what happened."

"I cannot believe this," continued Raye, "I cannot believe this. I cannot believe this."

"And I know this has got to be a whole lot of stress you have to live through, but you're going to have to. . ."

Raye interrupted angrily, "I did not hurt my baby." But she would not look them in the eye as she continued, "I have never hurt my baby."

S·I·X

IT WAS A TYPICAL MILD OCTOBER DAY IN THE SOONER STATE. The 68 degree morning, warmed to a somewhat cloudy and breezy 71 degrees. A day a two-year-old would want to spend outside playing.

While the temperature rose outside, rage boiled inside. Inside the house on the hill where Kelsey lived, the smile, frozen on the pink stickers, faded. A stirring anger, a churning hatred, a developing rage exploded in that house. It exploded at the littlest member. Kelsey couldn't defend herself from the evil human force about to take her life.

Mike Porter would usually bring Kelsey down to the master bedroom before leaving for work. Raye Dawn says that morning, he did not.

He left for work around 7:30 a.m. Raye Dawn got up an hour later and made her first phone call to her attorney, Greg Wilson around 9:00 a.m. Her round of phone calls included her mom, Brandon Watkins, Kelsey's attorney, and Jean Bonner, Kelsey's in-home caseworker, who told Raye Dawn she would be running a little late.

Between 9:30 and 10:00 a.m., Raye Dawn went upstairs to wake Kelsey; she was asleep in her bed. Raye Dawn thought it was strange she had a brightly colored beach towel under her head, so she called Porter at work to ask if he put it there. She says he told her he did not and figured Kelsey must have gotten up in the middle of the night and put it there. She also told him Jean was running late.

Michael Porter's lawyers would question Raye Dawn about that towel. Neither Porter nor Raye Dawn could explain why the towel was there or what it had been used for. The OSBI did not take the towel into evidence. Kelsey's mother would later testify she still had the towel somewhere.

Kelsey woke up in her own bed. She was lying on the towel. She had a small purple bruise the size of a nickel and a band aid on one finger.

Raye Dawn says she went back upstairs because she heard Kelsey moving around, "It's time to get up. Jean's coming to see you."

Raye Dawn says Kelsey sat up and said, "Ouch."

"What's the matter?"

Kelsey said, "Mommy I try to throw up."

Raye Dawn did not take her temperature; she did not take her to the doctor; she did call Gayla who suggested Raye Dawn make Kelsey something to eat because she had been sick. It had been a month since Kelsey had strep throat.

She stumbled downstairs for her cream of chicken soup and tea in her sippy cup breakfast. Raye Dawn and Kelsey sat in the bedroom, watching TV while Kelsey ate. She only finished half. Raye Dawn says Kelsey sat in bed picking her toenails while mom put her make-up on for Jean's visit.

After she left that day, Jean would write a report saying the house was clean and that Raye Dawn bragged Kelsey had eaten a "whole bowl" of soup; she wasn't sure whether it was cream of mushroom or cream of chicken.

While Jean was there Raye Dawn told Kelsey to stop picking at her toe. So the tiny blonde climbed out of her mom's lap and into Jean's. Kelsey showed Jean her baby toe on her right foot was red and sore. Her baby toe had no toenail polish. When Jean asked what was wrong with it, Kelsey told her, "I keep picking at it."

Kelsey wanted to watch, "Stuart Little", so Raye Dawn popped it in the VCR. She figured it would get Kelsey in the mood because a couple of hours later she was supposed to go with Gayla to see a movie. Jean could tell Kelsey was happy and excited about the trip to the movies.

Exactly one hour and sixteen minutes after Jean arrived, Raye Dawn says she looked at the house phone as she and Kelsey walked the caseworker outside. As Jean pulled out of the driveway, the mother and daughter were sitting on the porch steps looking at a turtle in the driveway.

It was the last time Jean would see Kelsey alive. She would get another report a couple of hours later saying Kelsey was dead.

When Bonner left she said Kelsey was fine. Something out of the ordinary was definitely going on behind those four walls. Who would tell? Not Kelsey. She wouldn't be able to.

Did the terror start once Jean shut the door? Who was the terrorist? For at least an hour and a half, Kelsey was alone at home with her mother, Raye Dawn.

Three people know what happened that day, one is dead, the other two point fingers at each other. We can only guess how Kelsey spent those last few hours of her life because Raye had lied under oath before.

She told the court she helped Kelsey move the turtle onto the deck. Kelsey didn't want to feed it because she thought there was a snake inside. Raye Dawn tried to explain to her that it was just a turtle. She left Kelsey on the deck with the door open while she went inside to get a drink.

When she walked back outside, Raye Dawn says Kelsey had gotten some leaves off the bushes and was throwing them at the turtle. When she was out of leaves, Raye Dawn says Kelsey followed her back into the kitchen and said, "Mommy I had an accident."

Between 1:30 and 2:00 p.m., Raye Dawn took off Kelsey's clothes, leaving the two-year-old wearing nothing but a black t-shirt. No diaper.

Raye Dawn says she tried to feed Kelsey lunch but she was being stubborn as usual. Raye Dawn insisted, "You have to eat something."

When Kelsey refused, her mom sent her to time out.

Kelsey went to time out in her room; Raye Dawn went to the bathroom. When she finished, Raye Dawn heard little footsteps coming down the stairs. Kelsey's little voice said, "Mommy, I want some berries."

Raye Dawn says Kelsey meant she wanted raisins. The toddler took the big steps slowly. Once she made it almost all the way downstairs, Kelsey fell into her mom's arms. Raye Dawn caught her and they both laughed.

While Raye Dawn put a Thanksgiving table cloth on the table, Kelsey helped decorate. Raye Dawn says Kelsey sat on the floor and put festive stickers on the window.

When they were done, Raye Dawn got Kelsey a box of raisins from the pantry and then told her, "Mommy is tired, I'm going to go lay down."

Raye Dawn says Kelsey said, "I lay by you."

Before they got into bed Raye Dawn says she called Porter to tell him they were lying down to take a nap. The two went into the master bedroom around 2:00 p.m. Raye Dawn says she knows the time for a fact because when they got in the bedroom, Montel Williams was already on. Montel comes on at 2:00 p.m. on Channel 43.

———

Kelsey took the box of raisins with her to the King size bed. She took each raisin out individually and would close the box each time. Raye Dawn says she told Kelsey to close the box, but the two-year-old was, well, just being two when she said, "Mommy, I have to get some."

"Well get some," replied Raye Dawn.

Raye Dawn says they laid there for a minute before Kelsey said, "Mommy I love you so much."

"I love you too Kels," said Raye Dawn.

Mommy and daughter drifted off into sweet slumber. Did Kelsey ever wake up from this afternoon ritual? We will never know.

Kelsey fell asleep on her back, under the covers. Raye Dawn says there were four or five pillows on the bed; Kelsey had one underneath her head and possibly a pillow on each side of her.

In Meeker, Kelsey's step-dad finished his day. Mike Porter jumped in his car and headed east on Highway 62.

Before he left work for the day around 2:30 p.m. Michael Porter called one of his best friends, and employee, Mike Taber. Mike and Mike had been friends for 17 years. Taber had worked for Midwest Industries before Porter's parents died and continued the job once their son took over. Porter told his friend to come over to look at some tires Taber was thinking about buying. Taber says Porter told him that if he wanted to see them, he would have to come out to the house right after he got off work at 3:00 pm. Porter insisted if Taber couldn't make it right then they'd have to do it another time. Taber told Porter he had to pick up his son from school but would probably stop by right after that.

When Raye Dawn woke up from her nap she says Porter was standing at the edge of the bed. Raye Dawn slipped out from under the covers watching carefully to see if Kelsey would wake up. When she didn't, Raye Dawn said she would go pick up Whitney from school. Many people say she never made that trip alone. October 11, 2005, she insisted. Kelsey was sleeping; there was no need to wake her up. They had been in bed 40 minutes.

Raye Dawn left Kelsey at home even though earlier that day she told her mom she would take Kelsey along. The plan was to drop Kelsey off with Gayla at work. That way Gayla didn't have to drive to Meeker to pick her up for the movies. Raye Dawn even told Porter that morning she would take Kelsey to Shawnee to pick up Whitney.

Raye Dawn wanted to show Porter the turtle Kelsey was playing with earlier so they left the bedroom and walked downstairs. When they couldn't find the turtle, Raye Dawn got ready to leave.

Around 2:50 p.m., the phone rang. It was Porter's best friend, Wendell Kelley. Raye Dawn answered in a huff. She handed the phone to Porter and then grabbed the keys to leave. Raye Dawn got into the truck and started backing out of the driveway.

Porter remembers Raye Dawn rolled down the window and said, "Take care of my baby."

He nodded his head and rolled his eyes.

Raye Dawn told her husband to, "Take care of my baby!" Raye Dawn claimed that's what she told everyone who watched Kelsey. Wendell says Raye Dawn was obviously aggravated he'd called.

Two kids create a lot of laundry. Porter was accustomed to washing clothes for his daughters and his wife. Sometime after Raye Dawn left to pick up Whitney he walked past the master bedroom and he heard a low sounding noise. A noise he later described as a guttural sound. The noise was coming from the bed where his two-year-old step-daughter was sleeping.

Michael Porter

Agents asked Porter to recall everything he could remember about October 11, "You talked to Kelsey?"

Porter replied, *"And she talked to me. I said, 'Are you being good for Mommy?'*
And she said, 'Yeah.'
And I said, 'Well, Daddy is going to be home after a while.'"

Michael's voice cracked as he continued, "And she said, 'Okay. I love you Daddy.' We did not do this. You have to help us."

"Well you keep saying 'we' and I understand why you're saying we, okay. I understand that. But you don't know what happened when you weren't there, and Raye Dawn doesn't know what happened when she wasn't there."

"We know when you came home, the baby was asleep. What is rational thinking going to tell you about something like that? Rational thinking is probably going to give you the same thought process that I have. Could someone else have come in and done that? Not very likely, but I guess it's possible."

"As outlandish as that seems, it's more possible than Raye Dawn doing it."

"That's emotional thinking. Emotional thinking isn't going to get this thing resolved."

Porter grabbed his heart, "I know what happened when I was there and I did not hurt her and I know Raye Dawn didn't hurt her."

Tanner pressed further, "Well you know you didn't, okay, but you weren't there when Raye Dawn was with her alone."

"No, no," exclaimed Porter.

"What is going on with your heart right now? Do I need to call an ambulance, Mike?" asked Tanner.

"No," Porter leaned to the edge of his chair, put one hand on either cheek and began rocking in his chair and twitching his right leg up and down.

"Mike do you need me to call an ambulance?"

"No, Steve. This is wrong."

"What's wrong, Mike?"

"This is wrong. This is wrong."

"What's wrong, Mike?"

Porter cried, "This is wrong."

"What part of this is wrong?"

Porter took his pointer finger and began hitting his leg, "Nobody hurt her. We did not hurt her, Steve. This is wrong."

Porter stood up and walked toward the door pacing back to his chair. Again, the camera recorded Raye's voice screaming in the next room. Porter either didn't hear it or didn't care.

"Steve, I don't have it. We don't have it in us to hurt children, Steve. I don't have it. I have children. I can't. We don't have it in us to hurt children. It's not..."

"Let me ask you this, Mike. You've known Raye Dawn for a year."

"Never. Never," exclaimed Porter.

Tanner interrupted, "You've known her for a year."

"Never, never. Steve this is wrong. I'm telling you this is wrong. We could not have hurt her Steve. This is wrong. You have to help us. This is wrong."

One hour forty-five minutes into the interview, Porter grabbed his heart again, and paced the room, "Oh shit, this is wrong. This is wrong. We loved that baby more than you could imagine."

"I don't disagree with you," said Tanner.

"Then how could we, how can you hurt something that you love? How can you do that? How can you hurt, how can you do it?"

"I don't know. That's what we're going to try to figure out. And I'm telling you. . ."

"That child was not intentionally hurt."

Tanner explained, "The Medical Examiner has determined that it could have been caused by squeezing. It could have been caused by blunt force trauma, a strike."

"No."

"That's what the Medical Examiner says."

"No."

"It wasn't caused by you, Mike?"

Porter looked at him as he said, "No, sir."

"Who's the other one that it could have been caused by?"

"I don't know. When I had her up and I was shaking her, I was shaking her up. I was doing this and she was falling back on my shoulder every time. I don't."

"Let me put this into perspective, okay. Let's say that I believed 100% of what you're telling me, okay. When you picked up. . .when you came home and Kelsey was asleep and three minutes later you heard her grunt and you went in and picked her up and started carrying her around, she already had those injuries. If I believe you 100%, she already had those injuries before you even came home."

But Porter shook his head, "No, no. It's not possible."

"Well, if we were to believe you 100%, which I don't have any reason not to believe you, those injuries were sustained to Kelsey sometime between 1:30 and 2:30 or 2:45 p.m. when you got home," said Tanner.

95

"No. Steve, I'm not...I can't...I know...I know in my heart what happened," Porter replied as he grabbed his heart again and tried to monitor his breathing.

"What?" asked Tanner.

"When I got home," finished Porter.

"Okay."

Porter continued, "And I know in my heart that Raye Dawn would ever hurt that child. And you're asking me. I can't."

"No, no, no. Because Steve, I know what you're saying, but if you're telling me that me or Raye Dawn intentionally did something to harm the child, you're wrong."

"I'm not saying you intentionally did it."

"Well non-accidental means that it wasn't an accident. And I can tell you that anything, whatever happened to that child, it was not done."

"Non-accidental, let's talk about that for a minute and let's talk about intentional, okay? Somebody doesn't spank their child thinking that they're going to end up dying. Somebody doesn't do some of the things that...the injuries that she had, thinking that that baby is going to die. They don't know that that's going to happen. They don't know that that's going to be the result of that little short period of time when they lost control. But that's not intentional Mike."

Raye Dawn Smith

Raye told agents she gave Kelsey Children's Tylenol Cold and Cough the night before.

Raye explained, "She sat in the kitchen floor, on the green rug, looking out the window at one point. And I said, 'Kelsey what are you doing?' And she said, 'Waiting on Grandma. Grandma coming to get me.' I said, 'Well, she will in a little bit. Not right now.' And she said, 'I want her to come get me.' And I said, 'She is. She's coming later.' And I said, 'Mommy promises.'" Raye's voice cracked as she told agents she missed her baby.

Za began to try to reason with Kelsey's mom, speculating Raye could have lost her temper when they were decorating for Thanksgiving. Za said, "I'll tell you what I think. I think it was when she was sitting on the floor in the kitchen when she was talking to you because earlier when you were talking about that, you were all upset."

"Because she's not here anymore," explained Raye.

"Did she break something on the table when she was putting that table cloth down?" asked Garrett.

"No."

"Did maybe something come off?"

"No."

"Did she knock something off of a counter top that might have caused the problem?"

Raye Dawn whined, "No, no, no."

"What was it?"

"I cannot believe this," whined the mother.

"Did you step on her? Was she on the floor and you accidentally stepped on her?"

"No."

"What was it? You did something to your daughter."

Raye screamed, "I did not. No, I didn't," and gasped for air.

"What could it have been? Was she on the floor? Were you jumping on the bed?"

"I did not hurt my daughter."

"Did she fall off the bed? What happened? You know what happened."

"No, I don't," screamed Raye as she slammed her hand against the chair.

"You know exactly what happened," insisted Garrett.

Raye Dawn's little temper tantrum continued, "No, I don't."

"Tell us what it was."

"I don't know."

"Was it an accident?"

"I don't know what happened."

"Well, either you're going to let us know it was an accident or it was intentional. Either you intentionally cold-bloodedly killed your daughter. . ."

Raye cut him off as she stood up and screamed, "Oh, my God."

". . .or you accidentally stepped on her or something happened. We need to know what it was."

For the infinite time, Raye repeated, "I did not hurt my daughter."

"Then who did?"

She could have pointed her finger at the only other possible suspect. Instead, she repeated, "I don't know."

"Raye, then what happened?" asked Za.

"I don't know. That's what I came up here for you all to tell me."

"We're telling you. We've told you this is the same conversation that we've been having for the last hour." They had been talking for two and a half.

Raye flailed her arms and replied, "I know.

"On the way back. I just kind of had a feeling something wasn't right. I don't know. That's when everybody said, 'Well, what do you mean?' I said, 'I can't explain it.' It's just

I can't explain it. But when I passed by my mom's work and her car wasn't there, I knew something was wrong. I didn't know. . .what it had to do with, but I just knew something had to be wrong because my mom is always at work."

Garrett asked, "What made you think that?"

"I don't know, that's what I can't explain. I don't know," said Raye.

S·E·V·E·N

October 11, 2005
From Debra Winn to DHS parties
"This is to notify of a child death in Lincoln County. The child is Kelsey Smith-Briggs, a custody child. The new referral number is 100942."

KELSEY SMITH-BRIGGS. The name became a number; a number with a secret. No combination of numbers reveals exactly what happened during the final hours of her life. Moments so horrific the little girl, whose smile had diminished day by day over the past 10 months, finally froze in anguish forever. She could not survive the final blow.

Raye Dawn says when she left to pick up Porter's daughter Whitney from Sequoyah Elementary school in Shawnee, Oklahoma Kelsey was sleeping, breathing, and appeared normal. Lawyers asked her when she left the house that day to pick up Whitney, "To your knowledge, had anyone abused her, hurt her, sexually abused her, or anything?" She said no.

Raye Dawn says it takes between 20 and 25 minutes to get to Shawnee. No one but Porter and Raye Dawn know exactly what time she left to pick up Whitney. Raye Dawn says it was not quite 2:50 p.m. because Porter got home at 2:45 p.m. She claims she drove the speed limit to Shawnee and by the time she arrived Whitney was one of the only children left. The teacher walked Whitney out to the truck around 3:10 p.m. Raye Dawn's next stop was a couple of minutes down the street. She picked up the mail at the house she and Porter used to live in on Chandler Street. Raye Dawn was expecting a child support check from Lance and a letter involving Kelsey.

October 11, 2005, at 3:16 p.m., David Jenkins, a volunteer for the Meeker Fire Department received a page to a home three miles east on Highway 62 for a child not breathing. Jenkins knew the address as Ray Smith's old house. His daughter and Raye Dawn were friends in high school.

When Porter discovered Kelsey was not breathing his first frantic call was to Raye Dawn's mom. Raye Dawn claims when she drove by and noticed Gayla's car wasn't at work, Raye Dawn had a sinking feeling something was wrong with Kelsey.

About the time Raye Dawn made it to Whitney's school, Michael Taber began the rough, bumpy trek up the Porter's driveway. Taber arrived at the exact time they had discussed on the phone a half hour earlier.

When Taber got out of the truck he noticed Porter was crying and appeared to be very upset. He was juggling the phone and a dying baby. The 911 operator was talking to the side of Porter's body. He was struggling to hold the phone to his ear as he screamed, "Oh my God. She's not breathing. What do I do?" Despite countless requests from the media and family members, no one knows exactly what was said that day. The 911 call was never recorded.

Taber knew something was seriously wrong when he saw Kelsey's face, "She looked like a baby doll. Her color wasn't right. It just wasn't right." Her eyes were halfway open and glazed. Her blue eyes had a dead, whitish color to them. Kelsey was not responding to her step-father's screams.

Taber grabbed the phone and told the 911 operator there was an emergency. He gave her basic directions. The operator told them to try to stimulate the baby by talking to her and rubbing her back.

Taber says he put his hand on Kelsey's back and started repeating, "Wake up Kelsey, wake up Kelsey."

That's when Gayla Smith pulled up the driveway and took Kelsey from Porter. Gayla put the dying two-year-old on the grass and tried to get her to wake up. Porter walked away from Kelsey into the grass, crying, "Oh, my God. Oh my God."

It took Meeker Fire and Rescue six or seven minutes to get to the address. It was more like ten before they made it up the driveway. David Jenkins and Greg Sebastian saw Gayla running down the driveway. She was holding Kelsey over her left shoulder. Gayla handed Kelsey to Jenkins who immediately recognized her as Kelsey Smith-Briggs.

Jenkins remembers Mike Porter screaming, "Oh my God," as he saw how blue Kelsey was. Jenkins took her to the back of the ambulance and shut the back door of the truck because he and Sebastian knew it was bad.

While it's not an exact science, doctors estimate 30 minutes after someone dies rigor mortis, the stiffening of the jawbone, sets in. At 3:28 p.m., Jenkins says rigor had not set in on Kelsey.

Kelsey had no pulse; she was not breathing; she had blue splotches all over her face. Everything from her lips to her tiny fingernails was blue. Her body was the temperature of the outside air, 80 degrees or so. She was not cold to the touch but Jenkins says at that moment Kelsey Smith-Briggs was clinically dead.

When Prague First Response arrived at the scene they tried to put a tube down Kelsey's throat to infuse her organs with oxygen. When that did not work they put a heart monitor on her. It flat lined.

Between 3:30 and 3:40 p.m. Raye Dawn pulled up to the house with Whitney and spotted the emergency vehicles. She raced up the driveway as her dead baby's body was handed from one person to another. Raye Dawn started screaming, asking what was wrong with her baby. She tried to get in the ambulance but they would not let her. Raye Dawn begged to see Kelsey saying if she could just hear mother's voice she would be okay.

When Raye Dawn asked Gayla what happened, Gayla just kept shaking her head and finally said, "I guess she had a seizure."

Raye Dawn screamed saying they needed an ambulance, a helicopter, something to get her to Children's Hospital.

The First Response ambulance rushed the two-year-old to Prague Hospital. It was the closest emergency room. Raye rode in the front seat of the ambulance.

Taber called his mother-in-law, a good friend of Kathie's, to tell her the news. She immediately called Kathie and the panic began for the Briggs family.

Melissa Gibson, a young Physicians Assistant, met emergency crews as they ran Kelsey into the E.R. She was the most experienced employee in the hospital that afternoon and was running the show. When she saw Kelsey she immediately noted the girl's eyes were fixed and dilated; her stomach was bloated. Gibson says they tried to put a different tube down Kelsey's throat in hopes of releasing the air in her stomach. Gibson remembers seeing two small bruises on Kelsey's face and shin not thinking they were anything out of the ordinary; however, this was the first child that would be pronounced dead under Gibson's care. The Physicians Assistant admits her primary goal was resuscitation, not noting bruises.

Gibson came out of the room to tell Raye Dawn they were still working on her daughter, but it was not looking good.

Finally, she had to break the news to the young mom, "I'm sorry but there's nothing we can do."

When the Smith's pastor, Charles Pearcy, arrived at the hospital he says Raye Dawn was sobbing, "Why did God take my baby?" Pearcy reached out to her and said, "Let's talk to Him and ask Him."

Pearcy remembers hearing what he would later describe as a really loud emotional noise in the hallway. The sound was agonizing and gut rendering. As the pastor approached Kelsey's step-father, Porter was throwing himself at the wall and beating the floor, saying, "Why did God do this? Why did he take Kelsey from me?" The pastor reached out to comfort him and Porter screamed, "No, no." At one point, Porter was so overcome with emotion he passed out.

All of the people in charge of protecting Kelsey were joined by OSBI agents at the hospital that afternoon: Yolanda Hunter, Donald Wheeler, Wes Priest, Carla Lynch, Porter, and Raye Dawn.

No one at the hospital called the Briggs family.

Yolanda Hunter called Donald Wheeler, who called Jean saying Kelsey apparently had a seizure and had been rushed to Prague hospital.

When Jean got to the hospital she saw Porter leaning against the wall. His eyes were red and moist from recent tears. He said OSBI agents were talking with Raye.

Jean walked inside and saw Raye Dawn sitting on the floor in the corner of a waiting room, surrounded by her friends and family. She stood up and gave Jean a hug. She told the caseworker she fed Kelsey some raisins and they took a nap. After Kelsey drifted off, Raye Dawn said she went to sleep as well. About a half hour later, she says Porter woke her up and told her it was time to go pick up Whitney. She got out of bed carefully so she wouldn't wake Kelsey.

Jean later noted, Raye Dawn's eyes were dry but her cheeks were stained with tears. Raye Dawn appeared to be in shock as she told Jean, "I'll wake up and then this will all be gone."

OSBI agents interviewed Jean about the hour she spent at the house.

While she was at the hospital Jean stopped to talk to Porter who didn't say much. His eyes welled up with tears a couple of times and he said seemingly to himself, "I don't know what's going to happen now."

Prague hospital nurses talked to Raye Dawn about an autopsy. She mentioned it to Porter who said he didn't want them to cut Kelsey open. Raye Dawn demanded the autopsy anyway saying she had to know what was wrong with her baby. She signed the piece of paper that would later lead investigators to arrest Porter for First Degree Murder. Little did Porter and Raye Dawn know, an autopsy would have been done with or without their signatures. Under Oklahoma law, an autopsy is standard procedure in any suspicious child death.

Nurses allowed Raye Dawn to hold Kelsey's body. She rocked her dead baby for an hour and a half before her family had to tear her away from her little girl's body.

People at the hospital remember seeing Porter and Raye Dawn talking. Raye Dawn would later tell investigators she and Porter did not talk until the ride home.

Investigators never declared the house where Kelsey was killed a crime scene. Raye Dawn left the hospital with Porter. They drove back to the big house together to gather some things. Either one of them had plenty of time and opportunity to destroy any potential evidence that could have left a clue about who killed Kelsey.

The mother, whose baby died while in the care of her husband, says she never thought to ask Porter what happened while she was gone. Raye Dawn told the courts she only asked Porter one question during that 20 minute drive back home. She asked, "Mike, when did she get a pull-up on?"

Raye Dawn said she noticed when she got out of the pickup that Kelsey had a pull-up on. She knew when they took a nap Kelsey was not wearing a pull-up. Porter explained he put one on Kelsey when he called 911. He thought the last thing they needed was for people to see her without any underwear. Raye Dawn replied, "I would have told them."

Raye Dawn Porter spent the night with the man who was supposed to "take care of her baby".

The next day, curious eyes spotted Porter and Raye Dawn at Walmart shopping for the new baby they were having together.

Michael Porter

Porter told investigators about the last conversation he had with Raye Dawn before she left to pick up Whitney, "She looked over at Kelsey and she said, 'I'm going to let her sleep.' And I said, 'Well, she's going to be mad at you.' And she said, 'Well, I'm going to let her sleep.' And she got up out of the bed, and we both walked into the kitchen. She put her shoes on and a couple of minutes later, she left. I'll never forget the last thing she said to me. She said, 'Take care of my baby.'"

Porter took a deep breath to hide the crack in his voice as he said, "I'm going to remember that the rest of my life. I don't know if I can do it, Steve. I hurt so bad right now. And Raye feels like that if she had been there, she could have got her out of it. So she said, 'Take care of my baby,' and she left."

"What was Kelsey doing?" asked Tanner.

"She was just laying. . .she was sleeping. I know that she was very deep into sleep because there was hardly a time whenever, if Kelsey is sleeping with somebody and that person gets up, she will wake up. I mean, she has been through so much in her life that she. . .she had, you know, separation anxiety for awhile. And that really affected her, and she was scared to death, you know, that she was going to be left or be taken away. So she. . .this day, she just didn't wake up. I mean, Raye got up. And I know I thought it was unusual that she. . .Kelsey didn't wake up. I mean she was okay. You know, that's the first time in awhile that I've seen Raye get up. . .and she'll tell you that. When she's lying with Kelsey and she gets up, Kelsey pops up. She wants to be. . .she wants to hang around with her mommy."

"And what position was Kelsey in?" asked Tanner.

Porter explained, "She was on her back and she was laying on a pillow. And I don't know if she had half of her covered up. And it didn't look like she had rolled around or anything, which was strange in itself, because she, you know, there are kids that are rollers and movers, and she will instinctively roll to her mom."

Tanner pressed for more details, "Was Kelsey breathing?"

"I didn't pay attention. I mean, I couldn't tell. I don't know. I didn't get down and feel her chest. I just knew, I noticed that she didn't get up and I thought, 'Man, she must be out.' She must have been tired.

"She was really excited that morning too. She was up when I came in and took her down to sleep with Raye in the morning, she was actually up waiting for me."

"Kelsey was?" asked Tanner.

Porter continued, "Yeah, I mean every morning when I come and get her the first thing I'll say, 'Baby you want to go lay'. . .and she was up out of that bed just jumping. And she

---

would have her legs wrapped around me and squealing. She was just so happy. And she'd say, 'Thank you, Daddy.'"

"From the time that she left, how long was it before you heard the grunt?" asked Tanner.

"I couldn't put a time on it. The only thing I can tell you is leading up to that is just empty space. But after. . .that's when it gets. . .after I saw her, that's when. . .no, I don't know, because I was just. . .I mean, I wasn't looking at a clock. I wasn't on a schedule. I don't know. I mean if I had to guess, I'd guess. . .I couldn't put it down to within five minutes, I don't think. Fifteen, 25 minutes, I don't know. I know the best way to tell you how long it is, is when I called Gayla was right after I picked her up. And I tried to wake her, and then I could tell that this was different. And my first reaction, I knew Gayla was closest. And as far as we live out in the country, I panicked and I just called Gayla and I said, 'Gayla, I need help.'"

Tanner asked, "After you walked by your bedroom door and heard Kelsey grunt, you went inside the room?"

"I ran into the room," said Porter.

Tanner continued, "And she was in the same position she was. . ."

Porter explained, "She was in the same position. Her head was kind of. . .I guess she wasn't sitting up, but her body was. I don't know what the word is. Is it flexion or. . .her body was in. . .she was. . .I mean she was flexed a little bit up, is what she was, like all her muscles were contracting. And she had her tongue out.

"As I picked her up, she was rigid. I mean, she appeared rigid on the bed. But when I picked her up and I tried to wake her up, I was on the phone with Gayla, and then she loosened up. And that's when I knew that. . .I mean, it was getting dangerous because she loosened up and she just. . .I mean, she had nothing."

"Were her eyes open?" asked Tanner.

"Yeah, her eyes were. . .they were open, but they were closing."

"As far as the breath and the chest compressions, I mean, you said you had some training in CPR but not a lot?"

Porter said, "No, I mean, not even enough to know if I was helping her or hurting her. But I do know that after two or three cycles of the compressions that I got a response. And the lady on the phone heard the response and she said, 'Is that her?'

"And I said, 'Yes, that was her.' And she said, 'Keep talking. Keep talking.' So at that point I thought that maybe she had. . .that maybe she had come back enough. And then I picked her up and. . .and I picked her up and I was talking to them and I was just trying to get them there," cried Porter, "When we went down the steps on the porch, she fell back. And her arms." Porter broke down, as he demonstrated how her arms fell back.

Porter continued, "By the time I made it to the door, I mean, it seemed like maybe that was the last that she had. When I went down the steps, she fell back and her head was. . .I mean, her head went all the way back."

Tanner asked, "Can you tell me. . .do you have any idea what that explanation would be?"

"There's no. . .there's no way that any of the things that I did trying to help her, that I could have hurt her?" asked Porter.

Tanner replied, "No, sir. We asked that question specifically to the Medical Examiner. There is absolutely no way that giving chest compressions would have caused the injuries."

"I mean, in her abdomen. . .Steve, I don't know. I don't know, she's so small."

"I don't know where I put the hand and where all I squeezed her and where all I was trying to get her to wake up. I know I was out of my mind with panic."

Porter leaned back, again, and put his hand on his heart, "Could I believe that some of the things that I was doing to try to help her, possibly hurt her? I've told Raye Dawn that I pray to God that when I was doing any of this stuff that I didn't hurt her. But at the same time, I can tell you that nothing that I did was intentionally to hurt her."

"Did you do anything to hurt her?" asked Tanner.

"Never," exclaimed Porter.

"Never?"

Porter said, "Intentionally. I mean, Steve, that's what I'm saying. In trying to help her, I don't know what I did. I don't know where all I grabbed her and where all I squeezed her and where all I tried to shake her to get her to wake up and where all I pushed. I don't know. But it doesn't sound like any of that matters to you.

"I don't know everything I did when I picked her up. Now, the time frame. . .but I mean, I do know every. . .I mean do I know if I did it too. . .I mean if I. . .I don't know if I squeezed her too hard Steve. I don't know. But if you're telling me none of that matters, then. . .I mean."

Tanner said, "What I'm telling you is those injuries were. . .to believe you that she was already in bed, then those injuries happened before you got home okay. Or you're not telling the truth about whether she was in bed when you got home and you did it. So that's. . .that's what we're thinking."

Porter speculated, "If I leaned on her and put my weight on her."

Tanner clarified, "Those types of things were explained to the Medical Examiner. I didn't explain the one about you leaning on her and stuff because I didn't know about it at the time, but the other stuff that you told me about shaking her. And you don't know how hard you shook her. And you don't know when she fell back like that when you went down the steps with her. If you grabbed her around the waist or if your hand was still under her butt and stuff like that. Those are the things that I've explained to them."

"I weigh 275 pounds," said Porter.

"Yes, you do. You're a big fellow."

Raye Dawn Smith

"I had feelings when she would just be awake, when she would wake up in the middle of the night," Raye said.

"But she didn't wake up," said Garrett.

Raye chided back, "I don't understand why a maternal instinct is getting turned around to thinking you did something wrong."

Garrett answered, "Because your daughter got hurt from 1:15 to 2:45 p.m. when she was with you. And you claim you don't know anything that occurred and you were with her the entire time and she's laying in bed with you.

"Even if you, even if I believe that you didn't have anything to do with what happened to Kelsey, and the reason I can't believe that is because there was no one else there, I still don't understand how you would not have some kind of explanation as to what might have happened that caused your child to die. Not be sick. Not take a trip to the hospital. Die. Die. And you have no explanation? You have nothing to say? The best that you have is, 'I don't know'?

Garrett continued, "If you won't tell us what happened, then you're making us think that you killed her on purpose."

"I don't know what happened to my daughter!" screamed the exasperated mother.

"How did she get her injuries?" asked Garrett.

"God, I don't know. I thought you all was going to tell me what happened to her."

Garrett continued, "And we did. We told you exactly what the Medical Examiner said. I read everything off my notes to you that I made yesterday and what I found out today. I've told you that."

Time and time again, Raye Dawn told investigators she did not hurt her daughter. Hours into the interrogation, Raye paused after she said, "I didn't kill. . ." and corrected herself saying, "I did not hurt my daughter."

The OSBI agents did not pick up on Raye's misstep. Garrett and Za continued, "Those injuries took place by somebody squeezing her too hard. They might have hit her in the stomach; they could have kneed her in the stomach; they could have kicked her in the stomach."

Raye Dawn started making sounds that appeared to be sobs, but no tears were visible. Garrett ignored her display of emotion and continued, "It's taken somebody applying lots and lots of pressure. That's what killed Kelsey. And you know, we don't think you did it intentionally. We think it was an accident."

"I didn't hurt my daughter," insisted Raye.

"We really think it was an accident. We don't think you woke up that morning intending to hurt her. We don't think you did it on purpose," said Garrett.

Almost trying to convince herself, Raye repeated, "I did not hurt my daughter."

Garrett got stern, "The Medical Examiner is telling us that you had to have been the one who killed her."

"There is no way!" screamed Kelsey's mom, "There is no way. How can you all say that?"

"We know it was an accident. We just need you to tell us it was an accident."

"I did not hurt my baby!" exclaimed Raye.

"This was not meant to happen," chided Garrett.

"Stop it!" screamed Raye Dawn.

"What did she do that upset you so much?"

"I did not hurt my baby."

"Raye Dawn look at me," interrupted Garrett.

She growled, "There is no way."

"Look at me. What took place?"

"Nothing. I did not hurt my baby. How can you sit there and ask me that?"

Garrett answered, "Because it's my job. And I've got to know because the ME is thinking you killed her and I don't think that."

Raye Dawn never outright denied killing Kelsey. That one time she said, "I didn't kill. . ." but never finished her thought.

Raye Dawn swore on her daddy's grave twice.

Garrett gave Raye another opportunity to blame Porter, "Do you want us to believe if you didn't do this, then somehow from the time that you go to get Whitney, that your husband, the guy you love, who is the father of the baby you're going to have, that he did something like this to Kelsey?"

"No," answered Raye.

"Do you think for one second that he did this to your daughter?"

Raye did not hesitate and quickly replied, "No."

"You didn't want this to happen," said Garrett.

"I did the best I could," cried Raye.

"I know. I believe that. And we know you didn't want this to happen to Kelsey."

Raye Dawn continued, now crying what appeared to be real tears, "I didn't."

"Raye these are the first real tears you've had all day and we feel for you. We know that you didn't want this to happen," said Garrett.

"I've cried and cried and I've cried," exclaimed Raye.

"And we're sorry they didn't give you the help. We really are. And we'll try to make it better for the other people who are in your situation. Were you scared that she was going to die on you? Were you scared that her health was bad?"

Raye explained, "That's why I had her checked from head to toe. I had blood work done. . .I had a bone density test done...she was supposed to have another one done because it came back inconclusive."

"But what about you? You've got to take some responsibility. You're the adult. You're the mother."

"I feel like I've failed," cried Raye. But she refused to take any further responsibility for the crime.

LANCE AND RAYE DAWN ON THEIR WEDDING DAY.

KELSEY AND RAYE DAWN

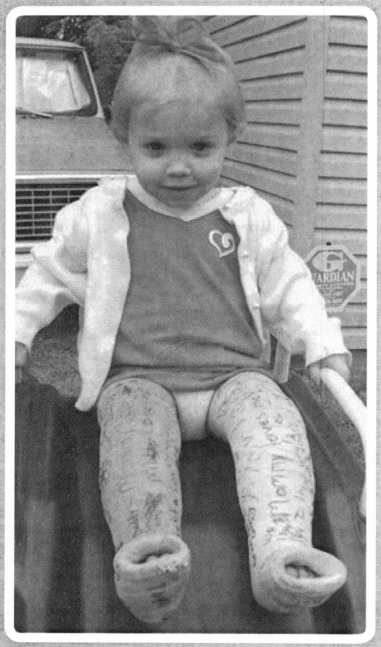

KELSEY'S TWO BROKEN LEGS

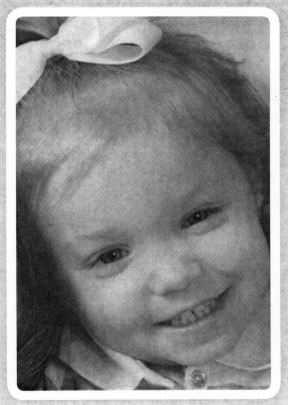

KELSEY'S BIG SMILE

MICHAEL PORTER AND RAYE DAWN SMITH'S MUG SHOTS

LANCE STANDING BY HIS DAUGHTER'S GRAVE

E·I·G·H·T

EVERYONE IN THE BRIGGS FAMILY LEARNED OF KELSEY'S DEATH OVER THE PHONE.

Jeanna was at work when her mom called hysterical. In a tone she had never heard her mom use, Kathie said, "Get home now. Kelsey is not breathing." Jeanna grabbed her purse and left Tinker Air Force Base in Midwest City to begin the 35 minute panicked drive to Meeker. While she was driving, Jeanna called her husband to tell him the news.

Shirica was sitting at her desk in the insurance office, just two blocks from Prague hospital when her mom called. Shirica took a chance and called a friend who worked at the clinic attached to the hospital, in hopes of finding out how Kelsey was doing. Shirica's friend could have been fired for giving out patient information, but Shirica knew the Briggs would not be welcome at the hospital.

The next 30 minutes felt like seconds for Shirica, as her phone continued to ring. Everyone was calling for an update. Her friend called back saying a couple of women were comforting Raye Dawn and that Porter seemed agitated. Shirica cannot imagine what her co-workers were thinking as she bounced between phone calls, finally demanding her friend get Kelsey's condition.

Kathie was on hold as Shirica took the call from her friend, who still regrets telling Shirica that way. All her friend said to Shirica was, "I'm sorry." At the hospital she heard someone tell Raye Dawn that Kelsey was gone and heard the mother begin screaming, "My baby! My baby!"

Shirica instinctively clicked over to her mom and said, "Mom, she's gone." Another regret. She never should have told her mom over the phone. She still replays that moment in her mind, wishing she had driven home to tell her in person. The sound that came through the phone will haunt Shirica for the rest of her life. It was painful. Horrendous. And the phone went dead.

Kathie was looking outside the front door when she learned the news. All she remembers is instantly falling to her knees. Kathie banged the phone on the floor in anguish, screaming, "Why!" and yelling, "No, God, please no." She doesn't know why the first phone call she made was to Teri Sigman.

Her fingers trembled as she dialed Teri's number. Teri was on her way home from work. All Kathie could manage to say was, "Kelsey is gone." The next call she made was to her husband, Royce. Kathie regrets not waiting the few extra minutes until he got home. The drive for him was the longest of his life.

Scared for her mother's life, Shirica called Jeanna. Jeanna was passing the Meeker cemetery when she learned of Kelsey's death. She knew she had to get to her mom as quickly as possible, so she turned on her hazard lights and called her husband to tell him Kelsey had died. Randy Fowler screamed, "No," and told her to pull over. Jeanna wanted to stop, but couldn't because she knew her mom was alone and she had to get home.

Shirica thought Robynn may have been closer than Jeanna, so she called her younger sister and told her to go to Mom. The conversation was brief; Shirica didn't tell Robynn, Kelsey had died.

Jeanna beat Robynn home that afternoon. She found her mother on the floor convulsing, screaming, and sobbing. Jeanna's feet were frozen at the door. She didn't know what to do but stand there and watch. She had never seen her mom cry before. Her mother was the one who comforted them. She didn't know how to comfort her comforter.

Jeanna stood by the door as Robynn pulled up and rushed inside, throwing herself on the floor and holding her mother.

Shirica doesn't remember driving home. She had to call her ex-husband and tell him to pick up the kids. Once she got to the driveway of the house she grew up in, she allowed herself to realize Kelsey was gone. She broke down sobbing. When Robynn's little girl, Ashton, started tapping on the window of the car, Shirica knew she had to pull herself together for the children. Robynn brought the kids because she didn't know Kelsey died.

Royce immediately decided he would catch the first flight to Georgia to tell Lance in person. He knew his son was in too delicate a frame of mind to learn the news of his daughter's death over a payphone.

By the time Royce pulled up to his home, he was too late. Lance already knew about Kelsey's death.

Inside, Robynn answered a phone call. Lance's voice greeted her with a hello. It was almost a sad fate that he called in the midst of their grief. The girls were so focused on getting to their mom; they hadn't thought about Lance yet. At first, they didn't want to tell him. But the emotions were overwhelming and they were hardly able to comprehend the news for themselves.

Kathie took the phone and pressed it against her ear. Her voice cracked and her words sounded foreign to her own ear. She did not know how to say it. Once she told him his daughter was dead, she did not know how to comfort him. In hopes his sisters could help, Kathie put the phone on speaker. The sounds coming from the other side of the line were not human.

The line went dead. Lance learned about his daughter's death standing at a payphone in Georgia. They knew Lance never should have been told over the phone. Jeanna immediately began calling the Red Cross to get him on a flight home. She called the base where he was stationed and told security they had to find her brother. The red tape associated with the military only added to her frustration. She works on a military base and knew they would have to drive to every pay phone to find him. Picturing her brother far away learning that news, was eating her alive. Finally base security found Lance, handed him money collected for his flight, and took him to the chaplain before his trip.

Royce's parents offered to go to the hospital to see if they could get information. When they walked into the hospital, Gayla greeted them with angry screams. She called for security and demanded they leave. Security escorted the 80-year-old couple out of the hospital.

Soon friends began stopping by with food. Before they left for the airport to pick up Lance, a family friend, Michelle Webb, came over and asked to lead a family prayer. Their weakened bodies stood and joined hands. Michelle did not rehearse what she would say that night; but her words were almost prophetic, "Let that which was done in darkness be brought into light."

No one in that room knew how Kelsey died. The Briggs believe Kelsey spoke to them through Michelle that night. The family would repeat that prayer in the years to come but it was never answered. Other than Kelsey, only two people know who was hurting her in the darkness.

The family headed to Will Rogers World Airport in Oklahoma City to pick up Lance. At the airport, their bodies were close but their minds were far away. Each of them sat in silence, lost in their own thoughts. When Lance's plane arrived, a seemingly endless line of people walked out of the terminal into the waiting area. Lance was one of the last people off the plane.

The Briggs family still wonders what the other passengers were thinking. Nearly a dozen people were standing there, waiting for a soldier to get off a plane. There were no flags, no cameras, only tears. And he, unlike so many others, survived the war. The other passengers and their families would hear that soldier's story on the news in the months and years to come, but would they realize they were a part of that intimate moment, when a soldier had to be carried out of the airport because his heart was broken?

Lance collapsed in Royce's arms. He begged his family to tell him they were lying. That it was not true. Royce helped him over to the wall where he leaned against the stone. Royce held him as he cried. He wanted his daughter. He sobbed as he told them about the stuffed camel he bought in Iraq and brought back for her. He had been saving it for months.

Royce took him off to the side as the rest of the family waited for his luggage.

Ashley came to the airport with her parents. For Lance, she was an unwelcome guest. He saw her but could not bring himself to acknowledge her presence. He could not understand why she would make the trip. She was no longer a part of his life. She walked out on the little girl she once claimed as her daughter.

Once they got to the van, Lance called Carla Lynch, the woman who was supposed to bring Kelsey to the airport to meet him. He was angry but the girls were proud he held himself together. He wanted to get information about his daughter's death. At that point everyone was speculating she died from a seizure. Lance mentioned that he wanted to ask Judge Key why he gave her back. That phone call would be construed by DHS as a threat against the caseworkers and the judge's life. It was another effort to deflect blame from their mistakes.

Lance would not go to his parents' house that night. He wanted to go to his home. He wanted to be with Kelsey's things. Ashley didn't go home with him that night or ever again. Lance spent the night alone. Without his wife. And without his daughter.

Ashley had left Kelsey's room exactly the same.

It was the second blow in less than a month, and Lance could no longer handle the pain. He lost his daughter and his wife.

He walked to the store that night and bought a case of beer. He stayed home to drown his sorrows, alone.

That night he drank until he passed out. He did not stop from then on.

Lance Briggs drank every single day for the next 9 months.

1:42 a.m. rolled around and Kathie sat down at her computer to write yet one more email. This one announced Kelsey's death to every television station in Oklahoma City and the lawmakers who did not protect her granddaughter. She did not expect a response. She hadn't been able to get anyone to listen; this time would be no different.

Sent: 10/12/2005 1:42 AM
Subject: Kelsey Smith-Briggs
"I recently wrote to each of you asking for help. My son was in Iraq and his two-year-old daughter was in DHS custody because of abuse. Well, my two-year-old granddaughter died this afternoon. I picked up my son at the airport, and it was the hardest thing I have ever had to do. The OSBI is investigating her death and now I am asking you, any of you, to make sure this investigation is done properly. I feel my little Kelsey deserves for the truth to finally come out. If just one person would have listened to my cries for help earlier, our precious little girl might still be here."

Within 24 hours phone numbers for every television station in the state popped up on the Briggs Caller ID. Reporters began calling, asking the family for interviews. To accommodate all of the calls, Jeanna had to change her cell phone package from hundreds to thousands of minutes.

An Iraqi war vet, government failure, and a beautiful dead baby-it was the perfect combination to feed the competitive Oklahoma media.

One of Oklahoma City's veteran, aggressive reporters knew better than to call. She just knocked. Having covered big stories in small towns for years, Cherokee Ballard and her photographer figured it would not be difficult to track down the Briggs home. It might take a stop in the town diner or the local gas station, but she knew the best way to get an interview with mourning families is to just show up. As she expected, the family was not difficult to find. The day after Kelsey died, Cherokee spotted a sign on the side of the highway marking the Briggs home. It read:

God Bless
SPC Lance Briggs
U.S. Army. Fighting in Iraq

That sign would soon be replaced by a large picture of their dead granddaughter. It read, "Justice for Kelsey."

As Cherokee got out of the news vehicle, Jeanna spotted her through the door. Jeanna was surprised Cherokee Ballard was at their door and rushed to tell Kathie. Jeanna answered the knock and explained the family was not ready to do an interview. Cherokee immediately respected their wishes and walked away. It was her compassion for their grief that made them grant her one of their first interviews.

For days to come, someone had to be in the Briggs home to answer the phone. Family, friends, and people they had never met were calling nonstop. The caller ID would overflow with the numbers of people touched by the story of their precious little Kelsey.

Many of those calls were from reporters. Britten Follett, another reporter in Oklahoma City had spoken with Jeanna a couple of times since Kelsey's death. Her producers were waiting for the Medical Examiner to determine a cause of death before running a story. There was still a chance Kelsey died of a seizure.

When the phone rang that afternoon, Kathie, Royce, Lance, Jeanna, Royce's parents, and other family members were sitting in Kathie's living room. Jeanna was sitting in front of the fireplace in a child-sized rocking chair. She answered the phone.

"Hi Jeanna. It's Britten Follett."

Britten continued without hesitation, "Since the Medical Examiner says it was a homicide...blunt force trauma to the abdomen...we're going ahead with the story. Do you think you or someone in the family would be able to do an interview?"

Jeanna knew her brother was staring at her, trying to judge her facial expressions. Jeanna tried to keep her composure as she apologized to Britten explaining she would have to call her back.

Just like they learned of Kelsey's death over the phone, they learned of her murder from a 24-year-old girl they had never met. As Britten hung up the phone, she realized no one had told the family Kelsey was murdered. A wave of nausea came over her knowing her words would change their lives forever. She instantly wished she could have taken back the phone call. As a reporter, she often found herself approaching grieving families to ask for interviews. This was different. She thought they knew. She couldn't understand why no one had called to warn the family this delicate information was about to be released.

The room was silent as Jeanna said, "Britten says the Medical Examiner said the cause of death was blunt force trauma to the abdomen, homicide." Sobs and screams once again pierced the silence. Lance ran out of the house screaming, "They killed her. They killed her. They killed my baby." The family followed Lance outside wondering how they could comfort their soldier. His Grandpa Briggs reached him first and tried to console him.

This news was not a shock to Teri. The First Lady of Oklahoma, Kim Henry, and first cousin to her husband had called the night before. She told them Kelsey did not die of natural causes. She had called them several times a day since Kelsey's death. Once it was ruled a homicide and she knew the state could be held liable, the calls ended. The First Lady would no longer return their calls either. Kim Henry's in-action cost her Governor husband some votes from his own family.

An afternoon spent comforting Lance turned into an evening of comforting the grandchildren. The girls were at Kathie and Royce's house preparing to tell their children about Kelsey. Once they learned Kelsey had been murdered, they couldn't put it off any longer. News travels fast in a small town and the children needed to hear this from their parents.

Shirica took her little ones home that day after school. Crying herself, she sat them on the love seat. Shirica sat on the floor with one hand on each of their legs.

Her voice sounded foreign, so did her words, "I'm going to tell you something that's going to be the worst thing that you have ever heard in your whole life."

She looked into Kyle and Bridgette's innocent eyes and told them Kelsey had died. No one close to them had died. They started screaming, "No! No!" And then Bridgette shut down. She stopped talking and showed no emotion.

As Bridgette detached herself from the situation, Kyle barged outside and started running up and down the sidewalk. He didn't know how to deal with his feelings. Kyle and Kelsey were close. Kelsey called her cousin, "My Kyle." Kyle asked for Kathie, the one person who was not in any condition to be around her grieving grandchildren. When Shirica told her son that grandma couldn't see him just yet, he asked to talk to the police. He wanted to help them solve the mystery. He wanted to help the adults. Kyle told his mother he knew Porter did it. He thought Raye Dawn was still very bad because she should have protected Kelsey. She was Kelsey's mommy. Shirica winced at her son's reaction. It was the hardest thing she's had to do as a parent, more difficult than telling her little ones they were leaving their father.

Kelsey's cousins Zachary and Ashton were sitting on the living room floor when their mom Robynn broke the horrific news of Kelsey's death. Zachary immediately started crying. Ashton began asking questions. At ages seven and eight, the kids immediately blamed Kelsey's mom. Mothers don't let their children get hurt.

The only cousin who was spared the turmoil of the time was Sadie. She was only 12-months-old and couldn't understand why everyone was so sad.

A few blocks away Jeanna and her husband Randy broke the news to Kelsey's 5-year-old cousin. Randy had been home with Eryn for a couple of days. They kept her home from school to shield her from what her classmates may have heard about Kelsey on the news. Randy knew Kelsey's death would change his relationship with his family forever. Randy's father and Raye Dawn's mother, Gayla, are brother and sister.

Because of the small town and family dynamics Randy and Jeanna knew they had to tell their daughter before she went back to school. But how? Jeanna didn't know how to deal with it herself. Much less, protect her little one.

Randy and Jeanna sat Eryn down on the couch and told her Kelsey was dead. The 5-year-old jumped off the couch, ran to her parent's bedroom, and locked the door. For a half hour Jeanna tried to talk to her daughter through the door. Finally she convinced Eryn to let just her in. Jeanna could barely keep from breaking down when she opened the door and saw Eryn crouched in a ball between the foot stool and the end of the bed. Jeanna held her daughter as she sobbed saying she didn't understand.

For months, Randy and Jeanna didn't tell Eryn that someone hurt Kelsey causing her to die. They don't know if they made the right decision. Eryn couldn't sleep at night because she was afraid she would stop breathing and die like Kelsey. Jeanna couldn't bring herself to explain that was not the way Kelsey died.

While Kelsey's family got ready for her funeral, Eryn took down the pictures of Kelsey in her room and wrapped them up. When Jeanna asked her what she was doing, Eryn said, "I just need them to be mine, so they're only mine when I want to look at them."

The Smith family wasted little time opening a bank account and putting an article in the paper asking for donations to pay for Kelsey's funeral and medical expenses. When the Attorney General's office got wind of the situation the A.G. immediately had the account closed. Kelsey's service was covered by the Victims Compensation Fund and medical bills were covered by the two medical insurance policies provided by Lance and Ashley and the state.

In the days and weeks that followed, many strangers would speculate about Raye Dawn's callous reaction to Kelsey's death. Raye Dawn's family stood by her side saying Kelsey's mom was just all cried out. Shirica posted this on the Internet:

"I can tell you what a grieving parent looks like. I saw one first hand on Oct. 11, 2005. I heard his voice on the phone when he was given the news that his precious baby girl was gone. The sounds that came from the phone were not the sounds of a human. They were sounds I will never forget for as long as I live.

The first thing he assumed when he knew bad news was coming was that something had happened to his mother, not his child. Parents do not automatically assume the news is going to be that their child is gone. Children are not supposed to go first.

He cried in complete disbelief. He said NO over and over. His words could not be understood.

He walked off of the airplane with blood shot eyes and tears that would not stop. He could barely stand. His knees could no longer hold him up. He had to lean on his own father. He asked if we had just played a cruel joke on him. His heart was literally ripped from his chest. He cried over and over how he just needed to give her the camel he had brought for her from Iraq.

He wanted to hold his baby girl just one more time. He was a broken man. He went home to her bedroom that night and touched all of her things and cried some more.

I sat next to this grieving parent at her funeral. He cried yet again. He could not speak. He could barely stand. His parents held onto him as if he were a child again. He could not begin to imagine standing up in front of all the people and speaking about himself. He would never be able to find the words. He walks up to the casket afterwards and hugs it. He does not want to let it go. That little box that sits at the front of the funeral home with his precious baby girl inside. He does not open it. He does not want the last memory of her to be this one. Instead he wants to remember her face as she looked so adoringly at him six months before.

He does not want to be seen in public. He wants to be left in peace with his memories. He then spends the next two days in the hospital for grief counseling because he cannot imagine another day without her here.

He just wants to hold her one more time. He wants to kiss her face one more time. He wants her to be able to lick his face one more time the way she did the last time he came home to see her. He wants to tell her he loves her. Instead he is left here with his broken heart and her memory.

He will have to hold onto those memories until they can be together again. He will have to continue to be strong the way she was for so long. He will have to try and make her proud the way she made him so very proud, the way she continues to make him proud everyday. He has to try and get by one hour at a time because getting by one day at a time is more than he can handle.

That is what a grieving parent looks like, or at least that is what an innocent grieving parent looks like."

Shirica's words brought back so many memories for Kathie, who wrote:

"The memory of that day will haunt us forever. Probably the hardest thing a person can do is tell a parent their child has died, especially when that parent is your own child. I had been called by a friend in town that Kelsey was not breathing and had been rushed to the hospital.

When the call came just minutes later that she had died I could not do anything but collapse on the floor and scream. I thought if I yelled "No" loud enough it would not be true.

I knew Lance would probably call any minute and when that phone rang I had to compose myself, forget my own pain, and be strong for my child.

Standing alone at a phone booth many miles from home is no way to hear devastating news. When he hung the phone up we no longer had a way to contact him. We called the Red Cross and found a number to his base and asked them to search for him.

Within five hours he landed in Oklahoma City. A soldier barely walking came towards us with so many uncontrollable tears. The strangers walking by could not imagine what was going on. This was not the homecoming we had planned, no American flags waving, no cameras, no children, just tears, tears, and more tears.

Now that day is in the distant past, and we must go on. Lance loved that little girl more than life itself. I only wish she had been born to two parents with that same feeling. He cannot understand how anyone could do this to his little girl, and why the adults in her life couldn't or wouldn't help her. He will go on, and he will continue to fight a war. This war won't be with his Army uniform on. This war will be for justice for his little girl. We are so very proud of Lance, Kelsey would be proud of him as well. God will guide him and with your continued prayers he will learn to laugh again."

Very proud mother of a soldier,
Kathie

A soldier who was cheated out of seeing his baby during the ultrasounds, watching his little girl's entrance into the world, choosing her name and the outfit she would wear home from the hospital; was also cheated out of choosing the outfit she was buried in, choosing her casket, choosing the plot at the cemetery, and watching as Kelsey was lowered into her final resting place.

Michael Porter

Tanner asked Porter, "You did nothing to that baby to cause the extent of the injuries that she had?"

Porter leaned over and said, "I'm going to be sick."

"Are you?"

"Yeah."

"Do you need to go to the restroom? Do you need to go to the restroom? Are you going to throw up?"

"Yeah."

"Don't throw up in here because they'll make me clean it," said Tanner

Tanner continued, "I think that it was probably an accident and that's why you're feeling so guilty about it."

"I'm not feeling guilty," scowled Porter.

"Oh, you're not? So it was an intentional thing? I mean. . ."

Porter cut Tanner off, "I'm not feeling guilty because what I was doing was trying to help her."

Raye Dawn Smith

"She's two years old. I mean, you need to help us. We need to try to figure out what happened to her. How she could have had those internal injuries? Are you really upset?" chided Garrett.

"How can you ask me that? I don't. . .I am in shock!" cried an exasperated Raye Dawn.

"Do you want to know how I can ask you that? I don't see a tear coming out of your face. There is not one drop. Look at me. There is not one drop," exclaimed Garrett.

"I have cried and cried and cried. And I'm in shock, I'm upset, I'm mad. I don't understand," screamed Raye.

"You wasn't crying Tuesday night," said Garrett.

"Yes I was," she said.

"You're like you are right now."

"I'm in shock. That was my daughter," said Raye.

Garrett asked again, "What happened to her?"

Four hours later, Kevin Garrett was no closer to answering that question.

———————

N·I·N·E

A FLY ON THE WALL INSIDE DHS WOULD HAVE BEEN DEAFENED BY THE SOUND OF FINGERS TYPING THE EMAILS EXCHANGED BETWEEN THE EMPLOYEES DIRECTLY INVOLVED IN KELSEY'S LIFE AND THOSE RESPONSIBLE FOR SOFTENING THE BLOW ONCE WORD OF HER DEATH LEAKED TO THE MEDIA.

George Johnson, the agency's media relations contact is a highly paid broken record. No matter what DHS does Johnson says the same thing, "Due to the confidentiality clause in child custody matters, I cannot comment specifically about this case." He usually goes on to say that there are thousands of children in state custody on any given day and the caseworkers are overworked and underpaid. He blames parents and says it is not the state agency's job to protect these children from the evils at home.

DHS Director Howard Hendrick and George Johnson received this email. It was a briefing of sorts on the case:

"There have been many e-mail communications from May 5, 2005, through September 6, 2005, to the director and many others concerning this child, but I am attaching the two that probably best summarize the whole situation. According to Debra, in a hearing June 14, since we could not determine with any degree of certainty who the perpetrator was from among 6 or so relatives, Judge Key did not accept our recommendation to continue placement with the grandmother, but instead placed with the mother and step-father, with limitations on the visitation of other relatives. His reasoning apparently was that if anything else happened to the child, at least we would know who the perpetrator is."

"I believe this has the capacity to be a very high profile situation, given the extreme criticism of OKDHS by all sides, and also due to the distant relationship to the First Lady."

They could not keep a two-year-old from being killed at home, but 24 hours after her death DHS began securing its locations in Lincoln and Pottawatomie counties, following what was perceived as a threatening phone conversation between a caseworker and Lance.

5:56 p.m.
Wednesday October 12, 2005
From: Mike Fairless
To: Cynthia Kinkade
Cc/Howard Hendrick

"Here's the plan: Agent supervisor Sherri Compton will supervise and roam between the two offices. She will be in Lincoln County in the morning then move to Pott County in time for the scheduled inter-views. Two agents are arranged for each location on both days.

Lincoln County-Rusty Rogers will be in Lincoln County. He is a new hire to us but is also an experienced cop and, as it happens, knows Lance Briggs by sight from his days as assistant chief at Meeker PD. He says Briggs is a "hothead".
Pott County-two officers running security
Both teams will check in with the respective county directors immediately on arrival and will alert the local PD in case they need assistance at some point. Agents will be armed and wearing body armor, but in civilian clothing with weapons covered. Their instructions should he arrive are to: 1) Immediately determine if he is armed. If he is to arrest him for bringing a weapon onto state property. 2) If he shows up unarmed and is behaving himself he will not be permitted further than the reception desk, but will be allowed to schedule an appointment for a later date and then asked to leave. Should he refuse the local police will be called, or we will arrest him, depending on his behavior.

We are obtaining a booking photo on Lance Briggs from a previous arrest so all agents will be able to identify him and work on additional intel. Also, we just determined a few minutes ago that Briggs' wife filed a protective order against him earlier today that they are looking to serve. I don't imagine he will take that well. That's about all I know at this time. I think we have it covered as well as we can given present information. If anything at all happens they will call me immediately and I will let you know."

Kathie blamed the extreme measures on the agency's guilt for not protecting Kelsey. Lance was at home, still in shock, and barely able to communicate basic needs. He couldn't eat and couldn't stop crying.

That same day DHS employee Wesley Priest called Kathie to ask if the family would come in for an interview. All of a sudden the state office wanted to know what happened to Kelsey. Kathie told him it was too late since her granddaughter no longer needed their protection.

But Priest insisted. Soon Kathie got a call from another employee who shared the news of the "secret" security and that they were out to get Lance. Kathie called Mr. Priest back and told him they would not be attending their appointment since the agency was more focused on security than fixing its fatal flaws.

Kathie says Priest was almost speechless. He asked, "How did you know that? It was a secret."

Lance and his family could only think about Kelsey. Confronting the agencies that failed her now seemed useless.

Later that day speculation began surfacing within DHS that Kelsey's death might not have been caused by a seizure. The office knew investigators were suspicious because of the history of abuse and inconsistent statements Mike Porter made.

Those involved in child deaths at DHS revealed the callous nature of the job through their personal emails. Protected by the cloak of secrecy surrounding DHS, the public has never seen these conversations.

From: Margaret Noble
To: Cynthia Kinkade and George Johnson
"This child death is going to be very high profile, I'm afraid. This is the child I went to Lincoln County about Cindy."

From: Kathy Sims
To: Cynthia Kinkade
"I think all of Oklahoma will know about this case after the news tonight and tomorrow. How is Margaret doing? I imagine this could be upsetting her."

From: Cynthia Kinkade
To: Kathy Sims
"It really is upsetting her. I'm somewhat surprised. I mean it's upsetting to all of us but it's not unheard of. I hope that doesn't sound cold, but I am considering telling her to go home for the rest of the day."

The same agency that did not protect Kelsey was now inquiring about the safety of Whitney, Kelsey's step-sister. Mike Porter had custody. But as of October 12, 2005, the day after Kelsey's murder, Judge Key was not willing to place the 9-year-old in state custody. He wanted more information. He needed to know for sure Kelsey's death was a result of abuse or neglect.

DHS child death investigators went to the house with OSBI. Neither agency saw anything unusual. Investigators reported discrepancies with time frames as to when Porter noticed Kelsey was not breathing and when he called 911.

One day after Kelsey's death, Kathie Briggs' letters began surfacing in the back of lawmakers' minds. She had written them begging for help in hopes of preventing this very thing. They too had better begin damage control. Otherwise, if it became public they had ignored the grandmother's plea for help; it could cost them elections. Representatives Kris Steele and Danny Morgan called the Briggs family directly. The Briggs would spend the months to come working with the two lawmakers on a law named after Kelsey, designed to protect other children from similar fates.

Morgan was the first Representative to call DHS inquiring about how she died.

Kathie Briggs wrote one more email to DHS and attached a picture of Kelsey that flashed on the news months before. Kelsey had been featured on a local meteorologist's "Hot Shots" and would be the face of child abuse in Oklahoma for years to come.

Kathie wrote Margaret Noble and Howard Hendrick at the DHS state office warning them there would be other child deaths if something was not done:

> "This is Kelsey, the little girl who won our hearts and the one we tried so desperately to keep safe and happy. Please remember her when the next grandmother or family member comes to you. Her life had a purpose and we seek to find out exactly what it was. If it was only to give us love and joy for two short years then she succeeded, however I feel it was more than that. My wish is that no other family feels the pain we are feeling right now."

Margaret was not sure how to respond. Two days following her death, DHS was already concerned about a lawsuit.

> Cindy,
> "The Director and I received this email this morning. Would it be appropriate for me to respond, offering my condolences?"
> Margaret
> RE:
> "Be mindful there may be a lawsuit down the road. I am sure HHH will send his condolences also." Thanks, Cindy

An internal email revealed Judge Key would not protect Kelsey from abuse but did protect his own children. The email reads:

> "While in Lincoln County we learned the judge has hidden his own children out someplace 'till this blows over. This is feeling a little like 1870 New Mexico, during Billy the Kid and the range wars, or maybe the Hatfield and McCoy's in West Virginia."

From: Cynthia Kinkade
To: Esther Rider Salem
"Yesterday the bio father Lance Briggs twice threatened the judge and our various staff. The threats were serious enough that the Director believed it warranted sending armed agents to both Pott and Lincoln County for today and tomorrow, at least. In addition, I am not letting Margaret see anyone in the lobby for awhile."

From: Esther Rider Salem
To: Cynthia Kinkade
"Thank you. Lincoln County already emailed me that the agents are there and they have held a safety meeting. I only hope none of this is needed."

None of the security guards were needed because in reality the threats were figments of the imaginations of insecure state workers. Lance Briggs again opted not to take the law into his own hands but trust the system that had failed him and his family time and time again.

The system was being reviewed by the agency directed by Janice Hendryx. The Oklahoma Commission on Children and Youth or OCCY is the only agency that oversees DHS.

This internal email summarizes the beginning of OCCY's investigation:

"Janice Hendryx said that they have been reviewing this case from every angle possible. I asked what they had found so far. Her response was pretty general. Lots of people were looking at this case. There was conflicting medical testimony on the broken legs. There were continuing injuries, but the mother always gives some type of explanation. There is some question on the thoroughness of the investigations of the continuing injuries. The big issue will be the ability of workers to determine what is abuse in relation to the continuing injuries? Ex...once when the child had a bruised and swollen nose, someone reported that the seven-year-old step-sib elbowed her in the nose in bed. Did the investigator ever question the seven-year-old to confirm this? Was there blood from the bloody nose in the bed?"

Kris Steele was the second Representative to inquire about Kelsey's case. Steele met with Janice Hendryx asking why OCCY was not able to prevent Kelsey's death. She recited the standard response: worker turnover, new workers being inexperienced and not completely trained and fully functioning.

She was not sure how to respond when Rep. Steele did not want to hear any of that.

The Briggs did not get an apology from any of the people in charge of protecting Kelsey. That is until they received a nine page letter from Carla Lynch, explaining her role in Kelsey's demise. The hand written note on the front page said, "If anything should happen to me. You have my side of things. I am sorry." Her final words point to Raye Dawn as Kelsey's murderer. "In close, it has been Raye Dawn from beginning to end. A leopard doesn't change its spots. This is my statement. No cover up on my part."

Michael Porter

Agent Tanner asked, *"Do you know what a polygraph is?"*

Porter nodded.

"What is it?"

"It is a lie detector."

"Would you be willing to take one?"

"I'm under so much stress right now, I don't want it. I don't want it to be based on that," explained Porter.

"Based on what?"

"Based on a polygraph."

Tanner explained, *"It's not fully based on a polygraph. It's based on everything. Polygraph is just a tool."*

"A tool which can be wrong," said Porter, *"I've taken. . .when I was in a custody battle before, I took one, and I failed on my name."*

"You failed on your name?" asked Tanner.

"Yeah. It showed I wasn't being truthful on my name. So I've had experience with them. I mean not. . .excuse me. . .not experience but..."

"So they had you hooked up and they asked you your name?" Tanner seemed surprised.

"And it indicated that I was not being truthful when I told them that I was Michael Lee Porter."

Tanner asked again, *"Do you want to do a polygraph test?"*

"I want to talk to my wife first. I want to talk to her. I'm sitting here telling you that for the rest of my life I may have to live with the fact that I might have done something to hurt my child, but that's not enough for you. I'm sitting here telling you that I have to live with that. I've already been living with that. I'm scared to death that I may have hurt her with what I did trying to help her."

"Give me a break. Come on Mike. You're reaching again. You're reaching for that thing in order to get it away from what really happened," said Tanner.

"No."

"You're reaching."

"No, I'm telling you everything."

"You're reaching. I don't believe you. Do you think anybody else is going to believe you? Probably not. I don't see how they could."

"People who give you the benefit of the doubt. Steve, I want to talk to my wife, and then I might talk to you again."

"Okay."
"Because I've told you everything that I know, Steve."

Raye Dawn Smith

Raye spent much of the interview leaned over, with her head in her hands, blinding her face from the investigators' gazes.

Agent Za said, *"I don't think you meant to, Raye."*

"And it probably didn't take but just a second," added Kevin Garrett.

"I didn't hurt my baby," replied Raye.

"Little babies are so fragile," said Garrett.

"You all tell me that. What do I need to do to prove to you-all that I did not hurt my baby? What do I need to do? What do I need to do?" Raye Dawn said in an indignant tone, her eyes, void of tears.

Za gave the mother a way out, *"Well, then, what do you think happened? Who do you think could have done this? I mean, we're being logical here."*

Raye clenched her fists and teeth, *"How do you explain the grunting and the. . .what Mike explained to me and what he seen?"*

"Raye, that's because of the internal injuries that she had. She was suffering, okay," explained Za.

"She didn't die immediately. And there was no way that she could have been laying in that bed with you and not letting you know that she wasn't feeling good," added Garret.

"Can you tell us why?" asked Garrett once again.

"I don't know what happened to my daughter. I don't know how many times I have to tell you."

"You don't have to tell me anything else because you know," interrupted Za.

"You've beat me up. I'm just wore out," added Garrett.

"I'm tired of hearing it," said Za.

Raye agreed, *"I'm worn out."*

"You know why and if you can't let go to tell us why, you know, I really don't know how you can walk out and be okay with it because it's going to get ugly you know," threatened Garrett.

Raye Dawn sat emotionless as Garrett stared at her and said, *"If what you're saying is the truth, then Michael killed her. One of you two done it. If you're 100 percent sure that you didn't do it, then Michael is the killer. I mean, good luck to you because you're married. If what you're saying is the reason you stayed in here the whole time is that you're not responsible for the death of your daughter, then Michael is a sorry son of a bitch, because he killed her. One of you two killed her. And if what you're saying is true that you didn't do it then he did.*

"Because if what you're saying is true, I'd be scared to death because you're sleeping with a guy that killed your daughter.

"Somebody will pay for your daughter dying. It's either you or it's your husband. I don't care. I'm going to come one of these days. Next time you guys see me and I'm taking one of you guys' asses to jail. That's the God's truth. That's going to happen."

Garrett stood to leave saying, "I don't think I could be married to somebody that killed my kid."

Raye said, "There's no way in hell."

"I don't know. Something bad happened to your daughter."

"This is not what I wanted to hear," responded Raye.

"So either you did it or he did it, and you're telling me that you didn't do it, so. . ."

"There's no way I could have ever laid a harmful hand on my daughter."

"What about Michael?" Garrett asked again.

"I've never seen him hurt her. He's just one of the most loving, caring people I've ever met," said Raye.

Raye whimpered as she said, "You was asking me awhile ago why I told her that I was sorry because I was telling her I was so sorry I couldn't protect her. I just feel like I failed. I never thought that was what you were going to tell me. It never, never crossed my mind."

"What's that?" asked Garrett.

"That she was hurt. I just never. . .she was having seizures. That's what they told me."

"We weren't there. Was there just a lot of stress going on in your life?" asked Garrett.

"I did not hurt Kelsey," repeated Raye Dawn, still no tears.

"Well, you might not have intended to hurt her."

"There's no way. How can you all say that to me?" yelled Raye.

"We're not saying that you intended to hurt her."

"There is no way I hurt my daughter. I've never hurt her," insisted Raye.

"Raye Dawn we're just saying there's a lot of stress in life, there's a lot of stress with kids. No one understands what it's like."

"Do you think Mike might have hurt her?" asked Garrett. Raye turns from them as she shook her head no.

"How do you know he wouldn't do it? Explain that to us," pressed Garrett.

"How can anybody hurt a child?" yelled the frustrated mother.

"Is there any reason why you can't tell us what took place?"

"You are going to have to tell the truth."

"I am telling you the truth. I swear to God. I put it on my daddy's grave," whined Raye.

"Her intestines were bleeding. She was hurt so bad that her intestines were bleeding."

"Oh my God. My baby," Raye stood and turned away from them, curling her body into the fetal position, against the wall.

"That is something that you had to have done," insisted Garrett.

"I did not hurt my baby."

"We're not saying you did it intentionally."

"I did not hurt my baby. I can't believe you're telling me this."

"We just need you to tell us what took place and why she got those injuries."

"This is ridiculous," interrupted Raye.

T·E·N

NINE DAYS AFTER KELSEY WAS MURDERED, KEVIN GARRETT ARRIVED AT
MIDWEST INDUSTRIES WITH HANDCUFFS.

A couple of hours before agents arrived at the office, Porter was busy
emailing friends, already building his defense.

> From: OKMagnet
> Sent: Thursday, October 20, 2005 8:23 AM
> Thank you so much for your kind words. This whole ordeal is just a
> total nightmare. My whole family is devastated...I just pray the truth
> will come out and Kelsey will get the justice she deserves. She was a
> very special child who was going to do some neat things...my heart
> breaks every time I think of her. Everyone who knows me knows the
> truth...let's just pray God allows the truth to surface. Please keep in
> touch and pray for my children...they are all that matters to me.
> Mike Porter
> President
> Midwest Industries, Inc.

Reporters had been alerted Porter would be brought into the Lincoln
County Jail around 11:00 a.m. Crews rushed to Chandler with satellite trucks,
ready to cut into the noon news with their first shot of the man investigators
believe killed the beautiful blonde girl.

While reporters waited outside of the jail, Kathie Briggs stood at the
back of her van. She parked across from Midwest Industries to see Michael
Porter escorted into the squad car in handcuffs. She hoped Porter would see
her that day. But he did not. She watched in silence as the man Raye Dawn
married was arrested by the state's top investigatory agents.

By the time the vehicle hauling Porter made it to the jail, the cameras were set, ready to roll. Kevin Garrett walked Michael into the booking area of the jail as photographers tripped over each other to get the best angle of the face that was avoiding all stares. The man who looked like anyone's next door neighbor traded the jean shorts and grey t-shirt he was wearing that day for a black and white jail jumpsuit.

Deputies snapped a grimacing mug shot of Porter, a picture that would be plastered all over the evening news. District Attorney Richard Smothermon filed a first degree murder charge that morning. Before noon, reporters got their hands on the arrest affidavit. It contained just enough detail to illustrate why investigators believed it was Porter who murdered Kelsey. The affidavit provided information from interviews with Michael Taber, Jean Bonner, first responders, Raye Dawn, Porter, and the Medical Examiner. Reporters scanned the document looking for new information to report on the noon newscast.

Britten's eyes focused on the last paragraph of the document. The words of the Medical Examiner, describing Kelsey's injuries were likely too graphic for news viewers during the lunch hour. There was no time for sugarcoating, though. Live on the air, Britten read from the report, "Kelsey died from blunt force trauma to the abdomen. Her death had been ruled a homicide. Kelsey had major abdominal trauma and it was non accidental abdominal trauma. Kelsey had a lot of bleeding in her intestines. Kelsey had bruising on the pressure points of ribs, front of chest, side and back. Kelsey also had bruising between the vagina and the anus. The Medical Examiner felt these injuries could have been caused by kneeing, punching, or squeezing. Kelsey also had upper lip bruising.

Moments after the report, Britten's Executive Producer called, upset she used the word anus on television. Britten could not understand what word she could have possibly used as a substitute. She was ill herself from the harsh reality of the little girl's last breath.

Kevin Garrett walked out of the jail to greet the young reporter. Garrett wanted to make sure she had picked up a copy of the arrest affidavit. Britten nodded yes. Garrett told her he was looking forward to seeing the complete Medical Examiner's report, saying this guy was a monster for what he did to that little girl.

Britten rushed back to Oklahoma City to interview Kathie and Royce at their lawyer's office. Jeanna had promised Britten the first interview with their family because they liked the way she wrote her stories. Britten and her photographer arrived at Burch and George Law Offices in the afternoon and met the family.

They were much younger than she expected. When you reference "grand-parents", Britten was expecting an older couple. She gave them both a hug, apologized for their loss, and thanked them for the interview. The small office was lined with hard bound books on shelves and a wooden table topped with glass. Britten tried to make Royce and Kathie feel at home in an office far too dignified for the couple from Meeker to be comfortable. Not knowing exactly what to ask first, Britten told Kathie to start at the beginning.

For nearly a half hour Kathie Briggs told the story she had written so many times, in so many emails. The story ended on August 27, 2005 when she described how the light was gone from Kelsey's eyes. She described the frustration she felt as she continued to write emails, to the Governor, the Lieutenant Governor, every lawmaker, every television station, and no one would listen. She told the camera that she did everything she could to save her granddaughter and it was not enough. Kathie Briggs only choked up once during that interview and would never cry for the camera again.

Royce, on the other hand, was a much different case. As soon as Britten asked him to describe Kelsey on August 27, 2005, he could hardly compose himself. Fighting back tears Royce said, "We weren't trying to steal her away from anyone; we were just trying to protect her."

The Briggs shared pictures of Kelsey's bottom from January 14, 2005 with the television station. Pictures of the bright red marks on her bottom, the ones Raye Dawn claimed she never noticed.

That night when Britten's lead story began, producers at the competing stations began screaming in outrage. They mistook the pictures of Kelsey's rear as photos from the autopsy table. Autopsy pictures are off limits for broadcast. Britten's video editor blurred the appropriate parts of the pictures so the station could show the beginning of the 10 months of documented abuse.

The next day, the Briggs family shared those pictures with Cherokee at the competing station. And so began what would later be called the media frenzy that sent Raye Dawn to prison. Nearly every day reporters would lead the newscast with a new story citing shocking new details about the death of two-year-old Kelsey Smith-Briggs.

Another station in Oklahoma City was the first to broadcast home video taken of Kelsey stumbling around in two casts, at daycare. The news report sparked the competing news directors to demand that video too. Soon Kathie was dubbing hours of home video of her dead granddaughter for television news stories.

That's when the Smith family decided to start a letter writing campaign of its own. Letters and emails accused the reporters covering the story of a bias against Raye Dawn. The Smith family had not done any interviews since the day of the funerals. Once someone in the family agreed to get a group together to talk on camera, producers immediately sent the reporters to Meeker to once again hear their side.

Gayla's cousin Sherri Heath, Raye Dawn's grandmother Mildred Fowler, Raye Dawn's Sister Janet, daycare provider Julie Sebastian, and an aunt all met at Mildred's house to defend Raye Dawn. They still believed Kelsey's death was an accident and that Porter had hurt her with chest compressions. Apparently they did not understand the definition of homicide.

The camera was rolling when Britten asked Mildred why Michael Porter had filed for divorce from Raye Dawn from jail. No one in the family seemed to have any idea that happened either. The women who portrayed themselves as such a close knit family did not know Kelsey had been murdered and did not know the man accused of doing it filed for divorce from Raye Dawn. Britten gleaned some additional information for her story that night. Britten closed her story by reporting, "Raye Dawn is pregnant with Michael Porter's baby."

Several days after he was booked into the Lincoln County Jail, Michael Porter went before a judge for his formal arraignment. Basically, the judge reads the charges to the defendant and they enter a plea of guilty or not guilty.

Michael told the judge he was not guilty; the words he did not speak that day would haunt a family. As deputies walked Michael into the courtroom, he made eye contact with the two women sitting in the front row. His eyes, filled with raw pain, looked straight at Shirica and her mom. They were caught off guard by the open display of emotion and had become accustomed to Raye Dawn's cool exterior. His face said I'm sorry. Michael shook his head and mouthed the words, "I don't know what to say."

The Briggs family walked out of the courtroom and said to each other, "He didn't do it."

Raye Dawn & Michael Porter

5 hours and 37 minutes into the interview Raye Dawn still denied either she or Porter had anything to do with Kelsey's murder.

"What are you thinking?" asked Garrett.

"Oh, God, help me," replied Raye.

"So what do you think? Do you think Mike could have done something like this?" Garrett asked again.

"He couldn't have," insisted Raye.

"Then you did it."

"I know I didn't."

While Raye was alone in the room, she stood up and leaned against the wall, praying, "Oh God, help me. I'm so sorry."

Investigators came back in the room, this time with Porter. Raye did not make eye contact with her husband. She stared at her lap. Porter would not look at Garrett as he pointed at the young couple and said, "So either you, or you killed her. One of you two, look at me. Mike, look at me. One of you two killed that girl, okay. My job is to find out who did that."

Raye put her head in her hands. Then she stood up and quickly ran out of the room mumbling, "I've got to go to the bathroom."

Porter stayed in the room with Garrett and they continued talking. Porter said, "She knows I didn't do it."

Garrett said, "Then that means she did it. I mean the Medical Examiner's Office does lots of autopsies every day."

"I told Steve that I could have been too aggressive. I told him that."

Porter began to get anxious again. As he started taking deep breaths, Garrett asked, "You're not having a heart attack on me or anything are you? Are you on medication or anything? Are you mad?"

"No."

"So anyway Mike, I mean look at it from our standpoint."

Mike said, "I'm looking at it from our standpoint as parents who know we would never harm our child. There's got to be some other explanation."

"So I mean, either your wife had done something or you had done something. I'm not saying it was intentionally, but somehow, some way, you know, Kelsey got hurt," *explained Garrett.*

"I want to talk to my wife," *demanded Porter.*

"Well, she had to go to the bathroom, I think. I don't know. But you know it kind of bothered me that Steve said you told him that you wouldn't take a polygraph. You failed one before on something on your name? Is that right?"

Porter nodded his head.

"I don't know. Do we have some eye contact? You never look at me. Is there a reason for that?" asked Garrett.

"I'm thinking. I'm going through what happened," replied Porter.

Finally Porter had to leave the room, saying he couldn't breathe. The recording device picked up only part of the conversation outside of the office. Raye Dawn shouted, "I don't know what to do." Tanner told Porter he couldn't coerce her into not cooperating.

Raye Dawn Smith

Raye Dawn and Porter traded rooms. After Raye Dawn ran out of the room...agents followed her into the other interrogation room. She told them, "This is the complete opposite of what I thought."

"What did you think?" asked Tanner.

"That she had a seizure," replied Raye.

"It's not what happened," said Tanner.

"I know," said the mother.

Tanner pried to get more information out of Raye, "What do you think happened Raye Dawn?"

"I don't know. My baby was fine all day. We talked to my mom, I don't know how many times that day because my mom was supposed to come and get her that evening. She was fine," said Raye.

Za asked, "Was Mike wearing the same clothes, like he did still have on his work clothes when you got back and when you saw him again after you'd left to go pick up Whitney?"

"I have no idea," said Raye.

"You don't remember?"

"I have no idea. I'm sorry. I mean, maybe if I went back home and looked."

Tanner, new to Raye's evasiveness, said, "All I'm saying is that what we're hearing from both of you guys is not the entire truth. And until we get the entire truth, we're going to have a big problem. But you want to know what I kind of think, you know, what I kind of think happened? Do you want to know?"

All Raye could say was, "I'm scared."

"Okay, well there was an accident that happened that caused these injuries to Kelsey. You and Mike finally got an opportunity to visit with each other and you just kind of decided that whatever it was you were going to try to cover up for each other. And the reason I tell you that is because some of the things that you're telling to these folks and that you're saying now is the exact same thing that Mike is saying. Typically when you have two people that witness something, they're not going to say the exact same thing.

Do you understand what I'm saying?"

Raye stared with a blank look, "I understand. But that's what I told you that we haven't really talked about it. Like, there are things that I didn't know because they hadn't . . ." she trailed off.

Raye continued, "Well, you all have already got me just, I'm twisted into a pretzel. I mean, I thought I just knew. You know I thought I knew what happened because that's what he told me."

"Who told you?" asked Za.

"Mike said she had a seizure," replied Raye.

"Why did you want out of that room as soon as he came in there?" asked Za.

"He just seemed so frustrated, and I'm not in the state of mind to deal with anybody. It was hard enough to know he was frustrated, and I can't deal with that right now."

"I'm curious to see what he's going to say to you. Do you see what I'm saying?"

"I understand."

"I'm curious if he's going to tell you to get an attorney."

"Did he say he was going to say that? I really don't understand why he's not cooperating. I mean, I didn't mean to raise flags or anything because I wanted out of there."

"No and you didn't. I mean, I can. . ."

Raye cut Za off, "It's just the frustration. Like when I'm upset about something, I can't handle other frustration, you know."

"Do you think you could go back in there and see what he's wanting to tell you?"

"I guess. I just don't. . .I don't know what I'm going to tell him."

Za said, "The bottom line here is that we need to find out what happened. And I think you can see our perspective that it was either you or it was him."

"I know. And that's what, you know earlier he kind of got aggravated with me because I said it was a normal day. I meant prior. I mean, it was just one of our days. We always had more. . .we just had fun when it was just us, like it used to be, so it was just a normal day."

"Do you think Mike is capable of doing something like was described, the blunt force trauma?" asked Tanner.

"No."

"You don't think so?"

Za said, "I'm going to take you back over there and just see what he has to say. I want to know what he's going to say. He asked to speak with you and we said okay."

"Right. So I mean are you all going to stay in there with us?"

"We can leave and just let you guys talk."

The group left the room and headed to the hallway. Most of the conversation in the hallway was too quiet to catch on the recorder.

Garrett's voice rose as he said, "One of you will go to jail. It may not be today, but there will be a day I'm taking somebody to jail. You can come down here and chat about it all you want. Go ahead and have a little chat, but if you want to find out what happened to your daughter. . ." his voice trails.

Raye and Za walk back into the camera's view as Raye asks to see her mom. Za assured her that Tanner is going to get her but Raye began to panic. She started pacing back and forth in the room, crying.

Za tried to calm her, "Raye, Raye, Raye."

"This is not happening. I will never forgive myself," cried Raye.

"It is not your fault."

"It wouldn't have happened, though, if. . ." her voice trailed.

"It's not Raye."

"Oh, God," she cried.

"If you didn't have anything to do with that, it is not your fault. It is not. Okay?"

While the camera did not capture the couple's conversation, Raye seemed shocked by Porter's behavior in the hallway. She asked Za, "Why did he say that? I'm confused. I'm scared. I'm scared. I feel like I've failed."

Za tried to comfort her, "I don't know. I don't know why he reacted like he did, other than the obvious reason. Have you ever seen him act like this before?"

"No," said Raye, "I guess I'm just shocked that he's acted like this."

"Right, what do you think that means?"

Raye continued, "And right away he said he didn't do this. I never said that."

"Has he ever said that to you before? 'I didn't do this. I didn't do anything?'"

"Not about this. He just told me that everybody thought he did it," said Raye, very quietly.

Za asked, "She never acted funny around Mike or acted like she didn't want to go with him or acted like she was afraid of him?"

"Well, it's not that she was afraid of him. Just sometimes she wanted to be with me, you know."

When Gayla came in, the agents left the room to give the mother and daughter a moment alone. The camera watched as Gayla rubbed Raye Dawn's leg and hugged her. Gayla's phone rang. Raye's brother Curtis was on the other end of the line. "They're just saying something bad happened to Kelsey.

They're saying somebody did it.

They don't think Raye Dawn did it.

They don't think Raye Dawn did it.

Raye Dawn's really scared.

We don't know what to do.

You think we should just leave?

You think we should just leave?"

When Gayla hung up the phone she got in Raye's face. Their conversation was too quiet to be captured by the recording device in the room. Raye shook her head and Gayla turned around quickly.

Before they left, Gayla asked Raye if she wanted to drive home with her. Raye replied, "No, Mike would be mad."

E·L·E·V·E·N

FOR ALL INTENTS AND PURPOSES, DISTRICT ATTORNEY RICHARD SMOTHERMON HAD TURNED A BLIND EYE TO RAYE DAWN AS A SUSPECT. Raye Dawn walked free, while Porter sat behind bars. People in Meeker began pleading with the D.A. and OSBI to at least consider Raye Dawn as a suspect. She was the one with a history of violence and anger; Porter had a business and two kids of his own.

From jail Porter filed for divorce from Raye Dawn to distance himself from the other potential suspect. In his divorce filings, Porter asked for everything in the home belonging to his son and daughter, including Whitney's journals. Inquiring minds wondered what secrets the little girl shared with her diary.

Debbie Hammons is related to both the Smith family and the Briggs. Without prompting from either side, she wrote a 12 page letter addressed to Kevin Garrett, Richard Smothermon, and the reporters who had begun covering Kelsey's case. The letter discussed vivid details about Raye Dawn's life with Kelsey; details lawyers did not ask her about on the witness stand at the June 15, 2005 hearing.

Details reporters would never be able to share with the public, since they were merely hearsay, but have haunted those involved with the case for years. The following are excerpts from her 12 page letter.

Dear Mr. Garrett and Mr. Tanner:

I have known Raye Dawn Smith Porter better and longer than most people that you've probably spoken to since the murder. I have known Raye Dawn since she was born. Gayla Smith has been like a sister to me and best friend for about 35 years, until this last February 3. The dispute between us was over Raye Dawn's actions toward Kelsey. Gayla and I spoke at least once daily and sometimes many more times if there was something going on in the family.

Raye Dawn always had to be the center of attention. She was the center of attention when in high school, as she was very popular. She's a performer, always craving the spotlight. She was coached well in her early years in many beauty pageants, in dance classes and recitals on just how to smile and win the people over. She's still practicing doing this very thing. Gayla would tell me about her drinking, her rages, fits of anger, many many times long before she even met Lance Briggs. Raye Dawn was running wild and was a loose cannon. Gayla told me when she once had a wreck in her Firebird on a dirt road somewhere east of Meeker one night and ran into a car. She'd been drinking and after realizing what had happened she ran into the field and hid the alcohol bottles before anyone arrived at the scene.

Gayla has told me about the many times that everything in the house would be broken and how Raye Dawn put her hand thru some sort of glass window at their house. She would just go crazy when she was drinking. Not the sweet little girl-like person that you see. I knew that unless she quit drinking so violently she would never be happy with anyone.

After Raye Dawn and Lance filed for divorce, they would still "visit" each other. I knew Raye Dawn was pregnant before she ever went to divorce court. Gayla had told me and asked me if I would keep quiet about it until the divorce was final. They did not want Lance to know that he was going to be a father and was determined that this child would not know "that family".

Gayla told me this past January that she would do whatever it took to get Kelsey back to Raye Dawn. She never was concerned about the injuries or where they came from. She was only concerned on Raye Dawn winning.

In June, after Lance got visitation with Kelsey, he and Ashley married. Raye Dawn was furious. She was so jealous of Ashley saying that Ashley always wanted everything that Raye Dawn had even in high school and now she's got her ex husband and is trying to get her baby. Gayla told me that the only reason that Lance married Ashley was to try to get more custody of Kelsey. She told me that Ashley was fool enough to go along with it because she cared so much for Lance and he didn't care anything for her. This threw even more fire toward the Smith's hatred of the Briggs family.

Several months later, Gayla called and told me on the phone, "If Raye Dawn doesn't kill Ashley, I'm going to". A few months later, Raye Dawn and Mike Porter would stalk Ashley outside her house when Lance was gone to the military. Ashley tried filing a VPO, but couldn't prove it.

Around the time of Lance and Ashley's marriage, Gayla started planning on sending Raye Dawn and Kelsey out of state to hide so that Lance would not know where they were. Gayla told me all of this along with the fact that Raye Dawn wanted to get a job at a strip club. Gayla didn't want Raye Dawn around if she did.

Gayla really wanted her to go and get out of the house. Gayla didn't like babysitting and always was commenting on them moving out. Most of this was due to the fact of Raye Dawn's continual drinking and the fact that she would stay out all night and try to sleep all day and Gayla did not want to "have to watch that kid," as she put it. I've been there and seen Gayla really slap Kelsey hard on the hands, arms and legs when she would touch something on a coffee table. She always talked about how Raye Dawn wouldn't pick up after herself or Kelsey and she was tired of doing it all the time and that Raye Dawn wouldn't watch Kelsey. I asked Gayla one time if Raye Dawn fed Kelsey and she said "I don't know, that's her job". Raye Dawn was in bed asleep and it was around noon at that time. Raye Dawn didn't have any patience with any child. She would scream at her if she didn't go to sleep. Gayla hit that child too hard for a little child just a little over one-year-old at that time.

Ray Smith got so ill that he was bedfast for several months before he died on 4-15-04. At first, they ordered a hospital bed for him and had it set up in the living room. Gayla didn't like it in her living room, so she called and had it picked up and put him in their king size bed. He eventually died in the same bed that Mike Porter found Kelsey in.

Gayla told me approximately a month before Ray died that "he wasn't dying fast enough" for the money end of it. She was tired of taking care of him. I would talk to her on the phone and I would hear him in the background calling to Gayla to come to him in the bedroom. She'd scream "shut up" or just ignore him. Ray would beat on the nightstand for them to come in there and finally Gayla would go. Gayla got so tired of dealing with the situation that she went on a long weekend vacation, going to Arkansas, and left the girls in charge of their dad. She was relieved when he died. Two hours after he died, I was there with her in their bedroom and she was going thru his shirts in his closet and asking his son, if he wanted this one or that one. It's like she couldn't wait to clear out his clothes.

During the time that Ray was so ill, Raye Dawn was still continuing her drinking and partying. The very day that her dad died, I went to the house as soon as I heard and on my way into Meeker I saw Raye Dawn coming out of the Rainbow Convenience store with a sack of beer. She had taken Kelsey over to Kathie's house (as she did frequently when she wanted to go out all night and drink), so she had thought this out and planned it. I tried to convince her that this wasn't the way her dad would have wanted it. She said that she "didn't know what else to do" and left. I didn't see her again until the next day, after she'd been arrested for DUI.

Before Ray died and before Raye Dawn met Porter, she had a "friend" in Meeker who would come out to the house to see Raye Dawn and they would talk on the phone for hours. He was married and Ray knew it. Ray was adamant that Raye Dawn NOT hang around, date, or talk to him in lengths. Ray got so mad about it that Gayla and Raye Dawn invented a code word that meant that it was him calling or she was going to meet him. When Ray finally was so sick that he never left his bed, the married man would sneak into the house. It was okay in Gayla's eyes for Raye Dawn to be seeing a married man.

The abuse to Kelsey started after Raye Dawn moved out of her mom's house. Gayla wasn't available to baby-sit and Raye Dawn had to deal with Kelsey on her own during the days that Lance didn't have visitation. Raye Dawn despised having to meet Kathie or Lance to give them Kelsey. I think that she thoroughly enjoyed the time away from Kelsey, but didn't like the one on one time with her. She and Porter were dating during this entire time. You know it had to have been hard to have dated with a little two-year-old child who is very active hanging around. Gayla didn't even want to baby-sit when Raye Dawn had to go to her classes on anger management, alcohol assessments, etc. One weekend I asked Gayla about Raye Dawn, if she was attending her classes and she said yes, that Porter was babysitting for Raye Dawn because "she" (Gayla) wasn't going to. When asked about this in court in June, Gayla lied and said that Porter never watched her. She was lying!

Gayla always remarked how they didn't believe that Lance was even in the Army that he was making this whole thing up and "if" he was, their only hope was that he'd get sent to Iraq and get killed. I heard this statement several times.

I was subpoenaed to appear for Kathie Briggs in court in June, 2005. Kathie's attorney didn't ask all the right questions, so therefore no one heard the entire story.

The Meeker police department testified in court in June that they had followed Raye Dawn home to make sure that she got home when she was driving drunk. Surely to God, Raye Dawn won't get off to walk free after her child has died under her watchful eye.

Thank you for your time.

Debbie Hammons

OSBI investigator, Garrett said the letter was void of any proof. Just because Raye Dawn wasn't winning mother of the year anytime soon, did not make her a murderer. Garrett felt Raye Dawn was not very smart, certainly not smart enough to frame her husband for the murder of her baby.

About a month after Kelsey's death, Britten received an email with information about Raye Dawn she could not ignore. The anonymous email popped into her inbox suggesting she go talk to a nurse who happened to be one of Raye Dawn's best friends. The author implied Raye Dawn had taken Kelsey to the nurse to get medical advice long before Porter was in the picture. The email said the nurse suspected abuse but never reported it. It was a decision that would force the nursing board to revoke her license if it surfaced now. The author of the email thought the girl would be honest if she was questioned about it.

The email provided no way of reaching the young lady. Britten's search led her to Edmond, a northern suburb of Oklahoma City. Edmond is dotted with soccer moms and upscale strip malls.

Britten was nervous as she walked up to the nurse's door. This sounded like the one opportunity she would have to see whether the D.A.'s decision to arrest only Porter was off-target.

When a young man answered the door, Britten explained who she was and asked for the nurse. A few moments later, a young woman, about Britten's age came to the door. The reporter asked the brunette if she would talk to her about Raye Dawn. The nurse quietly told her she did not want to get involved and shut the door.

The frustrated reporter walked away. Britten understood why the young lady did not want to talk to her, although her silence made Britten all the more curious about what she knew and what she was hiding.

A few days later, Britten had a message to call Agent Kevin Garrett. It was an incredibly odd message, especially since reporters were only allowed to speak with the agency's media relations contact.

The seasoned agent with the Oklahoma State Bureau of Investigation called the 24-year-old television reporter in hopes of gleaning a lead in the cloud of deceit. Garrett told her he heard she had an email that he might want a copy of.

Britten told him she had received dozens of emails since Kelsey's death and she needed more information as to which one he was referencing.

He was looking for the email that involved information about Raye Dawn and alleged abuse. Britten had no idea how Garrett learned about the email. She only had a few seconds to consider the consequences of sharing this confidential email with law enforcement. To protect the identity of the person who sent her the email, Britten agreed to read its contents to Garrett. Ultimately, Britten didn't see a problem in giving him the information, especially since she was not able to convince the nurse to talk. Maybe he could get more information out of the young lady.

Britten quickly realized the agent was trying to get information out of her. He asked Britten what she thought about the case and what she had heard about Raye Dawn. The conversation lasted for about 30 minutes.

Garrett told her he wished he could show her the taped interviews with Porter, where he exhibited all of the behaviors of a guilty party. Britten hung up the phone bewildered as to why she was being apprised of the details in this investigation. Based on her conversation with the lead agent on the case, Britten couldn't help but wonder if the investigation would ever shift in Raye Dawn's direction.

On November 15, 2005, Raye Dawn had more than a baby bump as she walked into the courthouse in an attempt to get custody of Kelsey's estate. Reporters from four television stations sat in the hallway of the Lincoln County Courthouse. Steve Huddleston, Raye Dawn's attorney, was waiting in the lobby when he stood up and announced he was going to get his client. It was a notice the media was not used to getting. A lawyer actually told them he was going to get the person they wanted video of. Nick Winkler, a young, aggressive reporter was waiting with a list of questions for the mother who had avoided the spotlight for weeks.

As she walked through the front door, Nick and his microphone quickly approached. The photographer positioned his camera in Raye Dawn's face and began walking backward as Nick fired questions, "Raye Dawn was Kelsey alive when you left her with Mike Porter?" Her lawyer interrupted saying, "We don't have any comment. We're just here for a court proceeding."

She looked straight ahead as she walked briskly down the long hall and around the corner. Nick continued, "Raye Dawn, who broke Kelsey's legs?" At that moment the mother of the dead baby began sobbing, trying to cover her face from the cameras. Nick had no mercy. He continued to fire questions, "Raye Dawn, you say you didn't see the bruises on Kelsey. We have pictures of the bruises. Raye Dawn? Raye Dawn, Kelsey told you Daddy Mike hurt my legs. Why did you let her go back into Daddy Mike's presence?" The photographer continued to record as he backed through doors and around three corners. Nick had time for one more question, "Could you tell us specifically what you did to protect Kelsey?"

When Raye Dawn entered the courtroom with her mother, the Briggs noticed she was extremely distraught. They could hear her sniffling and thought she was upset about the court proceedings. They had no idea she was crying about the reporter who could see through her act.

Nick says his adrenaline was rushing as Raye Dawn slipped into the courtroom out of the camera's glaring eye. He says, "Everyone in that little girl's life, including the media, had let Kelsey down and let Raye Dawn off the hook. It was my job to make sure that didn't happen again."

Nick understood there was a risk in questioning a so-called grieving mother on her way into the courtroom, especially since she had not been charged with a crime. Nick felt since no one in the Oklahoma media was willing to take a risk and do a story on Kelsey's case when she was alive, the risk of coming across as a bad guy was worth it. Especially if it meant the truth would come out. Nick says, "I felt many in Oklahoma wanted to hit Raye Dawn just as hard as Kelsey had been hit. So I hit her with the next best thing, a series of questions she couldn't answer."

Lance's attorneys also gave Raye Dawn an opportunity to answer questions. When they called her to the stand she pleaded the Fifth Amendment. Raye Dawn had an opportunity to fight for control of the estate, but instead, chose to protect herself.

Lance was awarded Executor of Kelsey's estate; however, that was only a mention on the evening news. The sobbing mother chased by the reporter was broadcast over and over. Nick's risk paid off. It was well received across the state. People began emailing the station, thanking him for holding the mother of this child accountable. The confrontation was so compelling, competing stations figured out creative ways to edit Nick out of their video.

Accountable in the eyes of the public is a different standard than in the eyes of the law. As reporters continued to dig for more information about everyone involved in this case, Raye Dawn enjoyed her freedom. OSBI completed its investigation into Raye Dawn and gave Smothermon an affidavit for her arrest. It sat in Smothermon's office for four months before he took any action.

When the criminal case seemed to be at a standstill, the focus of the local media turned to the overall system failure.

Nick discovered Governor Brad Henry, Judge Key, and State Representative Kris Steele sat on the board that oversees the CASA organization in Lincoln County. The board provided oversight for the organization that recommended the judge return Kelsey to Raye Dawn, where she was murdered. Key refused all interviews with reporters. A very nervous Representative Steele told Nick he sat on a lot of boards and had no direct involvement with the day to day operations of that particular board. When Nick called the Governor's spokesman to get a comment, he was told, "The Governor plays absolutely no role in the Kelsey case."

In an editorial meeting, Nick's managers restricted using the governor's picture on the screen with Steele and Key. The news director said, "We could cost the governor the election." The watchdog role of the media cowered in the face of politics. Governor Henry was re-elected in 2006 by one of the largest margins in state history.

Judge Key was conspicuously absent each time reporters showed up to cover protests at the courthouse. Members of the grassroots organization, now named Kelsey's Purpose, held rallies asking for the judge's resignation. The voices, holding signs with Kelsey's picture on them, screamed, "Justice for Kelsey!"

Kathie's family set up a website www.kelseyspurpose.org for people interested in the case to post comments. The pink wallpaper and bright letters appeared to be a website for children. Instead, Kelsey's Purpose became a grandmother's coping mechanism.

Someone created another website that would soon be coined the "bashboard". It was a place for friends, family, and strangers to take anonymous stabs at the two people who were home the day Kelsey died.

Still digging for information about what happened in the months leading up to Kelsey's death, Britten sent a letter to every state lawmaker and the Governor. The stack of letters was the beginning of Britten's four year odyssey to expose the problems ailing the agency in charge of protecting Oklahoma's most vulnerable. The letter challenged the public servants to release Kelsey's confidential DHS case file and court transcripts, arguing it was in the public's best interest to protect other children from the abuse. Legally, the court transcripts in Kelsey's juvenile proceedings were sealed and the state only had to release a summary of its involvement in Kelsey's life. The law does not specify what has to be included in that summary. Britten was determined to get more information about the recommendations that led to Judge Key's June 15, 2005 decision. She also wanted to know how the extensive list of state agencies could have failed the child.

Reporters tried to piece together the limited information available under open records. They searched campaign contributions and other familial relations that could have influenced the deadly decisions. The Oklahoma Commission on Children and Youth conducted a confidential investigation into DHS's handling of the case. The results of that investigation would later be leaked to the newspaper.

The contents of Kelsey's confidential DHS file never made the evening news; however, the damning nature of the mistakes noted inside the file sparked Lance to file a lawsuit asking for an overhaul of the Department of Human Services.

Protestors threatened an overhaul of the Lincoln County court system if Raye Dawn walked away without any charges in Kelsey's death.

The words Carnegie Library mark the outside of the building adorned with cement columns next to the courthouse in downtown Shawnee. Inside, sits a mounting case file and Richard Smothermon. The case was quickly morphing into a road block for a politician aspiring for higher office. The handsome District Attorney was aiming for the Attorney General's office. Smothermon knew the blonde two-year-old pictured on the picket signs outside his office could cost him his career.

Smothermon had another blonde and her mother in his office on at least five occasions. He met with Raye Dawn a lot and says he believed her at first. He believed her family too. He thought the Smith family to be good solid people, exactly the kind you'd find in Meeker, Oklahoma. Raye Dawn's family hired Steve Huddleston, a friend of Smothermon's, to defend her. Huddleston firmly believed Raye was innocent too. Smothermon and Huddleston talked about the case regularly. Though Raye Dawn would ultimately be charged with allowing Kelsey to die, some people involved in the case believe Huddleston's strong opinions rubbed off on the District Attorney. The delay in charging Raye Dawn gave her more time to develop her defense.

During the hours Smothermon spent questioning Raye Dawn about the case, he thought the story about the turtle was weird. Then Jean Bonner confirmed there was a turtle on the porch. Porter also confirmed Raye Dawn lured him out to the porch to see it. He thought the diaper thing was weird too. Most people thought it was odd she put a child who was still being potty trained down for a nap with a bare bottom. This too was confirmed by Porter.

Raye Dawn made one statement that left the blossoming D.A. puzzled. When she was driving back from picking up Whitney, she had a feeling that something was wrong because her mom's car wasn't at work.

Those feelings only happen in tragic romance novels, not real life.

Then Smothermon says he caught her in a lie.

During those meetings he asked her to tell him everything about Michael Porter, anything and everything that could help in the prosecution of his murder trial. Raye Dawn shared quite a bit, but she left out something he would use to bury her months later in her trial.

That, coupled with the fact Raye Dawn firmly denied ever abusing Kelsey. Raye Dawn couldn't explain the 29 bruises and abrasions on Kelsey's rear. Smothermon realized his star witness in the case against Porter was lying to him.

The nights became restless as 2005 came to a close; Smothermon began to question whether he put the right person in jail. Outside, the pressure continued to mount, and in this case, it was harder to ignore. It was a constant barrage. When Smothermon was in Oklahoma County, trying a case, prosecutors there told him he needed to charge that mother.

The outspoken Kathie Briggs became a staple on the District Attorney's Caller ID. At one point Smothermon yelled at the grandmother, "You can put as many people on my front steps as you'd like, but I'm not going to charge her unless I'm ready whether you like it or not."

The days after Kelsey's death were a whirlwind. Soon the Briggs faced their first Christmas without Kelsey. Kathie already had several Christmas presents for Kelsey. She wanted another little girl to have them so Kathie adopted an Angel from the Salvation Army tree.

Kelsey left behind a room full of toys. Lance searched his heart and knew other children would love them as much as Kelsey did. He packed them up and took them to his dad's family church. Kelsey's toys brought a smile to the faces of 50 children that Christmas morning.

The toy donations inspired Kathie to set up Toys for Kelsey's Kids. Each Christmas, boxes are set up around the country and the donations go to children in need.

Smothermon had a cardboard box of his own. The box was literally titled "crap" and was filled with stuff he felt he shouldn't have to put up with. It was filled with letters, screaming, "No deal for Raye Dawn!" and "You've got to charge her!" He read every piece of mail until he finally got to the point that he realized he needed to do what he thought was right, uninfluenced by other people's opinions.

Michael Porter's preliminary hearing had been postponed so the judge reduced his bond from one million dollars to $250,000. Legal analysts argued a judge would only allow the bond reduction if the case was taking a different direction and pointing to a new suspect. Porter bonded out of jail just before Christmas.

The night news broke that Porter was free; anchors introduced Britten for the lead story. Porter's bail was mentioned, but her report focused on exclusive information. Kelsey had injuries to her private parts the day of her death.

Viewers who saw Britten's report that night never realized it was a story they almost did not hear. Britten had to fight to report details that would become one of the most emotional parts of Kelsey's torture.

Earlier that day, in their editorial meeting, Britten's producers decided she would not report these exclusive details. Her bosses felt the public did not need to know about such intimate injuries surrounding Kelsey's death.

The young reporter stood by her information and argued it would become key evidence in the upcoming trial. She felt it was their obligation as a news organization to report this new information no matter how disturbing it was.

Britten won the argument. Her story aired and it cast additional suspicion toward Porter. Britten's sources could not confirm the two-year-old had been sexually abused but that something had been forced between Kelsey's legs creating a tear to her rectum. It was hard for anyone to believe there was any way a mother could cause such intimate injuries to her little girl.

Out of jail, Michael Porter spent most of his time at his sister's house and soon went back to work at the family's magnet company. It was hard to keep a low profile when everyone in town had an opinion about the case.

A few days after Christmas, his sisters dragged him to a movie at Quail Springs Mall in Oklahoma City. They thought it would give him two hours of relief from the constant barrage of stress. He reluctantly agreed. As they walked into the mall, Porter and his sisters ran into Raye Dawn and Gayla. Porter began shaking and later said he nearly had a cardiac arrest. Raye Dawn looked at the man charged with murdering her daughter and laughed. Porter said it was as if she found it amusing she had gotten away with it.

After Porter's release the bloggers assumed instant legal expertise and began speculating about Raye Dawn's culpability. The bashboard discussions almost always gravitated toward the likelihood of Raye Dawn being the guilty party. Some posts were simply rumor; others were based in truth. People who claimed to know Raye Dawn the best screamed with their typed words that Kelsey's mom was capable of murder.

Kathie and her family soon realized a blogger by the name of "True Justice" continued to mold the discussions back to Raye Dawn. The so-called anonymous nature of the Internet provided an outlet for the one person no one had heard from. Kathie began speculating "True Justice" was Michael Porter.

The words of "True Justice" were silenced by gag order, yet manipulative and convincing. Porter knew his lawyer Paul Sutton would likely drop him as a client if he found out Porter was sharing details about the case to the world.

Shirica called Michael's friend Wendell and asked him to pass along a message to Michael's sisters. She felt a connection with them as victims. There had been times when she wasn't always pleased with her brother Lance's behavior and knew their hearts had to be torn. Shirica knew Porter's sisters were innocent bystanders in the web of deception.

Mary Beth, Michael's older sister and the owner of Midwest Industries, called Shirica. Shirica says Mary Beth cried as she apologized for what the Briggs family was going through. Mary Beth didn't know Kelsey well because Raye Dawn and Porter kept to themselves, but she felt confident her brother didn't kill Kelsey. Porter's sisters had been inundated with hateful calls and Mary Beth had a difficult time dealing with the way her brother was being persecuted on the nightly news. Shirica says Mary Beth asked her, "I'm not asking you to save him. But if you know in your heart that something isn't going right. If there's something you know or find out that would prove my brother didn't do this, would you do something about it?"

Mary Beth and Shirica never spoke again but they did exchange emails or so Shirica thought. The emails quickly became educated about the case. Shirica thought it was odd because Mary Beth claimed she didn't know Kelsey well and hadn't spent much time with Porter and his new family. She justified this change of attitude believing Mary Beth was studying the case to help with her brother's defense.

Shirica soon discovered Michael Porter was writing those emails. She does not believe Mary Beth ever knew her brother had virtually assumed her identity.

The first email came on Thursday, December 29, 2005, at 3:59 p.m. One day after Kelsey would have turned three.

From: okmagnet
To: shirica
Subject: RE: Post
Let me say our family's thoughts and prayers are with you everyday. We can't begin to say that we know the depth of your heartbreak. The emotion of yesterday was unimaginable. The only thing that gives us any comfort is we know the truth-Michael did not do this. I know that is a comfort that your family does not have right now. We also understand that Kelsey was taken from your family by someone and the same person is now trying to take Michael from us. However, there seems to be a great lack of interest in prosecuting the guilty party. Not A SINGLE DAY GOES BY that Michael does not do things to support Justice for Kelsey - trust me. Michael will have his day in court-this we all know. We are all ready for that day, because the things of darkness will be brought to the light. What we should ALL be concerned about is the reluctance to prosecute other parties. We know what kind of person Michael is-proud, gullible, trusting, blind at times-yes. Capable of hurting a child-NEVER. The truth is there-search your heart for it. Please have faith that we will do everything possible to make sure justice is done. We will continue to support Kelsey and your family in our prayers and actions. We would like to keep the lines of communication open, and for that to happen our communications should be kept in confidence. I hope you will respect and honor this request. God bless you and your family.

Since Shirica suspected those were Porter's words, she addressed him directly in her reply.

From: Shirica
To: okmagnet
Subject: RE: post

I am interested in the truth and only the truth. I have strong opinions on what happened and I just need one thing confirmed to know for sure. It is tragic what we all have had to endure at the hand of Raye Dawn. I saw the look in court. I just want to explore that. I truly understand your fear to speak with me. I would not blame you for not contacting me. I was just in hopes you might trust me to do so.

The author of the emails assured Shirica she was in fact talking to Mary Beth, not Porter. Shirica asked "Mary Beth" if she could meet with her brother. Shirica saw innocence in his eyes in court but needed to hear it in his voice.

The two exchanged several emails that first day and continued to write at least once a day. Shirica told "Mary Beth" the OSBI agents questioned one of Raye Dawn's ex-boyfriends who told them Porter was very jealous of Lance.

From: John Smith
To: Shirica
Subject: RE:
As far as I'm concerned she can say what she wants about Mike because there are enough people who know it is bullshit. She is the alcoholic, she is the one who is a sex addict, she is the one with anger problems, she is the jealous one and she is the controlling, possessive one, and she is the one who killed Kelsey.
Everyone knows she didn't want to be pregnant, I know because she told me. I also know that the first three weeks after she found out she was pregnant with Kelsey she did everything in her power to try to kill Kelsey through drinking and drugs-which of course she blamed all on Lance too. I am tired of her being the victim-I will not let it happen this time. KELSEY IS THE VICTIM!!!! Raye Dawn is evil and the truth will come out. I AM DEVOTED TO THAT AND SO IS MICHAEL.

While the two were exchanging emails, *The Oklahoman*, the state's newspaper, published a three part series on Kelsey and the case. The Briggs had to prepare a statement. Lance had a hard time with it because he was concerned it would make him look like a monster. The author of the article told him Raye Dawn accused him of hitting her as a result of a fight about an order of French fries. Shirica shared her family's concerns with "Mary Beth" who claimed Raye Dawn was now accusing Mike of being abusive too.

> From: John Smith
> To: Shirica
> Subject: RE: hi
> But Lance knows it is a lie. He knows he didn't hit her over French fries...it is just so sad that she can do this. Mike never touched her but now she is saying that he abused her and she gave him so many chances. Please, if she would have ever tried to leave him he would have said 'Good Riddance'. He tried so hard to make that marriage work, but like I said, all she cared about was drinking, partying, and living the life that Kelsey took from her.

Shirica believed Raye Dawn was not being held accountable for her role in Kelsey's death and she thought Porter could help fill in the blanks. Kelsey's aunt drove to Oklahoma City on January 7, 2006. She thought she was meeting Mary Beth and Porter at the Quail Springs Dillard's. Porter started getting nervous when Shirica was running late. He left his sister's cell phone number in their last email. He did not want Shirica to call it because his sister did not know about the meeting.

With the same blind trust Porter placed in his wife, he placed his entire criminal defense in Shirica's hands. He trusted Shirica would not tell any-one about their meeting. For security purposes Shirica had already told her boyfriend about the meeting and on her way there she told her mom.

When Shirica spotted Porter, she was not surprised Mary Beth was not there. Shirica suspected she had been communicating with Porter directly all along. Shirica was not scared, just very nervous. She was even a little sick to her stomach about meeting the man charged with murdering her niece.

Shirica says Porter seemed beaten down, very fragile. She couldn't help but notice how thin he had become. She apologized for being late, but Porter said, "Do not ever apologize to me for anything."

To disguise himself, Porter wore a navy blue stocking cap. For an hour and a half the two walked laps around the second floor of the department store. Porter got emotional every time Kelsey's name was mentioned and couldn't bear to hear about Lance's pain.

Shirica knew Porter was manipulating a relationship with her to reach Richard Smothermon. Porter's lawyer did not want him to talk to the District Attorney. Porter was indignant that he could exonerate himself if he could tell the D.A. what really happened in the months leading up to Kelsey's death.

Porter spent nearly an hour trying to convince Shirica that the D.A. and OSBI pinned Kelsey's murder on him from the beginning. He felt they did not give him a chance to share anything about Raye Dawn. Porter told Shirica his deepest regret was that he loved Kelsey, but he didn't love her enough. He said he protected his own children from Raye Dawn but did not protect Kelsey. For that, Porter felt he failed her and deserved to go to jail.

He told Shirica, Raye Dawn was completely obsessed with Ashley. He said Raye Dawn and her sister-in-law Miste would drive past the house where Ashley was living, which happened to be the house Raye Dawn grew up in. The two continued to drive the route long after Ashley was out of the picture. Porter says they drove by the weekend before Kelsey died. Porter said one day he and Raye Dawn were arguing about her obsessive behavior and Kelsey heard Ashley's name. When Kelsey asked for her Mommy Ashley, Raye Dawn slapped her.

Porter explained no one in the Briggs family could comprehend the hatred Raye Dawn and Gayla had for their family. He told her about a listening device the Smith family planted in the Briggs house. Michael claimed he didn't have too many details about the device because Raye Dawn's family kept him out of the loop on such discussions.

Porter confided in Shirica, telling her something he had never told anyone about the case. The day Kelsey died, Porter told Shirica, he walked into the bedroom and found Kelsey naked in the bed, with her butt propped into the air with pillows. He intimated that Raye Dawn had placed her in that position to frame him.

Porter made eye contact with Shirica as he told her he did not kill Kelsey. At the time, Shirica was convinced Raye Dawn had taken Kelsey's life. That's why she believed Porter as he said, "I am willing to give my life for Kelsey. When I say that, I mean that I know that the sentence for failure to protect is life in prison and I am willing to accept that. But I am not willing to die for a crime I did not commit."

Four days after Shirica and Porter's visit, the pressure and tension mounted online. Jeanna demanded Raye Dawn be arrested. Her post read:

We do not want to have Raye Dawn arrested before the time is right. I know that everyone wants her arrested RIGHT NOW!! Trust me, I do too. However, I do not want her arrested before the case against her is rock solid for the appropriate crime. I do not want the OSBI and the DA to do to her what they did with Mike. I want her charged with the right crime with sufficient evidence to support it. God may have arrested Mike first, in order to open his eyes and get his heart and head in the right place for him to be used by God. I believe that God is using Mike to be Kelsey's voice and tell her truth.

Shirica forwarded the post to Porter.

From: John Smith
To: Shirica
Mike did read and "hear" it. I think that this post would echo Mike's exact feelings. Mike cried like a baby after reading that…it could not have been said better.

That day, the Medical Examiner's Office released its complete report on Kelsey's death. Shirica read it as soon as she got her hands on it and caught Porter in what she still believes was a lie.

Porter had told her he found Kelsey naked, her butt propped up with a pillow. The pathologist reported Kelsey was wearing a black biker rally t-shirt and a wet pull up. The pathologist says the t-shirt had vomit on it. Shirica says there is no way Porter put a t-shirt with vomit and a wet pull up on Kelsey.

She called her mom and Jeanna to share her discovery. If he lied about that, what else was he lying about? But it was not enough for Shirica to cut off communication with Porter.

From: Shirica
To: John Smith
Subject: DA
I thought the medical report may be hard to handle for you. It was for me. Have you read it?

From: John Smith
To: Shirica
Subject: RE: DA
The medical report was unbearable. I could not sleep at all last night, I prayed all night that God would allow the DA to hold RD accountable with the findings of the report. I cannot imagine what she had to endure. I do not understand how anyone could do that to Kelsey and the thought of Kelsey looking at Raye Dawn and wondering why, kills me. He needs to know that there is a lot more to this story than whatever he has been told by Raye Dawn. The truth for Kelsey is the most important thing to me and people need to hear it.

On January 12, 2006, Smothermon told the Briggs, Raye Dawn would not be arrested for several weeks because he had another trial to focus on. Since Smothermon was not grasping the gravity of this case, Shirica and others sent the DA hundreds of postcards. They let him know the case would make or break his career and urged him to make it a priority.

Shirica broke the news about Raye Dawn's imminent arrest to Porter in another email.

From: Shirica
To: truejustice101105
Subject: Discouraging News
Please do not lose your faith. I have this hope for seeing Raye Dawn in her stripes being paraded into court the way you were except I hope there are cameras in her face when they do it. I know that hope will come to light. I know it will.

As the case got closer to trial, Shirica would be criticized for exchanging emails with the man charged with Kelsey's murder. The Briggs felt Porter was their only link to what the end of Kelsey's life was like.

She wanted him to trust her, all the while knowing he was smart enough to detect ulterior motives. For weeks he managed to convince her it was his sister sending the emails. Shirica says she was grasping at straws; she had no desire to be his friend or to save him. It was a fine line though. To gain his confidence, Shirica had to convince him she wanted Raye Dawn to hang for the crime. Once Porter felt completely comfortable with Shirica, he stopped using his sister as a cover and communicated directly.

From: truejustice
To: Shirica
Subject: RE: Discouraging News
Knowing the extent of her injuries now kills me. Kelsey had no chance no matter what me or anyone else did. THAT SELFISH BITCH!!! How could I have done all that in 12-15 minutes?? Why would I do ANYTHING when I HONESTLY thought she was asleep? Why would I do anything to hurt her when I knew Mike Taber would be there any second?

Kathie had Smothermon's ear, at least more than Porter did. So Porter asked Shirica if he could contact her mother. Once he got in touch with Kathie he had no need for Shirica.

When Kathie saw truejustice101105 in her inbox, she knew who it was.

From: truejustice
To: kjbriggs
January 20, 2006 4:43 p.m.
We had been wanting to contact you for some time now. There are so many things that need to be said, but I will just tell you that I will answer any questions that I can for you. We know that you all want and deserve the truth. I know the correspondence must be hard and many people would not understand but here goes. Our prayers are with your family every day.

From: kjbriggs
To: truejustice
January 20, 2006 9:20 p.m.

First of all this is a little strange. Why we have a desire to communicate may seem strange, but when you grasp at straws for answers
you are willing to put yourself out there. Obviously I have many
questions and they start with last January all the way to October
11. I would like to sit and ask point blank questions and get very
honest point blank answers, but I also don't want to take advantage
of your situation. Basically there is nothing I can do to change the
criminal investigation. Facts are facts and that is what it is based on.
I am sure you know I am not convinced the proper person has been
charged with the right charge. I have been snowed by so many concerning Kelsey for so long that I have to remain skeptical of everyone.
I am actually looking for answers for the civil case at this point. I
feel there are a lot of people who did not act ethically and I want to
know who, what, when and why. If there was enough information
to put some others in jail for failing Kelsey then I would be willing
to talk to the DA about deals. I am sure you know who all I am
interested in, but mostly Gayla or any family member, Meeker police,
DHS, CASA, CHBS, Judge Key, Judge Combs, Greg Wilson and
Dr. Koons.

From: truejustice101105
To: kjbriggs
January 20, 2006 9:46 p.m.
Well here goes. This is the hard part. The criminal investigation is
being bungled severely. Every lawyer in the county knows this. The
DA is destroying his case day by day. We feel we have solid evidence
that Raye Dawn committed the crime. The DA has the same evidence and it is being ignored. Basically at this point it appears that
he has made the decision that rather than admit they may have made
a mistake he has chosen to continue on the current course which will
NOT get justice for Kelsey. Raye Dawn will not tell the truth about
what happened, and it is unfortunate that the DA does not see that,
but that is how it is. She was NEVER pursued as a primary suspect
in this investigation - even these last few months have been them
basically going through the motions.

For the next ten days, true justice and kjbriggs exchanged emails. Porter was making his case to the one person he thought could influence the District Attorney. Kathie mined Porter for intimate information about what happened in the months leading up to Kelsey's death. Porter was her only link to the truth; but for all she knew the black and white words popping up in her inbox were those of the man who was lying about what caused so many black and blue marks on her granddaughter.

Many people would judge Kathie's decision to meet Porter that day. Many people wondered how she could sit down in the same room with her granddaughter's suspected murderer. Kathie wanted answers. Answers Raye Dawn was never willing to give. Maybe she was searching for closure; maybe she was seeking the "true justice" that could not be found online.

Kathie was not nervous as she drove to the Porters' business to pick him up. She was confident there were no safety issues. At this time she firmly believed Raye Dawn had framed Porter for Kelsey's murder.

From: truejustice101105
To: kjbriggs
January 23, 2006 11:22 p.m.
How does 1:00 sound? I see no need in waiting. The more I put it off the more chance I have of talking myself out of doing it. Richard told Paul today that he still has every intention of arresting her, he just does not want it to be for too little. The thing is he can amend charges, but I believe that they can only be amended down, not up. If he does not charge her with murder then he never will.
To me, anyone who can't see that Raye Dawn is a sociopath is blind. I was at the funeral. I SAW her with my own two eyes. She can turn it on and off like a light switch. People in that family actually bad mouthed me because I was so distraught at Kelsey's funeral. It was surreal. You know the sad thing, there was so much evidence at the house that could have been used against Raye Dawn that is gone now, stacks of letters that she would write after she had sobered up from one of her drinking rages, so many things that because Kevin wanted to arrest me so quickly will never come to light. I could have handed her to them on a silver platter, but since they let her clean

out all the evidence like they always do, all I have left is my word, which is damaged because I stood behind Raye Dawn even when I had doubts. I will do my best to control my emotions tomorrow but I can't promise anything. I can't turn my feelings on and off like Raye Dawn. Although I did not kill Kelsey and I do not feel I should spend the rest of my life in prison, a part of me feels a great deal of responsibility and regret. I was already faced with the facts that I believed Kelsey died in my arms, but I would have coped with that because I knew I did everything I could THAT day to save her. But then for people to not only say that I didn't try to help her but that I actually took her life is almost impossible to take. The fact is Raye Dawn will always be the same person, she will never change. I am not the person I was when I was with her.

Kathie picked Porter up from work and took him to Shirica's apartment. The conversation in the minivan was uncomfortable. The two people tied together by a dead two-year-old had really never met. Kathie knew of him. She talked to him on the phone a couple of times but had never spent any time with him.

The first thing Porter asked Kathie was whether she was wearing a wire. Kathie explained that he's probably not used to honest people, but the Briggs do not operate like that.

Kathie told Smothermon she was meeting with Porter. Porter made her promise she would not reveal anything about their meeting to his lawyer. Kathie felt it was her job as a mother to tell him the meeting was probably not a very good idea. But he wanted to continue.

Kathie brought Porter one of Kelsey's teddy bears to give to Whitney. All of Kelsey's cousins had something of hers, and Kathie wanted Whitney to have something too. When she handed over the teddy bear Michael lost it. He had to go to the bathroom because he was crying so hard. She says it was hard to tell whether they were tears of guilt or emptiness.

Kathie told him she did not want to talk about October 11, 2005. She was just looking for information on their civil case. The criminal stuff was between him, God, and a jury.

Kathie asked about the Smith family's relationships with DHS and the judge. Porter made sure to tell her about Raye Dawn's hatred for her family and her anger about Lance coming home. Porter told her about one time Kelsey got a beating for calling Ashley, "Mommy Ashley". Porter says Raye Dawn was not going to allow Kelsey to go to school in Meeker because she did not want the Briggs to be able to see her. He told her the reason Kelsey's hair fell out all of a sudden was because Raye Dawn got mad and pulled it out.

He confirmed Kathie's suspicions that Judge Key made his decision before the trial to give Kelsey back to Raye Dawn. He remembered the Smith family hiding the listening device in Kathie's home. Porter told Kathie, Raye Dawn would sit across the street from the Briggs home with a video camera, recording each person who would come and go.

Kathie knew she could not believe everything he told her. He lied under oath before, why should he tell the truth now? She was very reserved about what she shared but felt she had nothing to lose by meeting with him. While she did not have sympathy for him, at the time, Kathie did not believe he was the person who murdered her granddaughter.

In the end, Kathie thanked him for meeting with her and took him back to work.

In January, Richard Smothermon held a news conference making a plea to the public for any information in the case. Kathie and Jeanna drove to Shawnee to hear what Smothermon had to say first hand. Jeanna wanted to meet the man she had been speaking with on the phone. The two walked into Smothermon's office and Jeanna introduced herself, announcing she was there because she did not want her mother on television that evening. Smothermon told her Kathie could do interviews if she wanted, but Jeanna explained she wanted to make sure the public heard the plea from him, not Kathie Briggs.

Jeanna and Kathie sat behind all of the cameras crammed in the small conference room and listened as Smothermon admitted Raye Dawn was a big part of the investigation. Smothermon announced he needed more information. He asked anyone who had any knowledge Raye Dawn had abused or neglected Kelsey to come forward. The smallest of details could help secure his case.

Smothermon's plea landed him in hot water politically. In the days that followed, the public became frustrated and began calling television stations saying their tips were not taken seriously and the District Attorney's office had not returned their calls. Smothermon called the stations defending himself saying all of the tips were being handled by OSBI.

A few days after their meeting Kathie decided it was best to end her communication with Porter.

From: KJBRIGGS
To: truejustice101105
Subject: Re: (no subject)
Date: Mon, 30 Jan 2006 20:47:55 EST
I have been thinking since we met. I don't think it is a good idea and I am not comfortable with this. You could be baiting me for information, you could be lying to me to get me to lend reasonable doubt with your information. Basically I am doing the same thing. I am using you to find out what happened to my granddaughter. It is wrong of me. You might be innocent of murder, you might be guilty. I was not in that home that day and it is wrong for me to assume a position either way without all the evidence. If you are innocent it is wrong for me to put you in a position to lose your attorney. If you're guilty it is wrong for me to give you my time. You avoid every question and that tells me you are just baiting me more and more. Basically my trust is very little. I cannot change what happened in the criminal aspects of this case. I want to know who failed Kelsey from January until October 11, 2005. I will have to trust the court system and our DA to do that. I want Justice for Kelsey and I cannot get it by doing anything unethical.

Porter made another plea to his only link to the District Attorney and tried to answer the questions he had not.

Subj: Re: (no subject)
Date: 1/30/06 8:54:57 PM Central Standard Time
From: truejustice101105
To: kjbriggs
I understand. But just know that I want the same things as you. I will answer any question that you have and I have told you that, but I would prefer not to do it by e-mail at this time. I will leave my offer

on the table. It will remain there. If you choose to never take me up on it then I understand. I am sorry if you felt I was avoiding your questions, I certainly have not tried to. So much has been lost because people would not communicate. It would be a shame if we still could not after everything. I am in no way baiting you. I told you in the beginning I do not want nor do I expect any help from you in any way. My offer for help in holding people accountable stands and will stand. No matter what happens to me I will not stop until I have exhausted every means I have to make sure people are held accountable. Please know that. Again, I have not and will not ever try to bait you. To what end? 12 people will decide my fate, and you will not be one of them. I know that. I will die knowing I DID NOT hurt Kelsey, and there are people who can not say that for themselves. I am sorry I have not made my true intentions clear to you. I certainly understand your lack of trust, but I made my offer for help to you with a pure heart.

Subj: RE: Answer
Date: 1/31/06 3:33:47 AM Central Standard Time
From: truejustice101105
To: kjbriggs

And I am not sure which questions you felt I was avoiding. I can't go back through and check e-mails because I delete them after I respond. But here are a couple questions I know you had. Number one, yes Raye Dawn had a cell phone. Yes Raye Dawn had a toddler bed/crib. The bed had side rails that you could raise or lower. She had the side rail removed and used it like a normal bed for Kelsey. She claimed to me that that night she had turned the open side towards the wall, so Kelsey would had to have climbed over the high side that was facing out. I had NEVER seen her do this before. Her story on the collarbone has already changed so many times who knows what happened. We were at Wendell's house when Kelsey leaned on the unlatched screen door. That was one of the very few times I ever saw Kelsey fall or hurt herself. Miste lied about the zoo because Raye Dawn asked her to. Kelsey did NOT hurt her foot at the zoo. Craig Key told Greg Wilson at least three weeks before the court hearing that "He was going to fix things". Basically Greg made it clear to Raye Dawn that it was well in hand and all she had to do was show up. You were there, you knew the Judge had his mind made up. The Judge came up to Raye Dawn in the hallway and said "I created this monster, now let me take care of it." I heard this with MY OWN EARS. I do not ever want it said that I was not willing to do whatever it took to make sure the people who failed Kelsey are held accountable. If you have any more questions, then feel free to ask them, AND I WILL RESPOND IN WRITING. I WILL ASK NOTHING OF YOU. I care more about justice for Kelsey than myself, I would have thought I made that very obvious. If I do not hear from you then I will know that you do not feel I can help you in this cause. Thank you for your time.

Ultimately, Shirica and Kathie learned very little about Kelsey's life before she died. Through the emails they learned a lot about Porter's character. As it turned out, the words written in those emails would land Porter in prison.

By February, everyone involved in the case had a lawyer. Lance's attorneys had named defendants in the multi-million dollar lawsuit. The District Attorney summoned a multi-county grand jury investigation into Kelsey's case. People in the legal community speculated Smothermon would take the easy way out and hand the case over to the grand jury. Then jurors would decide if Raye Dawn should be charged.

While Kathie spent the week preparing for her testimony, studying the dates and times of each injury, Michael Porter reached out to her again.

Subj: Good luck this week
Date: 2/20/06
From: truejustice
To: kjbriggs
I just wanted to tell you I will be praying for you this week. I hope the Lord will allow the truth to come out in that courtroom so people can be held accountable. You will be one of the only chances for Kelsey's voice to be heard in that room. Raye Dawn will be working against you and the truth, but you already know that. Good luck and God Bless you.

Smothermon had a different plan. He never intended to call Kathie to testify before the grand jury. The only person called to testify was Dr. Kelli Koons, Kelsey's pediatrician. Grand jury dealings in Oklahoma are kept completely confidential. No one leaked the fact that the District Attorney did not use the grand jury. He sat upstairs and talked with Kelli Koons about the case, privately.

On February 23, 2006, the very next day, Smothermon surprised everyone with another news conference. This time he announced charges against Kelsey's mother, "I'm filing tomorrow morning, two felony counts against Raye Dawn Porter in the case of Kelsey Briggs. I'm filing one count of Enabling Child Abuse and one count of Child Neglect."

Smothermon denied ever considering murder charges against Kelsey's mom. He said, "Either she knew that Porter was abusing her, or she should have known. And the law makes no distinction of whether you knew or should have known. If she truly didn't know, she missed a lot of red flags."

Smothermon told reporters Raye Dawn neglected Kelsey. He had evidence to prove she drove while under the influence of alcohol with Kelsey in the car.

Raye Dawn's charges muddied the water as to whether she would testify against Michael Porter. Smothermon said, "She can either quit cooperating and we'll go to trial or she can do the right thing and continue cooperating and a judge or jury will take that into consideration."

Smothermon gave Raye Dawn until the next morning to turn herself in to the Lincoln County Courthouse. Raye Dawn's family escorted the eight months pregnant mother-to-be into the door of the Lincoln County Jail. She was inside before the photographers waiting outside could get a good shot. Deputies booked Raye Dawn into jail; but she was never handcuffed or forced to wear stripes.

Tension was high as the Briggs family sat outside the courtroom. It was the day they had been waiting for. As they sat making small talk, Raye Dawn's grandmother, Mildred Fowler, approached the bench Kathie was sitting on. She leaned down just inches from her face and asked, "Do you sleep at night?" Kathie remembers sitting in silence for several seconds as she contemplated her response. At the same time Mildred's gentleman friend was pushing his chest into Lance's chest. Lance could not understand why the elderly man, he had never seen before, kept repeating, "Who do you think you are?" From this moment forward the District Attorney's office provided security for all court proceedings.

The rest of Raye Dawn's family waited until moments before her scheduled court appearance to escort her across the courtyard between the jail and the courthouse. When they walked outside the Smith family was greeted by a hoard of media outlets waiting for a shot of Raye Dawn. To protect Raye Dawn from reporters' questions, her family formed what could only be described as a human shield around Kelsey's mother. As the family approached the courtroom, the family and friends surrounding Raye Dawn shoved reporters and put their hands in front of television cameras. There would be no Nick Winkler show this time. Cherokee Ballard shouted, "Raye Dawn did you love Kelsey?" Britten asked, "Raye Dawn, who broke Kelsey's legs?" Raye Dawn walked silently. Gayla's boyfriend shouted, "Ask Kathie Briggs!"

So they did. After the hearing, reporters asked Kathie Briggs how she felt about the reference that she somehow knew or allowed Kelsey to be abused. Kathie told them she understood they were trying to deflect attention away from Raye Dawn. Kathie knew she was an easy target because she had custody of Kelsey when someone broke her legs.

The Smith family blamed everyone but themselves. Diverting attention from Raye Dawn seemed to be their only defense.

Kathie could not fathom why Raye Dawn was getting special treatment once again. Had she gotten to the D.A. too? Kathie sat down at her computer a day after Raye Dawn's court appearance and shared her thoughts with Smothermon.

Subj: Kelsey Briggs
Date: 2/25/06
From: KJBRIGGS
To: Richard Smothermon
After spending the day still in disbelief I have decided to express my thoughts to you.

   Yesterday our family was treated as if we had no business being in court. Outside of Kelsey, Lance is the victim in this crime and you did not speak to him, nor did you acknowledge him. My son went home crying, he felt his daughter's life was worth nothing when the one person who could have protected her paid $2500 for her freedom. Then to think the one person that could represent Kelsey and our family would not even fight to get a higher bond. Lance stated there was really no reason for you to be in court, all you did was agree to Huddleston's every move. Raye Dawn was treated like royalty.

What is wrong with our system? Are any of you going to realize that for nine months a baby was abused and now she is DEAD? You act as though someone just misplaced their doll and we have lost a vital member of our family.

You have been told by the Smith family we have a vendetta and I think that clouds your judgment. Kelsey was not a prize we were trying to win, she was a child we were trying to save. We are not some Podunk family from Meeker. My son has served his country, all three of my daughters are college educated and all are good parents. Our family owns several businesses in Shawnee and the surrounding area. You say you are our attorney, but aren't you also working for the Smiths? Raye Dawn has a choice in who represents her, he is getting paid to do his job. We do not have a choice, we have to put our faith in the very system that let us down time and time again. You want us to trust you and we try, but you do not stick by your statements.

I don't know what your plans are for Raye Dawn, but I can tell you our family does not want a deal made. We want you to prosecute this case in front of a jury. We feel that she still should have more charges filed. She should have been charged by your office in January and Kelsey could still be alive. Kelsey was failed then and she deserves justice.

It concerns me when you are referred to as "lets make a deal Smothermon" from our legal community.

You said your case was strong against Porter and you did not need Raye Dawn. You also said your case was strong against her. So please do not let us down. She did not give Kelsey a deal and she does not deserve one either.

You stated you always wanted to be a prosecutor and now is your chance to prosecute one of the state's biggest child abuse cases. We cannot help Kelsey anymore, but you can.

Raye Dawn Smith

A week after her husband was arrested for murder, Raye Dawn showed up at OSBI headquarters again. This time Raye brought her lawyer. Steve Huddleston spent nearly an hour talking with Agent Kevin Garrett, laying out his defense, before his client ever came in the room.

Raye traded the casual look from a week earlier, for her conservative, grieving mother attire. She walked in wearing her name tag over her left breast, a white button down collared shirt, and black cotton gaucho pants. Her blonde hair had been straightened, parted, and tucked behind her ears. Raye was dressed to impress the man who arrested her husband.

Raye immediately started looking at the stack of pictures Huddleston brought for Garrett to see. Pictures of her daughter's smiling face. Raye Dawn's face was still "all cried out."

Raye came for this interrogation armed with pictures and stories. A week earlier she couldn't imagine a scenario where her husband could have been capable of murder. Now that he had been arrested and she was free, Raye Dawn managed to recall some details she left out of their conversation a week prior.

Garrett began with the uncomfortable conversation about the sexual abuse, "Did your mom tell you anything that I told her?"

"She just said she had a rip somewhere," *replied Raye.*

"Inside between her rectum and the vagina, there's a tear. I saw photographs of the tear and it's a separate incident."

"Wait. Is this on the outside or in the inside?" *Raye didn't seem to understand the description.*

"Inside. There's bruising on the outside, there's also bruising around the anus, but on the inside there's a tear. Of course, I'm going to want to ask you, you know, how did she. . .do you know of any way that she could have gotten that kind of injury?"

"And I went back and I've thought and I've thought, and she never said anything about anything. So is the bruising like. . .you said the bruise is on the outside?"

"Yeah."

Raye Dawn shook her head and said, "He's sorry."

"It even looked to me like there was a bruise on the cheek, you know, where maybe if you were holding it open or something, you know. You know, just thinking on how that could have occurred kind of makes me sick at my stomach and I'm sure being your daughter it makes you pretty sick, you know."

Raye continued, "You know, and I go back to thinking that here recently, you know, every time I would leave, something would happen. Like you know, I wouldn't be gone maybe 10 or 15 minutes. But now that I look at it, something you know, would happen every time."

"What would that something be?"

"He said the lamp fell over and hit her in the face. By the time I got back, she had a bruise on her face. Can I tell you one incident that really ticked me off?"

"Sure."

"That whenever she had soap in her eye and she had rubbed it, you know, red, and she, the sun kind of hurt her eye, so we couldn't go to Frontier City like we had planned on going, and which that upset everybody. But I went somewhere and I came back. And Mike, Bubby, Whitney and Kelsey are all back there in our bedroom on the bed. And Kelsey, I think, is sitting on Mike's stomach. And he had her eyes taped shut and her mouth taped shut and they were all laughing at her. I walked in there and I was like, 'What the hell are you doing?' and I just jerked her up and took her out of there."

"When was that?"

"It was when we were supposed to go to Frontier City."

"What kind of tape did he use?"

"Like masking tape."

"Masking tape?"

"Like the clear, well, the clear kind of stuff like you use for like Christmas paper."

"That's more of a scotch tape kind of thing, isn't it, the clear?" asked Garrett.

"Okay," agreed Raye.

"Masking tape, I think is like white."

"Well, this was the clear stuff," clarified Raye.

"Okay. He taped her eyes shut and put it over her mouth."

"And when I asked him, when I said, 'What the hell are you doing?' He was like, 'Well, she was laughing until you came in here. She wasn't laughing because she couldn't see me because her eyes were taped shut."

"Was she crying?"

"No she was just sitting there," said Raye.

"Okay," replied Garrett.

"And I called my mom about that too."

"You didn't mention this the other day when I interviewed you. I don't think I've ever heard of anybody doing that to a little kid before. That's a new one," said Garrett.

"That made me really mad," said Raye.

As for all of the bruises, Raye says, "They would just kind of. . .I thought they just popped up because you know, I would even ask you know, 'Mike, do you know where this came from?' And he was like, 'I have no idea.' But it was just like these little round ones. And she even had one that Tuesday because Jean asked her about it, you know. Of course, Kelsey, she ignored it because she got tired of people asking her. But I guess she did."

179

"*Do you consider yourself an observant person?*" asked Garrett.

"*Sometimes, no. I'm kind of dingy,*" replied Raye. "*I just thought she was bruising easily, like if she just, you know bumped into something. That's why I was taking her to the doctor and having blood work done to see if there was a reason. My mom was afraid she had leukemia, is why she was bruising easily.*"

"*I mean, you didn't have a red flag come up?*" Garrett asked.

"*Yeah, because I was getting aggravated because, you know, I even asked Mom. I said, 'Everything is coming back normal and above normal. What is going on here?' Now I even asked Mom that. I don't know. There has got to be, you know, we knew there had to be an explanation.*"

Garrett continued to press Raye for explanations, "*Well, on these bruises on the face, is there a chance that, have you ever grabbed her by the face or anything that might have caused the bruise?*"

"*No, Mike used to, when she wouldn't eat, he would kind of do this,*" Raye demonstrated how Mike would massage her jaws.

"*So he would rub her jaws.*"

Raye continued, "*To try to get her to chew. When I saw him doing that, I told him, I was like, 'Don't be doing that.' I told him to quit doing it because she doesn't like it.*"

Raye's memory improved drastically since her last visit. All of a sudden she remembered multiple stories that cast suspicion toward Porter. Raye said, "*I went to my grandma's, I think it was, to get water or something at my grandma's and come back. And Porter said, 'Is there a bump right there?' And I said, 'It's red. Why?' And he said, 'Well, Kelsey fell down the stairs.' And I said, 'When? Why? What happened?'*"

"*At the new house?*" asked Garrett, "*He said she rolled, like all the way down them?*"

Raye answered, "*No. I think he said maybe half-way. But that one, I wasn't too sure about. I called my mom on that one.*"

"*Even Mom said last night, she said, 'That raised a red flag to me.'*"

Raye continued, "*You know he told me he hated me sometimes, and all I care about is that 'thing in the back.'*"

Garrett asked, "*He was calling Kelsey a 'thing in the back'?*"

"*Yeah. Yeah, that made me mad too. And I called my mom,*" said Raye.

"*Okay. So what good does it do to call Mom? Does she just kind of help things?*" asked Garrett.

"*She just, she's somebody for me to talk to. I talk to her. He used to make fun of me because I called my mom, you know 50 times a day.*"

T·W·E·L·V·E

THE FIRST WEEK OF 2006, REPORTERS SAT IN THE MEDICAL EXAMINER'S OFFICE AWAITING THEIR COPY OF THE FINAL AUTOPSY REPORT. The Chief Investigator for the Medical Examiner's Office walked out with a stack of papers, still warm from the copier, and handed them out to each reporter. He told reporters the injuries to Kelsey's vaginal area were not necessarily caused by sexual abuse. It could not be ruled out, however. It was the pathologist's opinion that those injuries could be caused by a punch or a kick, as well.

The headline of *The Oklahoman* the next morning read, "Autopsy Shows Extent of Kelsey's Fatal Injuries." The Medical Examiner says Kelsey died of "blunt force trauma" to the abdomen, but also suffered blunt force trauma to the genital area, head, torso, arms and legs.

Dr. Inas Yacoub went to school in Cairo, Egypt and had been with the Oklahoma State Medical Examiner's Office for a couple of years. She examined Kelsey's body.

Much of her report was written in very technical medical terms; however, the diagrams illustrated the sheer terror of Kelsey's final day. Yacoub marked the bruises with small black dots on the diagram of a child's body. Arrows pointed from the bruise to the margin of the page, documenting the size of each bruise. Six arrows pointed to Kelsey's private parts. The pathologist described a tear to Kelsey's pelvis between her left ovary and pelvic wall.

Kathie knew her granddaughter's last moments were horrendous but the diagrams were difficult to stomach. Her afternoon shopping trip was interrupted by reporters asking for her reaction to the report.

This was another report that was released to the media before the family had seen it. News of the possible sexual abuse was not a shock. Kevin Garrett called the Briggs home in the days following Kelsey's death to warn them about this information. Garrett explained injuries to Kelsey's private parts could have been caused by an object. This is why Kathie still believes either Porter or Raye could have been the perpetrator.

Yacoub believes the impact to the abdomen pushed the tissue together, bruising and tearing the tissue through her abdomen area. The pathologist reported significant trauma to the pelvic area between the vagina, the uterus and the rectum.

Kelsey's upper lip was torn; there were bruises to her lower right abdomen. Yacoub noted at least seven bruises all over her legs, a very large bruise on her left leg and left thigh, and several small bruises on her right leg.

Kelsey's body had bruising around her anus, a scrape on her back; her brain was swollen; and she had several bruises on the back of her head, between her hair and her skull. Yacoub says those would have been caused when Kelsey's head hit a hard, solid surface.

The pathologist noted Kelsey was wearing orange nail polish and her baby toenail had been ripped off.

Dr. Yacoub examined the injuries under Kelsey's skin and found recent hemorrhaging, with no evidence of healing. She says she did not see any evidence of an old injury that decided to open up, which means the injuries had to have happened within minutes or hours, not days.

In Yacoub's medical experience one trauma could not have caused all of the injuries. Yacoub would later testify, "Kelsey Briggs died at the hand of another; I ruled it a homicide."

One of the two people who could have been responsible for the murder was scheduled to bring another child into the world. Doctors induced Raye Dawn on April 11, 2006. Six months to the date after Kelsey's death. DHS whisked Curtis Blaine Shelton Smith into the safety of Raye Dawn's relatives. Sheltered from the tumultuous life he was born into, Blaine was only a couple months old when he was rushed to the hospital. The child's medical records were kept private but Porter indicated the baby boy was being treated for effects of fetal alcohol syndrome.

As the state prepared to prosecute Michael Porter for Kelsey's murder, Richard Smothermon approached both the Smith and the Briggs family with a delicate subject. He wanted to unearth Kelsey's body from its final resting place for a second autopsy.

He explained Porter's attorney had hired an expert witness to refute the findings of Oklahoma's Medical Examiner and he felt he needed a witness of his own. Dr. Dean Hawley is a forensic scientist from Indiana who has been paid to testify as an expert in hundreds of criminal cases across the country. Hawley wanted to do an autopsy of his own.

Both families reluctantly agreed. The same funeral home that buried Kelsey six months before, dug up her body.

Smothermon promised he would stay by Kelsey's side for the entire autopsy.

That day, as Jeanna drove home from work she couldn't help but turn her head and look at the cemetery. She saw Kelsey's casket coming out of the ground. Not knowing what else to do she picked up her phone and called Smothermon on his cell phone, sobbing.

Between gasps for air Jeanna said, "Make sure they take care of her... and when they put her back...they say a prayer and don't just drop her back in there." Smothermon promised Kelsey's aunt again he would not leave her side and would say a prayer himself before they buried her again.

Shirica was lying in a doctor's office hooked up to a machine and an I.V. The room was dark and she was alone when her cell phone rang. It was her mom calling to tell her Kelsey's body was being pulled from the ground.

Shirica spent two hours on the table crying. She had no idea what the doctor must have been thinking when she came in every few minutes to check on her. But Shirica couldn't stop crying. She did not expect Kelsey to be unearthed that day, but rain was on its way and the funeral home needed to do it before the ground was saturated.

Cherokee and her photographer drove by the cemetery that afternoon in hopes of confirming the tip Kelsey's body was being exhumed. Cherokee had the opportunity to have an exclusive story for that night's newscast. The District Attorney asked her to sit on the story. The Briggs family did not feel comfortable with the story being reported until Kelsey was back in her resting place.

Smothermon stood by Kelsey's side as Dr. Hawley performed a second autopsy on Kelsey's body at OU Children's Hospital. Smothermon and six others watched as Dr. Hawley placed Kelsey's body face down on the autopsy table and removed the tiny shirt, skirt, and tights the two-year-old was buried in. Once he was able to remove the clear plastic wrap encasing her body, Hawley learned her body had deteriorated during the six months she had been in the casket.

One of the people observing the autopsy was John Cooper, an independent Medical Examiner from Texas, hired by Porter.

Hawley was looking for DNA or evidence of a sexually transmitted disease in Kelsey's vagina. Yacoub did not take specimens to test for either one. Hawley says the injuries Yacoub took photos of on the day of her death were no longer evident. Hawley looked inside a plastic bag of organs but could not identify the body parts he needed to look for DNA. Kelsey's vagina, uterus, ovaries, bladder, and anus were not there. Hawley needed those parts to test for the presence of bodily fluids that would likely be present if Kelsey was sexually abused.

Even without Kelsey's reproductive organs Dr. Hawley was able to note some evidence that would prove helpful in Smothermon's case. Dr. Hawley showed Smothermon there was some calcification to Kelsey's private parts, indicating to him she had been injured there before and was healing.

Hawley studied the tear to Kelsey's pelvic wall and the purple bruise on the back wall of her rectum to determine if those injuries were caused by sexual abuse. Smothermon believes it could have been caused from Porter's penis. The tear was so significant it could not have been caused by a finger nail.

Smothermon says Hawley pointed out evidence of some type of infection in Kelsey's vaginal canal, but said it was too late to test for a sexually transmitted disease, a test that should have been done moments after her death at the Prague hospital or on the autopsy table. The hospital was apparently more concerned with giving Raye time with her dead child than gathering evidence in a murder investigation. No rape kit was done on Kelsey's body. A simple test would have exposed any evidence linking Porter or Raye Dawn to the crime. A test would have prevented the heartache of disturbing Kelsey's body again.

The second autopsy was completed on April 27, 2006 the day the Governor Henry proclaimed "Kelsey Briggs Day" in the state of Oklahoma.

Kathie had a hard time concentrating on Kelsey's Purpose that rainy day. She knew her granddaughter's body was being unearthed. Kathie and Shirica drove to Shawnee to meet with one of the groups handing out Justice for Kelsey stickers and child abuse material that afternoon. No one there knew what was taking place a few miles away. Kelsey's grandma and aunt looked up at the rain that day thinking each drop was a tear from Heaven.

The grandmother held back tears when the D.A.'s office called to report the autopsy was complete. Kathie tucked her cell phone back in her purse, took a deep breath, and once again put on her public face. It was time to go back to work for Kelsey and other abused children.

Jeanna was still rattled by seeing the tiny coffin and could not put on her public face for Kelsey's day. She stayed home and added to all of the other tears coming down from heaven that day.

Since Hawley's autopsy was finished, Smothermon's only other duty was to place the camel Lance bought for Kelsey in Kuwait inside her casket. Lance wanted it buried with her the first time but the two services made it impossible. With a stuffed animal from her daddy in her arms, Smothermon stood next to Kelsey's casket as they lowered it back into the ground.

Hawley prepared a pathologic diagnosis of his own agreeing with Yacoub that Kelsey died of blunt force injury to the abdomen. Hawley went a step further saying Kelsey was a victim of forcible sexual assault.

The ruling took Smothermon to Michael Porter's living room. The District Attorney obtained a search warrant to pursue a hunch. He was looking for additional evidence on Porter's computer to support Dr. Hawley's diagnosis.

OSBI agents seized Porter's computer at work and executed a simultaneous search at his house. Smothermon believes someone warned Porter they were coming. Inside his house agents found numerous disks and other evidence a computer had been there. Porter had internet service but agents could not find a computer.

Agents found an enormous amount of pornography stored on Porter's work computer. Smothermon says it was everywhere. They found websites and searches all dealing with anal sex. Porter used the online alias, "Big Daddy". There was an online conversation where Smothermon says Porter talked about his enormous penis.

The stash of anal related pornography combined with Dr. Hawley's testimony was enough for Smothermon to add new charges against Michael Porter.

In July of 2006, Smothermon filed alternative charges against Kelsey's step-father. The jury now had a choice of First Degree Murder or Child Sexual Abuse. These additional charges delayed the preliminary hearing again to give the defense more time to prepare its case.

On August 23, 2006, Michael Porter and his lawyer made no effort to skirt the cameras. They walked along the sidewalk as reporters asked Porter about the sexual abuse charges. Porter walked in silence next to a very smug Paul Sutton.

A section of the courtroom had to be reserved for the Briggs family in hopes of avoiding another unpleasant encounter with the Smith family.

The courtroom was packed as four witnesses broke down an hour by hour account of what they say happened October 11, 2005. Mike Taber took the stand describing the scene at the house as he pulled up the long driveway to look at tires. Taber told the judge he was life long friends with Porter and could not imagine him capable of hurting Kelsey.

David Jenkins, the first responder, described Kelsey's body as gray, almost like a baby doll. She was dead when he arrived.

The star witness was Raye Dawn Smith.

Raye Dawn took the stand dressed in a black suit with her blonde hair pulled back into a clip. Porter rolled his eyes and shook his head as the tearful mother told the same story she concocted for the OSBI agents. Porter's lawyer went through a series of detailed questions about the number of pillows placed on the bed and how they were arranged around Kelsey's body. He argued his client did not have enough time to kill Kelsey and the evidence clearly points to Raye Dawn.

This was the first time reporters heard Raye Dawn's story about the turtle and the strange items she fixed Kelsey for breakfast. It was also the first time reporters heard Raye Dawn's meek, tearful voice.

Smothermon made it clear to the judge the state was in the process of negotiating a deal with Raye Dawn's attorney to reduce her charges. Raye Dawn testified she had not been made aware of the details of that agreement and that is not why she decided to testify.

After Dr. Dean Hawley took the stand, the young Judge Dawson Engle announced there was enough evidence against Porter to go to trial. Dr. Hawley told the court he had no evidence to prove who did it. He found no semen or bodily fluids inside Kelsey. He did say Kelsey's injuries at the time of her death were consistent with forcible sexual assault from the back to the front.

To avoid another Nick Winkler style questioning the judge banished television cameras to the front lawn of the courthouse. After the hearing,

Lance Briggs approached the cameras to make a statement. Lance said, "A lot of testimony I heard today was hard to hear. We have complete faith in the D.A. He's gonna do his job and I just want everybody to remember Kelsey."

Raye Dawn's Grandmother Mildred stood nearby and listened to the makeshift news conference. Cherokee asked if Mildred wanted to say anything. After a moment Mildred decided to make a brief comment, "Today I was here to support my granddaughter and the District Attorney and pray that justice would be done to the man that took my little great-granddaughter's life and deceived our whole family and that he would be locked up where he belongs so he can't hurt another child."

When the cameras cleared and the families headed home the Briggs had time to take in what they heard and did not believe.

This was the first time Kathie and her family heard Raye Dawn's account of what happened October 11, 2005. That afternoon Jeanna called Smothermon on behalf of her family. It was one of the hardest calls she made throughout the court process. Jeanna called to express her family's disappointment with Raye Dawn's testimony. Jeanna told the District Attorney her family could not support prosecuting a man based on a fabricated story. Jeanna told him they would not stand by quietly if Raye Dawn's lies put Porter behind bars for murder. Even if it meant sacrificing Porter's conviction. The call tore them apart. But how could they know he was the one?

As both sides continued to prepare for trial, Porter's lawyer was building that reasonable doubt. Sutton's expert witness submitted an autopsy evaluation of his own. Dr. Cooper reviewed much of the same information Smothermon gave Hawley. The doctor from Texas arrived at a much different conclusion. It was his opinion the second autopsy provided no new information. Cooper says the agents at the autopsy told him Hawley's goal was to find evidence of sexual assault. Cooper says no such evidence was encountered. If Dr. Hawley truly perceived otherwise Cooper says he did not mention it in his presence.

Cooper praised Yacoub's autopsy saying it was expert, thorough and very nicely documented, saying her findings were right on the mark. Cooper says Hawley's sexual assault hypothesis was a contrivance concocted at the behest of the prosecuting attorney in order to make the case for the attacker having been a male. Cooper says, "The fact is that the injuries found at the autopsy could not have and did not kill Kelsey within the 20-25 minutes that Mr. Porter was on the premises and had access to the child on the day of her murder."

From a pathological perspective Cooper says people do not usually die of blunt force trauma that quickly. In child abuse deaths involving abdominal trauma, typically there are several internal injuries. Cooper says often times no one suspects how seriously the child has been injured for an hour or two until the child finally goes into shock.

Cooper says he can state to a reasonable degree of medical certainty Kelsey survived two hours or more after being beaten. It is not conceivable she could have died within half an hour of sustaining the trauma.

Cooper believes Kelsey was beaten with a blunt object and kicked to death. In his opinion the perpetrator could not have been Michael Porter because the autopsy and laboratory evidence exonerate him.

Which expert witness would the jury believe?

Raye Dawn Smith

"Did she ever not want to go to Mike? I mean, that would be a behavioral change. Did you ever notice anything like that?" asked Garret.

Nonchalantly, Raye Dawn said, *"That's like how she was whenever he would just pick her up, you know, when she would kind of start crying or pucker up. She did that."*

Raye Dawn contradicted herself when she said, *"She would start crying, and I was like, you know, to even go to the kitchen. This was before June. But I mean, just to get up and go to the kitchen, she would start crying."*

Raye Dawn, played with her hair, *"Like kind of cry, but she wouldn't. . .I never did really see any tears. So the way I looked at it was she was trying to get my attention, was the way I looked at it."*

Garrett asked Raye if there was anything that frustrated her about Kelsey. Raye said it was irritating that Kelsey would not swallow her food. Garrett asked, *"Would you discipline her for something like that?"*

"She would just have to sit at the table until she swallowed."

"Okay. But you wouldn't spank her. . ."

"No."

"Or anything like that? No time out?"

"No."

"Okay."

"I might have put her in time out for not swallowing before. I believe I did," explained Raye.

"So what else would she do that might. . .would upset you?" asked Garrett.

Raye answered, *"If Mike was, you know, say, like, putting her into the bath or helping her change her clothes, sometimes, you know, she would let us know she didn't like it. I was like, 'Kelsey what is wrong with you?' So then I would just take her."*

"She wouldn't want to take a bath?" asked Garrett.

Raye told Garrett she could not understand why Kelsey did not tell her Mike was hurting her, *"She's talked as long as I can remember. I mean, I think that's why I get so mad now and upset, is because I thought she would have told me or she would have told my mom that something was wrong."*

"Told you what? What do you mean? Tell you what?"

"Like if the reason we're going through all this problem or whatever happened to Kelsey, if something was going on, why wouldn't she have told me?"

"So you're saying then, if Mike was abusive to her or doing something bad to her, she would tell you? Is that what you mean?"

"Yeah. That's what I was thinking. Wouldn't she have told me?"

"And she never did, apparently?" asked Garrett.

Raye answered, "She never said anything. The night before, she was put in time out, not by me, because she was sitting with me on the couch. We were watching TV and I got up to go do something. And anyways, I came back and I said, 'Come here, Kelsey.' And he was like, 'She's in time out.' I said, 'For what?' And he said, 'When I picked her up, she started pouting.'"

"And this is going to be Monday?" asked Garrett.

"Uh-huh," said Raye.

"October the 10th?"

"Uh, huh."

Garrett asked, "Was she okay staying with Mike, or did it upset her?"

Raye answered, "Sometimes she'd be okay. But that was a ways back, she might be okay, kind of. But then she got to where she would throw up, like when I'd come back. I was like, 'What in the world?' And he was like, 'She just looked at me and just threw up.'"

"Is this recently?"

"From, you know, when we moved into mom's house and then."

"And when was that?"

"Back a ways. We were in the process of moving in before we signed the papers, because mom stayed with us a couple of nights."

Garrett asked, "Has Mike ever told you that maybe she got sick whenever he was giving her a bath?"

"I haven't thought about that. I don't remember. I haven't thought about that," said Raye.

"Well, can you think about it now?" asked Garrett.

"I don't think she ever threw up in the bathtub," answered Raye.

"You don't remember Mike ever making a comment that she had thrown up or got sick while he was giving her a bath or a shower or something?"

"If she did, it was before because I don't think she ever did in the bathtub," said Raye, "You know, it got to where towards here recently that she would. . .I'd come back and I was like, 'What is going on?' And he was like, 'She just threw up.' And then sometimes. . .because I wouldn't leave for very long. I never left her for very long."

Garrett pressed further, "Now did she throw up whenever she was with you?"

"The only time I remember her throwing up when she was with me was when she was sick," said Raye, *"Like sometimes there was a pan, or you know, sometimes he'd have the towel down. And after. . .to where she had thrown up on the couch or he had changed her clothes."*

"How many times did this happen?" asked Garrett.

"There were a few," said Raye.

"How many is a few?"

"Maybe less than, maybe less than ten."

"Less than ten?"

"Uh-huh."

"Okay. Eight times?"

"I don't know for sure," said Raye.

Garrett continued, "Well, that's a lot, isn't it? I mean, did you think that was kind of odd that when your daughter was with you she seems to be fine. And then when you go to take a movie back and she's with Mike, she seems to have some kind of stomach problem and she's throwing up?"

"What I thought was. . ." Raye stuttered, *"This is. . .because I. . .you know what I thought it was. . .was that she had been jerked. . .you know they took her away back in the day."*

"They? You mean DHS?" asked Garrett.

"Well, when Kathie did her guardianship," said Raye.

"Kathie Briggs?"

"I just thought it was, you know, her having separation anxiety and that she was just worried I wasn't coming back," said Raye.

"Okay, so now today, looking back on these vomiting incidents, what do you think is causing her to vomit?" asked Garrett.

"I think she was scared to death," answered Raye.

"Of?"

"I think she was scared of Mike."

Garrett looked at his notes for a minute before asking, "Mike, during the week when it came bath time or shower time. . .it mainly would be a bath that he would give the children. . . that he volunteered to do it at least half of the time?"

"Yeah, I guess," said Raye.

"I mean, is that close?"

"Yeah, that's probably close," said Raye.

"If she was hungry, what would she tell you?" asked Garrett.

"Mommy, I'm hungry."

"*What about if Michael's beating me? I mean, did she ever say anything to you to indicate that maybe he was too forceful in discipline or anything? Did you ever get anything from her on that?*" *asked Garrett.*

"*She never said anything,*" *said Raye,* "*No, she didn't. She didn't throw fits really. She was just a good kid. All I remember is her kind of puckering up sometimes.*"

"*Puckering up? What's puckering up?*"

"*Kind of like, you know, she wanted to cry,*" *said Raye.*

"*So did she like Mike?*" *asked Garrett.*

"*She acted like she was just crazy about him,*" *said Raye,* "*I mean, you know, when I'd call on the phone, sometimes she'd say, 'I want to talk,' and she'd talk to him you know. And before she got off of the phone, she'd say, 'Love you,' you know. He seemed to be so good to her. He seemed to be crazy about her.*"

Garrett continued, "*Because earlier you were kind of making me feel like he's the most perfect guy. I mean, he likes to bathe the children all the time and anytime you ask him to do something, he does it. But he's just a typical guy.*

"*And it just seems like to me that before you answered stuff a whole lot easier than you are today. You really seem like you're thinking. Are you feeling okay today? Is something bothering you? Are you on medication?*" *asked Garrett.*

Raye paused before she said, "*I just want to get over. . .I want to make sure I get everything right. I just want to make sure I get everything that, you know, because there's a lot of stuff, you know, that now I pay attention to it, it raises red flags now.*"

"*Meaning?*"

Raye answered, "*Like when, supposedly, she would have seizures. I was always asleep and he was always up. Sometimes he was watching TV or sometimes, because his computer was in Kelsey's room. Sometimes he'd be in there at the computer and I would throw a fit about that.*"

"*His computer was in Kelsey's room in Shawnee?*" *asked Garrett,* "*Did Mike, was he a subscriber to Playboy or any pornographic stuff?*"

"*Not that I knew of,*" *said Raye.*

"*I'm going back to that injury, the anal injury, you know.*"

"*Right.*"

"*Sex toys? Any of those in the house. Vibrators, things like that?*" *asked Garrett.*

"*We had one, but it was never used.*"

"*He never used it or anything like that?*"

Raye Dawn shook her head no.

"*Okay. What about anal sex? Was Mike into anything like that?*" *asked Garrett.*

Raye Dawn looked down and shook her head, no, "Not to me."

"Has he said anything about that with anybody in the past, girlfriends or relationships or anything?"

"Uh-huh."

"What did he tell you?" asked Garrett.

Raye answered, "He just said he had."

"Okay, with?"

"Previous."

"Did he say who he was with?"

Raye shook her head no, "Because I didn't really care to hear about that crap. But, like, he had mentioned it to me."

"Mentioning what, that he wanted to?"

"Right."

"And you told him no?"

"Right, this is really. . ." Raye Dawn trailed off in a nervous giggle.

"I'm sorry. But with the injury that your daughter's got, I mean I think it might be something that maybe he's into. So if he told you that he wanted to do that with you and then other people, it might be important to know who those people are so I can ask them," explained Garrett.

"Right."

Raye Dawn told them that she believed it was probably Whitney's mom.

Raye asked, "So this tear, supposedly, that's on the inside, how old is this?"

Garrett answered, "It's fresh. It's a separate incident. It's a separate incident. It's a separate injury."

"Okay."

"So whatever happened to her stomach didn't cause that. You've got two different things, two different injuries and they're both recent," explained Garrett.

"Like that day?"

"Yeah."

"Was there blood on her Pull-Up?" asked Raye.

"I don't know," answered Garrett.

"Because I mean I went and looked that house over up and down and it seemed like there might have been a couple of blood spots by the bed. And I asked Mom, I said, 'Was she bleeding somewhere?'"

Garrett continued this line of questioning, "You only have one vibrator there at the house? Did he know where it is at?"

"Well, see, because we got it from Shawnee. I wanted to throw it away."

"Was it his idea to get it?"

"Uh-huh, that was a long time ago."

"Okay. Like when you first started dating him?"

"No, it was maybe a little further than that. Because I had found it somewhere, we were cleaning out the house, and anyway, I chunked it in the dump."

"So you think you threw it away?" asked Garrett.

"I just did here recently," answered Raye.

"When's recent? Since your daughter died?"

"Yeah. I mean, I know where it is," said Raye.

"Where do you think you found it? Where was it, in the bedroom?"

"That's what I'm trying to think."

"Was it in the master bedroom?"

Raye appeared to be deep in thought, "Where did he put it? Because we still had boxes, so I don't know if was in a box and I just took it and threw it in the back when we were cleaning the house out. I'll have to ask my sister where we found it at."

Garrett continued, "Okay. So that might not have been something. I'm just trying to figure out, you know, if that is the case, I mean there's other things that could cause that, but there's always the potential that, you know, that might be the instrumentation."

T·H·I·R·T·E·E·N

L AWYERS STUDIED PICTURES OF K ELSEY'S TINY BODY LYING ON THE AUTOPSY
TABLE.

Smothermon studied Kelsey's mounting case file, searching for his smoking gun.

Voters studied Kelsey's smiling face delivered to their mailboxes.

Her name invaded voicemails, "My name is Kathie Briggs, grandmother
of Kelsey Briggs. Kelsey lost her life after Judge Craig Key returned her to an
abusive home against the recommendations of DHS and the DA's office."

The grandmother from Dale, Oklahoma spent the legislative session at
the Capitol lobbying for child abuse reform. Kathie also campaigned for
Sheila Kirk, the only candidate running for judge against Judge Craig Key.

After Kelsey's death Kathie promised she would make sure Judge Key did
not have the opportunity to send another child to their death. Kathie laughed,
saying she would campaign for Satan if he was running against Judge Key.

Kathie and Sheila, an attorney in town, spread Kelsey's story across
Lincoln County. Sheila mailed out full color flyers. On one side was the
picture of Kelsey looking up at Lance in his fatigues. Flip it over, voters saw
the pink heart shaped sticker that said "Justice for Kelsey."

Sheila had a vested interest in Kelsey's life. She had been asked twice
to be Kelsey's court appointed attorney. Both times she refused, explaining
her experience with Raye Dawn painted a conflict of interest. She was Raye
Dawn's attorney in her divorce from Lance.

The strong willed attorney promised the justice Judge Key failed to
uphold through his backroom deals. She pointed out Key broke Oklahoma
law when he ruled against DHS recommendations and gave Kelsey back to
Raye Dawn.

A story Sheila and Kathie told to every voter who would answer their door. The women transformed grassroots politics to red dirt politics. It was a two woman, thousand flyer crusade to oust the infamous judge.

Most Lincoln County residents wanted to hear Kelsey's story. Many wanted to share their hugs with the grandmother they had watched on television. Despite hundreds of news stories, there were still voters who did not know Judge Key was the one who returned Kelsey to the abusive home.

Like everything else in this case the election was hardly void of controversy. Once the flyers with Kelsey's picture arrived in their mailboxes, Raye Dawn's family began taking out editorials in the local newspapers praising Key's decision. The war of words went back and forth. Nearly every day a new full page ad or editorial emerged, taking sides in an election where the only "issue" at hand was a dead baby.

The election was something to keep Kathie's mind off of the looming trial. As Election Day grew near Kathie felt the pressure compounding. She had worked too hard and ultimately had to trust the democratic process. She soon had more faith in voters than the criminal justice system.

On Election Day, the campaign planted people at each polling place. They were instructed to report the numbers the minute the polls closed.

Judge Key supporters made one last attempt to taint voters before seven in the evening. A high profile defense attorney, who would later endorse Judge Key's book, went on the most watched local news station. Live on television he said Judge Key would win the election by a landslide, because the "Kelsey factor" was not enough to cost him the election.

The lawyer's strong opinions sweetened Kathie's next phone calls. The ecstatic grandmother called Cherokee and Britten to announce Lincoln County elected its first female judge in state history by 1,811 votes.

Kathie wanted her taste of victory to continue through February. February 12, 2007, to be exact.

Richard Smothermon's days were filled with interviews and nights filled with research. Bringing his work home took on a new meaning. He was bringing the file home to his prosecutor wife, Connie. Connie worked in the Oklahoma County District Attorney's Office as an Assistant D.A. for years. Now she's a law professor at an Oklahoma university. At home she worked tirelessly beside her husband, helping him prepare for one of the most monumental cases of his career.

Smothermon's wife could not sit beside him at trial. So he knew he needed help and couldn't count on anyone in his office to get the job done. He had good prosecutors but no one with a specialization in child abuse or murder.

He needed help. He wanted a prosecutor who could dismantle anyone on the witness stand. He knew he needed to call Pattye High. High worked as an Assistant District Attorney in Oklahoma County for years. Smothermon knew she was looking for a new job. The two had worked together prosecuting Judge Donald Thompson. Thompson was convicted of using a penis pump to help the time pass during trial. Smothermon knew High was a hard nosed prosecutor who earned a reputation as a bulldog in the courtroom. Smothermon was aware they had differing opinions about Kelsey's case.

In the months after Kelsey's murder, the two spent a lot of time together preparing for Judge Thompson's trial. When Smothermon asked High what she thought about the Kelsey case, High made it no secret she strongly disagreed with his charges. She felt Porter was not alone with Kelsey long enough to prove beyond a reasonable doubt he was the killer. High also felt Porter did not have a motive. In all of the child abuse deaths she prosecuted during her 17 year career, there was never a case where the caretaker came home one day and decided the child was going to die.

If she were the prosecutor, she would have filed First Degree Murder against both Raye Dawn and Porter and tried them together. To ensure both of them were held accountable, she would have filed an alternative charge of First Degree Murder-Permitting Child Abuse. She would have asked the jury to choose the killer and then sentence him or her to death.

Despite their differences Smothermon called High anyway. High was interested in the case but made it clear she wanted her opinions about the case taken seriously. She knew Smothermon was too far along in the process to go back on his charges against Porter, but she wanted to make sure Raye Dawn was held accountable for her role in Kelsey's death. High took the job.

Smothermon wanted the Briggs' approval before bringing High on the case full time. He wanted the family to feel comfortable with his second in command. So he called Jeanna, the family member voted to be liaison with the D.A.'s office, to set up a meeting.

Jeanna and her husband Randy were getting ready for a little addition to their family when Smothermon proposed the idea of an addition to the legal team. Royce and Kathie took their nine months pregnant daughter Jeanna to her doctor's appointment at 4:00 p.m. on January 18, 2007 so they could go straight to their scheduled introduction with High.

Jeanna's baby had other plans. When Jeanna arrived at the doctor's appointment, her blood pressure was too high for her to wait until January 24, 2007, the day her cesarean was scheduled. The doctor told Jeanna to go home and pack; she was giving birth in the morning, fifteen hours away.

Moving the delivery up a week would give Jeanna more time to recover before Mike Porter's trial. Jeanna was concerned she might have to miss the trial. Her entire family would be attending the trial and she would have no one to watch her newborn. She had asked the doctor to move the cesarean up but the doctor refused stating she could not risk the health of a live baby for the death of another baby.

Jeanna recognized High's name from the newspaper. She remembered reading that High had assisted Smothermon during the Judge Thompson trial.

They had heard good things about High and figured if she could send a judge to prison she would be beneficial in this convoluted case.

Jeanna had a hard time concentrating that evening. She was trying to focus on what High was saying but was distracted. She was making a mental note of things she and Randy needed to pack when they got home.

The freezing temperatures and looming ice storm were no match for the warm exchange inside the restaurant that night. Kathie loved High instantly. The attractive, confident and respectful mother of three hated Raye Dawn for not being a good mother to Kelsey.

High was blunt and Kathie respected that. She did not sugar coat anything. Kathie had heard so many lies she appreciated anyone who was a straight shooter.

High had no concerns about her ability to enter the high profile case this late in the game. There were boxes of documents and evidence to sift through. High says Smothermon already knew the case so she had to dig in.

The more High read about the case the more she was convinced Porter was not the killer. She met with two of Oklahoma's leading child abuse experts about the physical evidence Dr. Hawley said pointed to sexual abuse. High says neither of them believed Kelsey was sexually abused. They felt the most likely explanation for the injuries to the little girl's private parts was a hard blow to the bottom.

High was unconvinced Kelsey was sexually abused and felt a lot of time had been spent making a monster out of Michael Porter. She believed Porter was equally responsible for what happened to Kelsey. He was guilty, just not of murder. It was hard for High to understand why Raye had not been strongly considered as a suspect. Then again, she knew in child abuse deaths there is a bias in favor of mothers. No one can fathom a mother hurting her child. High knew better. Mothers snap just like fathers and step-fathers.

The more High learned about Raye Dawn the more she began to suspect Raye Dawn was evil. In High's opinion, the fact that Raye Dawn knew Lance was coming home could have been trigger enough. There was no way Raye Dawn was going to give Kelsey to Lance. If it came down to Lance having Kelsey or nobody having Kelsey, High believes Raye Dawn would have picked nobody.

While the prosecution team prepared for trial, so did Paul Sutton and his wife. The couple had spent months preparing Porter's defense. Sutton could not prove Raye Dawn was the murderer. The lawyer was confident he could instill reasonable doubt with a jury. He and Porter poured over Kelsey's case file and Porter's memory looking for little details that would implicate Raye Dawn.

Sutton quickly discovered Raye Dawn's life was laden with shortfalls. The attorney and his client developed a list of questions for each witness. Most of them focused not on Porter's behavior but Raye Dawn's.

Sutton planned to call a long list of witnesses in hopes of confirming under oath some of the information he gleaned from Porter and the other people he interviewed.

Sutton wanted to know if OSBI agents checked the washer and dryer for clothing the night of Kelsey's murder. He also wondered if they took the pillow cases and the top sheet that had been taken off the bed into evidence. Sutton did not believe they checked any of the bed coverings for DNA, bodily fluids, sweat, blood, or vomit.

Sutton knew his client was a big guy and also assumed agents had not measured Raye Dawn or Porter's hand or thumb span. There were bruises on Kelsey's body that appeared to have been caused by small hands.

Sutton wanted to know why Gayla's cell phone records reflect her talking to Raye Dawn during the time Raye Dawn and Kelsey were napping. Porter told his attorney Gayla often ran errands for the company, so it did not make any sense that Raye Dawn would immediately think something was wrong when she noticed her mom's car was not at work.

Sutton was going to use Yolanda Hunter to tell the jury about what Raye Dawn and Gayla said at the hospital the night of Kelsey's murder. Yolanda was shocked when they announced Kelsey's death was probably for the best because of everything she would have to go through with the Briggs family.

Sutton planned to use Raye Dawn's closest friend, her sister, to build his case against Raye Dawn as a parent. Porter told his lawyer he had a number of conversations with Rachelle about Raye Dawn's lack of patience with kids.

Rachelle spent the days following Kelsey's killing with Porter. After the OSBI interviews on October 13, 2005 Porter stayed at the house and Raye Dawn stayed with her mom. He was the prime suspect in the murder of a two-year-old and Rachelle was not afraid to stay with him.

Sutton's "smoking gun" sat in a plastic evidence bag. The black t-shirt Raye Dawn told everyone Kelsey wore all day, Sutton believes, was just one of her many lies. After the murder Kelsey's CHBS worker, Jean Bonner, told him that Kelsey was "fixed cute, in an orange short set." She noted Kelsey's shorts were pinned because she had lost weight. It was a much more logical outfit for Kelsey to be wearing on the day of a DHS visit. Porter explained Raye Dawn always made a point to make sure Kelsey was dressed to the nines when a caseworker was coming.

Prosecutors found the orange short set soiled with urine in the dirty clothes hamper at Raye Dawn and Porter's house. Sutton planned to question Raye Dawn about why she claimed Kelsey was wearing the sweat suit all day. Sutton agreed with Assistant District Attorney High, who suspected Kelsey's accident triggered Raye Dawn's rage.

The secret behind the orange short set died with Kelsey. As the trial rapidly approached and caseworkers were served with civil lawsuits, Bonner "forgot" what Kelsey was wearing. Sutton never learned why Bonner changed her story.

Sutton decided Porter himself would take the stand. He would recount what happened that day to cast doubt on Raye Dawn's explanations of the previous injuries. Sutton learned Porter started going to the doctor with Raye after Kelsey broke her legs. Porter wanted to make sure Raye was telling him the truth.

Sutton could prove Raye Dawn lied about one of Kelsey's injuries. One night Raye Dawn came home drunk. When she tried to get in bed with Porter and the kids she kicked Kelsey in the nose. Raye Dawn threw a temper tantrum because Porter kicked her out of the bedroom. She kicked and banged on the bedroom door until she finally gave up and began running around the house naked.

Sutton planned to dismantle Smothermon's key witness on the stand. He knew the D.A. would call Raye Dawn, and Sutton had a list of questions waiting on cross examination.

To show a history of rages Sutton planned to ask Raye Dawn, "Did you ever get suspended in high school for hitting a teacher?"

"How often did you give Tylenol or similar medication to Kelsey? For what reasons?" Raye Dawn may have convinced DHS Kathie was drugging Kelsey, but Porter told Sutton it was Raye Dawn.

"Did you ever give more than a proper dosage because you felt she was stressed or wouldn't settle down fast enough?"

"When was the last time you gave Tylenol or any medicine?"

"How many times have you been pregnant?"

"What did you do for Kelsey's 2nd birthday?" Porter told his lawyer that he bought Kelsey a cake because Raye Dawn had spent all of her money on beer, blowing off Kelsey's birthday, saying it was no big deal.

"Why days later were the bed, slide, and hairbrush still in the same place when Meeker Police came and took photos?"

"Why did you avoid DHS in January when you knew they were trying to contact you about Kelsey's bruises?"

"Who was Kelsey's pediatrician since birth?"

"When Kelsey would hold food in her mouth and or refuse to eat, what did you do?" Porter says Raye Dawn would say, "Eat your food you little bitch. You're not going to do this with me."

"What movie was Gayla taking Kelsey to at 5pm on October 11? Where? Why wasn't she dressed and ready to go? Why a t-shirt only?"

"Why would Kelsey need a nap at 1:30 p.m. if she had awakened at 9:30 a.m., 4 hours earlier?"

"Did you run out of time before Mike Porter came up the driveway and that's why Kelsey didn't have on a pull-up?" Porter says Raye left the pull-up on the island in the kitchen.

"Who picked out your vibrator, from Christie's Toy Box, the sex toy store, in OKC?"

"Do you remember showing Mike Porter how it worked in the car on the way home? Do you still own it? Where is it now? What happened to it? When did you dispose of it?"

Jurors and the world would never hear the answers to those questions.

As the discovery phase of the trial continued, Smothermon told Sutton he had copies of all of the emails Shirica and Porter traded. In them, Smothermon told Sutton, Porter confessed he was at least guilty of Enabling Child Abuse.

Sutton realized his client had lied to him. Porter never told his lawyer about his conversations with Shirica or Kathie. Sutton would have shouted from the rooftop that he believed Mike Porter was innocent. Defending a confession is another story.

Sutton felt betrayed and realized his client knew a lot more about those 10 months leading up to Kelsey's death, than he had revealed. Sutton called Smothermon asking for a plea agreement sending Porter to prison for 10 years.

By law, Smothermon had to call the Briggs to let them know Sutton and Porter were considering a deal. The family always knew a deal was possible but didn't expect anything to happen that close to trial. Smothermon told the family to think about a sentence they could live with.

When Smothermon denied the 10 year plea agreement Sutton called back and asked for 20 years. The Briggs felt 30 years was the minimum sentence they would consider.

This time Smothermon called a family meeting. Jeanna had just given birth to Austin but needed to be a part of these discussions. They had been afraid the D.A. would go behind their backs and were relieved he wanted their blessing.

The D.A. explained two deals were on the table. Porter could plead guilty to manslaughter and go to prison for 25 years. The other option was Enabling Child Abuse for 30 years.

While he claimed to be confident Porter would be convicted if they went to trial, Smothermon slipped in a shred of reasonable doubt. In a prior meeting, Smothermon told the Briggs family that Sutton mentioned a new piece of evidence that would let Porter off the hook. At this point, the D.A. did not know what this new evidence was or if it was concrete.

New evidence aside, the Briggs entertained the plea agreement because they were strongly convinced reasonable doubt during trial would set Porter free. The drawback to accepting a plea deal was that many of the details would be buried with Kelsey. They didn't know if they could live with the unanswered questions that would never be disclosed in court.

The O.J. Simpson case kept running through Kathie's mind. She didn't know if she could shoulder the burden of rejecting the deal and then losing the trial. She didn't want Michael Porter to walk.

Smothermon said, "It's up to you. You're the ones who have to live with this."

Porter was not willing to live with the manslaughter sentence. Since the beginning, he maintained his innocence in Kelsey's death. Porter believed accepting a plea involving manslaughter would be admitting he had a hand in her killing. Porter refused, even though it meant less prison time.

It was 30 years and enabling or they go to trial.

Yet another sleepless night for the Briggs family. Ultimately the family left the decision in Lance's hands. Lance decided he did not want to have to sit through a trial.

Smothermon's goal was to get a conviction on Porter's record. Sending him to prison was a victory no matter what the crime. In Smothermon's mind, the sentence is most important, not the crime on his rap sheet.

Lawyers would criticize Smothermon for that attitude. Lawyers felt it was his responsibility as a District Attorney to prosecute Porter for the crime Smothermon believed he committed, not just make a good deal.

Pattye High was torn by the plea deal. If she was wrong about Raye Dawn and Porter was the killer, 30 years in prison was hardly enough for Kelsey's brutal murder. This way, no jury would have the opportunity to decide if Raye killed Kelsey and left her for Porter to find, or if he did it after Raye Dawn left. If Porter accepted the deal, no one would be held accountable for Kelsey's murder. Kelsey did not die painlessly; she did not die quickly; she had been dying for years and High felt she could argue why the death penalty was justified. There was no question in her mind Kelsey's murder was heinous, atrocious, and cruel; one of the qualifications for the death penalty.

Porter agreed to the deal, knowing he would have a week to say his goodbyes, before his formal sentencing.

All of these negotiations were taking place in private, away from the public's prying eyes and the media's curious ears. As with all closed door decisions, there's always someone with loose lips and the will to tell.

January 29, 2007, before Cherokee was scheduled to come into work someone called her with a tip. A plea deal had been reached with Porter. While the call came as a surprise, Cherokee suspected something was brewing because it had been too quiet. Nothing had emerged about the case since before Christmas and trial was two weeks away.

She quickly jumped into reporter mode and started making calls. Kathie couldn't talk about it because of the gag order but her reaction confirmed the news. Cherokee raced to the Lincoln County Courthouse in hopes of getting a copy of the deal when it was filed with the court clerk. That's where she ran into Britten and her photographer, who had received a similar phone call. 4:30 p.m. came and went. The courthouse closed and no document was filed.

Cherokee's tip had a phone number attached. Michael Porter's home phone number. So she took a deep breath and dialed. The voice on the other end of the line was very polite. Porter addressed her as Ms. Ballard, saying he could not comment. Porter promised one day he would, just not now.

Kathie arranged for the reporters to talk to Jay Sigman, Kelsey's stepgrandfather. He was the only person on Kelsey's paternal side who was not under the gag order.

Sigman said that the family always knew a plea bargain was an option and if this punishment fit the crime they would live with it.

The news crews rushed to meet a very emotional Janet Gragg, Raye Dawn's half-sister. A tearful Janet asked why Porter should be allowed to take a plea bargain because this was not justice for Kelsey.

While Janet's interview helped piece the story together, both Cherokee and Britten wanted to hear from someone more intimately involved, Raye Dawn or her mother. Gayla agreed to talk for them both.

As time ticked by and the deadlines passed, the crews rushed to interview Gayla. They met her on a cold street corner in Edmond. On the bench outside the office of *The Edmond Sun* newspaper she sat with framed pictures of Kelsey and Raye Dawn. She was angry, yet tearful. Gayla was upset she had not been informed by the D.A. about a possible plea. She felt members of her family were not being treated like victims. She learned about the plea from Britten and Cherokee.

Gayla said they would continue to tell the truth like they had always done, but she did not know what the decision would mean for her daughter's case.

At the end of the interview, Gayla said, "Kelsey was lost in the battle."

It was not the cold temperature but Gayla's words that gave Britten chills that night. She was not sure whether Raye Dawn's mom was referring to the family battle between the Briggs and the Smiths. Maybe she was talking about the battle between Raye Dawn and Lance or maybe the system.

It was chilling because again it seemed as though Gayla was missing the point.

Within 24 hours, every news outlet in the state reported word of the deal. Porter was scheduled to surrender in less than a week.

The night before Porter's sentencing, he and Sutton agreed to sit down with Cherokee. Porter couldn't do an interview, but Cherokee knew this might be her only chance to talk face to face with the only person ever charged with Kelsey's murder.

When Cherokee and her photographer husband, Scott Travis, walked into Sutton's office Porter was not there. Sutton laid out the ground rules for the meeting. There would be no cameras, recording devices, or note taking. Cherokee was not allowed to ask anything about the case. Sutton was very concerned about his client's vulnerability. He did not want Porter to disclose anything that would jeopardize his plea deal.

Minutes later Cherokee was sitting next to the man many believe brutally killed his two-year-old step-daughter.

Porter directed his nervous twitch to a bracelet made of paperclips. Scott could not help but wonder if Whitney or Bubby made him the bracelet. He thought it was odd a grown man would be wearing a child's craft around his wrist.

Despite his size, Cherokee couldn't help but think Porter was somewhat childlike. His height and build were dwarfed by his vulnerability. He was quiet. Very soft spoken, yet respectful. He said, "Yes ma'am," a lot.

Porter knew he would almost be a senior citizen before he emerged from prison. His little ones would be grown. Porter told Cherokee how much he loved his kids. He fought back tears as he described Kelsey.

When she mentioned Raye Dawn the tears dried up. His face morphed from a grieving father to a stone faced ex-husband. He couldn't say anything specific about her but his demeanor reflected his hatred toward the only woman he ever asked to marry.

The meeting lasted no more than 10 minutes and Cherokee learned nothing more than Porter's raw emotions. She believed he was sad Kelsey was gone. He loved Kelsey and he wanted to tell Cherokee more but couldn't.

Porter shook her hand as he left, apologized for crying, and went about his last 24 hours as a free man.

The very next day, Friday, February 2, 2007, was bitter cold. The high temperature was 16 degrees in Oklahoma City; yet the sun was shining and the sky was crystal blue.

Britten and Cherokee wondered what it was like for Porter to wake up knowing this is the day he would go to prison for the next 30 years. This is the last time he would wake up in his bed as a young man.

They wondered if he regretted the deal or was the regret for failing to protect Kelsey?

News crews arrived in Chandler about 2:15 p.m. Photographers stood in the freezing cold to get video of the major players walking into the courthouse.

They spotted Michael Porter with his attorney at his side. Again the two did not dodge the cameras but walked silently by each lens. Porter stared straight ahead in his dark blue shirt and black pants with no tie. It was less for him to take off before he had to change into orange.

Inside the courtroom the air was thick. Deputies ushered each family in separately to designated seats. The seats did not separate the Smith and Briggs family. Lance, Kathie, and Royce Briggs shared the front row with Raye Dawn. Reporters sat in the jury box armed with notebooks to describe Porter's reaction for the rest of Oklahoma.

The judge called the hearing to order and told Porter to stand.

The man who had been charged with Kelsey's murder for 16 months wept out loud. He clenched his fists and tried to stare at the ceiling but the tears doubled him over.

Between gasps for air, he pleaded guilty to not protecting Kelsey and told the judge he would go to prison for 30 years.

The raw emotion was sobering for those in the courtroom that day. Torn by the anger over Kelsey's murder, people in the courtroom couldn't help but feel sorry for him. Some almost wanted to reach over and comfort him. Again, he seemed almost childlike.

Were they tears of guilt? Tears of regret? Or just tears? Porter was so overcome with a myriad of emotions Cherokee almost expected him to shout out something. She wanted to hear anything that would explain his anguish.

Ten minutes later deputies escorted Michael Porter, and possibly the answer to Kelsey's murder, out of Lincoln County in handcuffs.

Photographers got one, three second shot of Porter leaving before they rushed back into the courthouse to get reaction from the families.

The Enabling Child Abuse plea implied Porter had some sort of knowledge Raye Dawn was the abuser. It insinuates he allowed the abuse to happen and did not tell anyone. In his signed admission of guilt, Porter described the violence that took place three months before Kelsey died. He said he walked in on Raye Dawn punching Kelsey in the stomach and told no one about it.

Raye Dawn's family had plenty to say. Raye Dawn's lawyer, Steve Huddleston, told news crews he had issues that the man originally charged with Kelsey's murder would now share information about his client.

Smothermon began to question Huddleston's blind trust in his client. As a D.A. he had countless closed door conversations with defense attorneys. Smothermon says it was rare that both Huddleston and Sutton wholeheartedly believed their clients were innocent.

Gayla defended her daughter and did not hide her anger as she reiterated her granddaughter was murdered. When Britten asked who killed Kelsey, Gayla snapped, "Mike did."

Raye's sister and cousin both defended Raye Dawn's character saying she was a good mom.

Raye let her family go to the frontlines for her. Instead of defending herself, she ducked the spotlight. No one saw her leave the courthouse.

The Briggs family pointed the finger back at Raye Dawn. They told TV crews it was not over. They would not be satisfied until Raye Dawn went to trial.

Lance promised he would not accept a plea bargain for Kelsey's mom. He wanted a jury to decide if she failed to protect their daughter.

He put on a strong front for the cameras but Lance broke down in Smothermon's office. Lance didn't expect to be shedding tears over Michael Porter. His were tears of unanswered questions. Porter may have been stepping up and taking responsibility for not protecting Kelsey or copping out to avoid the embarrassment of a sexual abuse trial.

That night, no one in the Briggs family slept. At 4:00 a.m., Jeanna rushed to the bathroom overcome with nausea. She thought she was going to vomit. As she stood over the toilet, nothing came. She almost felt as though her family was responsible for sending a father to prison. She thought he was guilty because she couldn't imagine a father giving up 30 years of his life without fighting. Yet, that didn't make it easier.

She hadn't seen the new evidence against Raye Dawn. No one had. Except Porter's attorney, who discovered it on a website set up by Raye Dawn's family.

Nestled about three quarters of the way through the pictures was a shot of Kelsey at nine months. Kelsey was wearing a hat, shorts, and a crop top. In between her top and pants you could see a dark purplish mark just right of her belly button. Some argued it was a shadow. To the naked eye it was a bruise. The picture was snapped long before Mike Porter was in the picture.

This photograph became the so called "smoking gun" in the state's case against Raye Dawn. It highlighted abuse long before anyone suspected.

Abuse where the perpetrator could not have been Porter.

Porter was taken to an undisclosed location within the Department of Corrections. The D.O.C. was concerned for Porter's safety in the general prison population. Once Porter was secure, Sutton told Smothermon where to find the picture. It was taken by a photographer at the Sears Portrait Studio in 2003.

As soon as he saw it, Smothermon says he had no doubt it was a bruise on Kelsey's abdomen. Up until that point Smothermon says he had discussed a five year prison sentence in exchange for Raye Dawn's cooperation in the case against Porter. That day he called Huddleston announcing all deals were off the table.

He now knew while it might have been Porter who murdered Kelsey, it wasn't just Porter who hurt Kelsey all along. In light of this new evidence, Smothermon upgraded the charges against Raye to Child Abuse, or the alternative of Enabling Child Abuse.

A jury would never see that picture. Before Raye Dawn's trial, the judge in the case banned prosecutors from using the picture as evidence.

Every expert in the world could testify the mark under Kelsey's shirt was a bruise. No one could prove Raye Dawn put it there.

It was Raye Dawn's word versus the bruises on her dead baby.

Michael Porter

Had agents used more than Mike Porter's behavior in the interrogation rooms to make an arrest, someone might be charged with her murder. Had agents followed the 80/20 rule, limiting their part of the interrogation to 20 percent of the conversation, Raye and Porter might have been forced to say more than "I don't know." Had agents not interrupted Raye on numerous occasions, she might have revealed a key piece of information. And someone might be charged with Kelsey's murder.

If Raye and Porter revealed their secrets in those rooms, agents did not pick up on it. Porter looked up as Tanner said, "Maybe you could have been a bit more aggressive than you initially thought."

"If it comes down to that or. . .yeah, if it comes down to that or my wife doing it. . .I mean, it's not. . .she would never. . ." Porter's voice trailed off.

"It's kind of one or the other. It can only be one," responded Tanner.

Porter continued, "But what I'm saying is, I can't say with certainty that I wasn't too aggressive, and I can't say with certainty that I. . .that I, you know, wasn't . . .what I'm saying, I don't know how hard I did these things. I don't know how hard I. . .you know, how hard I shook her, and I don't know how hard I did that. I don't want to make it sound like I was just, you know, 'Hey Kelsey, wake up.' That certainly was not the case.

"And I've already. . .I mean, you say a significant amount of pressure. And you have to understand in the panic mode I'm in, that when I'm doing these things, they're sudden. They're not slow. They're not calculated, and they're not. . .you know, I don't stop and think, what do I do next? You know I'm down, I'm doing all these things because I think seconds matter. I'm not sitting back and thinking, you know, how hard do I need to do this? Or how fast do I need to do it? Or how slow do I need to do it? I'm just thinking about, you know, the next second, is what I was thinking about.

"And I can't tell you with any certainty that I wasn't too aggressive and that I didn't do anything that may have hurt her. But as far as anything intentionally to hurt her, no. I told my wife, I said, 'I pray to God that nothing I did harmed her in trying to help her.'"

"Why is it you don't believe me when I tell you what the Medical Examiner said?" asked Tanner.

Porter responded, "I mean, this whole time I was going a thousand miles an hour, and I'm doing these things suddenly and I'm doing them to get a reaction."

"Well, what would make you think that the injuries happened during that time frame rather than before you got home?"

Porter said, "Because I don't believe Kelsey was gone."

Raye Dawn Smith

"You're husband's lying," stated Garrett, "I mean, if you had nothing to do with it or were involved in it, then that means he's involved in it."

"Okay," said Raye.

Garrett continued, "Because I think I told you on that Thursday, the last time we had talked on the interview, that you know, one of you two had to have killed Kelsey, caused the death. I mean, and I still believe that to this minute."

"I wouldn't hurt my daughter. There's no way," insisted Raye, once again.

"You know that somebody's responsible for it."

Raye Dawn started crying, "What can a child do for someone to do this?"

"I don't know. That's news to me."

"I mean, I want that answer given to me."

Garrett asked Raye about the night after Kelsey's murder, "Did Mike go in the house?"

"Uh-huh and all the way home, you know, he kept. . .well, on the way out there, he said, 'You know I didn't do this.' And I said, 'I never said that.' You know, I didn't want to talk anymore because I'm trying to grasp what I. . ."

"But deep down you're thinking he did it, though, aren't you?" asked Garrett.

Raye agreed, "Yeah."

"Because like I told you before you left that day, one of the two of you had to have killed her, said Garrett.

"Right. And I'm sitting there, you know. . .I wanted to go. . .you know, like Mom said, 'You can ride with me or, you know, do whatever you need to do.' And so I go ahead and I drive. And he kept trying to talk to me and I was like, 'I don't want to talk. Just be quiet, I don't want to talk.'"

"Did he ask you, did he say that he did do it?"

"No. And I wish he would. But he like, he just kept saying, 'You know I couldn't hurt her.' And I was like, 'Just stop talking.' I didn't want to talk anymore. I had talked all day. And I had all this stuff going in my head."

F·O·U·R·T·E·E·N

A POOL OF MORE THAN ONE HUNDRED CREEK COUNTY RESIDENTS ARRIVED AT THE COURTHOUSE IN BRISTOW, OKLAHOMA. They nervously clutched their jury summons wondering why news crews from all over the state were staked out across the courthouse lawn. Armed deputies paced back and forth, greeting photographers and reporters with an order not to shoot any video of the jurors. Photographers were also ordered not to shoot through the windows of the courthouse.

They were not waiting for pictures of jurors. They were waiting for the tearful mother Nick Winkler had chased down the hallway in Lincoln County, peppering her with questions about who broke Kelsey's legs; the tearful mother who would choose when to shed those tears for the jury; whose tears, or lack thereof, may have sent her to prison.

The sky was overcast July 9, 2007; photographers brought the rain gear for the cameras, knowing they would be camping out on the courthouse lawn, waiting for glimpses of the major players.

There were two major entrances to the courthouse. It had almost become a game of hide-and-seek as to which door Raye Dawn would sneak in to avoid photographers. Throughout the eight day trial, they would have plenty of opportunities to get video of her.

That morning Raye Dawn walked in wearing a very matronly cut pink skirt suit with brown loafers and pantyhose. The outfit was rumored to be her grandmother's suit. The young mother tucked her blonde hair behind her ears. She would wear the same gold heart necklace for eight days of trial.

Reporters from the major television stations and *The Oklahoman* sat in the front row on the hard wood bench. They went through five or six notepads each. Their pens ran out of ink half-way through the trial.

In the courtroom Raye Dawn sat with her lawyers, Steve Huddleston and Tim Henderson, at a table facing the jury. The prosecutors sat between the podium where lawyers would question witnesses and the twelve faces responsible for Raye Dawn's fate.

Jury selection began promptly at 9:00 that morning with a pool of 22 people selected at random. One of the first questions Lincoln County District Judge Paul Vassar asked the potential jurors was whether they had seen any of the media reports on Kelsey's case. Only eight people responded, yes. One of them heard a mention about the case on the news that morning.

The voir dire, or juror questioning process, almost worked in Raye Dawn's favor. The way the defense phrased questions, Raye Dawn's lawyers did not care how jurors answered. They just wanted to instill doubt in the jurors' minds before the first witness took the stand.

After three hours of questioning, lawyers decided on seven women and five men. Seven were married; two were divorced, one was a widow. Nine had children of their own. One woman worked at a hospital. One spent 12 years at the Tulsa Boy's Home counseling troubled youth. Another woman watched Court TV all the time. One juror cried at least once a day. Another would fight for a life sentence for the mother.

Once the jury was selected nearly everyone from both families was forced to leave the courtroom. Lawyers asked for the rule of sequestration. Anyone who had been subpoenaed as a witness was not allowed to listen to the evidence. Lawyers agreed to allow one family member from each side to listen in. The family immediately agreed Kathie should be the one. When Huddleston objected they nominated Jeanna. Lance sat in the courtroom for opening arguments but Smothermon felt the testimony would be too emotional for him. So Kelsey's father sat outside with the news photographers for most of the trial.

The Briggs family set up homestead in an empty courtroom, away from the public and away from the Smiths. They sat and waited for updates. Nervous chatter passed the time.

Late that afternoon Richard Smothermon began the opening remarks that had been swirling in his head for a year and half.

"On October 11, 2005, Kelsey Smith-Briggs was murdered. She was beaten to death. Dr. Yacoub, the Medical Examiner who examined Kelsey's dead body, will testify she died from a blow to the stomach that caused her pancreas to burst; she suffered scrapes to her back, bruising to her genital area, bruises to her head, her torso, and all of her extremities.

"But that is not the beginning of the story. It's actually the final chapter of a horrible tragedy.

"October 11, 2005, Patti Jean Bonner, Kelsey's CHBS case worker will testify she left Kelsey at 1:30 p.m. with her mother and the child was fine.

"Between 1:30 and 3:27 p.m. when emergency responders arrived at the scene and Kelsey was for all intents and purposes dead, only two people were around Kelsey: Michael Porter and Raye Dawn. Only one of them inflicted all of the injuries.

What happened? That's your job to figure out."

Smothermon gave jurors a summary of the state's case and the testimony they would hear in the coming days. Witnesses like Raye Dawn's co-workers and doctors widely considered experts in child abuse would build a case for either charge: enabling or abuse.

Smothermon told jurors, "Michael Porter will testify he pleaded guilty to 30 years in prison because he saw Raye Dawn abuse Kelsey on numerous occasions and did nothing to stop it."

"The Briggs family, doctors, and DHS told Raye Dawn, Kelsey was being abused and Raye Dawn did nothing to stop it."

"She died from being beaten to death."

"Why? Because she did it or did nothing to stop it."

His tone was angry. His voice was invested in the death of the two-year-old as he closed by saying, "October 11, should never have happened; it was obvious she could have stopped this train wreck herself."

Raye Dawn's lawyer, Steve Huddleston, stood and began her defense by saying, "I'm here to tell you a totally different side of this case. These two families have a history of animosity. Raye Dawn married Lance Briggs in 2000. When they divorced, a long custody battle over Kelsey Smith-Briggs followed."

Huddleston spent the next hour losing jurors in a sea of dates, times, and numbers. He explained despite the pictures of bruises, Raye Dawn had never been charged with a crime, until now. She was cleared of abuse by law enforcement. Huddleston told the jury Michael Porter killed Kelsey.

"Make no mistake Michael Porter is responsible for Kelsey's death. My client has never been charged with murder. We're not here for a murder trial. Raye Dawn has always cooperated. Michael Porter has always been the only one charged."

"In fact the D.A. asked her to testify against Michael Porter and she agreed."

"Evidence will show my client is a young girl who escaped a bad marriage, was a single mom, who thought Michael Porter would be a good husband. Now she realizes she made a horrible mistake and he is not what he appeared to be.

"Kelsey was in the middle of allegations from both families and she suffered for it. There were two families making so many allegations that Porter stood in the shadows."

Huddleston blamed Kathie Briggs for the fact Raye Dawn was charged in the first place, saying she pressured Smothermon and reminded jurors Raye Dawn was being watched by a half-dozen state agencies nearly every day. If everyone else did not recognize Kelsey was being abused, why should Raye Dawn be charged with knowing?

Jurors left that night with Huddleston's words echoing in their minds. He closed by saying, "Kelsey was not abused by my client. She loved her daughter and her daughter was her life."

Tuesday morning jurors saw pictures of Kelsey's body on the autopsy table. Judge Vassar was forced to order everyone out of the courtroom when Raye Dawn started sobbing. Her sobs appeared to be on cue as they subsided once the jurors left the room.

After lunch jurors heard from the man originally charged with putting Kelsey's body on the autopsy table. High had interviewed Porter for several hours in the weeks leading up to trial. High says she believed Porter was telling the truth, otherwise she would have told Smothermon he had no business putting Porter on the stand. While High understood why Smothermon made the decision to call Porter as a witness, again, the two prosecutors disagreed. High felt his testimony would cause more problems than it was worth. She did not think they needed Porter to get a conviction. Smothermon knew Huddleston would point to Porter as the perpetrator regardless of whether he testified. Smothermon wanted jurors to hear from Porter himself.

Michael Porter walked into the courtroom wearing an orange jumpsuit. He had to raise both of his hands for the oath because they were handcuffed together. For the two hours Michael Porter was on the stand, Raye Dawn did nothing but glare at her ex-husband. She did not cry; she did not shake her head; she just stared at the man she left her daughter with the day she was murdered.

Smothermon began by boldly saying, "Mr. Porter you were originally charged in this case correct?"

Porter shook his head up and down saying, "Yes, with murder and sexual abuse."

"You know I believe you murdered her and sexually abused her?" said Smothermon.

"I know that is your opinion."

"You were aware of all the evidence against you when you pleaded in this case. Why did you plea?"

"I made a promise I would make a plea if I ever was charged with the crime I committed and that's enabling."

Smothermon said, "I still believe you to be guilty. Why are you here?"

"There's a lot of truth that needs to be told."

Michael Porter proceeded to tell the jury about three instances where he witnessed Raye Dawn abuse Kelsey. The first was in January of 2005. Porter says Raye Dawn brought Kelsey over to his house in Shawnee. Raye Dawn was in the bathroom and she started yelling at Kelsey because there were toys all over. About 10 seconds later Porter says he saw her holding Kelsey by her arm and swatting her about 10 times.

In July of 2005, once they were married, Porter says he was cooking outside and the kids were in the playroom. Raye Dawn was sitting in his chair in the living room while Kelsey ran back and forth from the playroom to the living room. Raye Dawn stood up and said, "Come here Kelsey. Come here."

Porter says he heard a door slam. Twenty or thirty seconds later he heard crying but could not find Raye Dawn. Then he says he realized the crying was coming from the bedroom. He opened the door to the bedroom and heard her say, "Don't you ever do that." She had her leg over Kelsey, holding her down. Michael Porter says he watched her hit Kelsey twice with a closed fist.

Porter says he walked into the bedroom and said, "Get the fuck away from her," grabbing Kelsey and carrying her down the hallway. He says Raye Dawn followed him. He told her if she did it again, she was gone. He says she told him if she leaves she's taking Kelsey threatening, "All I have to do is blame everything on you." Porter says he threw the keys at his wife and she let them hit her in the head.

The third time he says he witnessed Raye Dawn abuse Kelsey was the Sunday before she was killed. Porter says they were having a garage sale that weekend. Raye Dawn's brother and his wife came over. When Raye pulled up in the truck, he saw her jerk Kelsey out of the truck, drag her up the steps to the house and throw her in the chair.

When he asked her what happened he says she told him, "She's being a little fucking brat."

Richard Smothermon asked him why he did not tell anyone about these incidents. He told the jury he was protecting his wife. Smothermon told him it was hard to believe anything he said because he admitted to lying before. Michael Porter did not flinch when he said he lied a lot for his wife but that was over. He was there telling the truth.

Smothermon asked, "Do you believe you were responsible for Kelsey's death?"

"Indirectly."

"Do you believe Raye Dawn has culpability in Kelsey's death?"

"I know she does. If you're asking me, she's responsible."

Richard Smothermon asked Michael Porter what happened October 11, 2005. He said, "I got up at 7:30 a.m., went to wake up Whitney, helped her pick up her clothes. I didn't take a shower that morning; I carried Kelsey down the stairs to our bedroom because Kelsey didn't like the stairs. I took Whitney to school and got to work around 8:30 a.m.

"I talked to Raye Dawn several times that day and knew Jean Bonner was running late. I left work around 2:45 p.m.

"When I walked into the bedroom, Kelsey was on her back in the middle of the bed and Raye Dawn was closest to the door. When I knelt down by the bed Raye Dawn's eyes popped open and I said, 'You guys go back to sleep. I'll go pick up Whitney.' She said, 'No I'll do it.' She took me downstairs to show me the turtle Kelsey was playing with."

Smothermon asked if he thought it was odd Raye Dawn wanted him to see this turtle. Porter said, "At the time no, but now I do. She was trying to get me out of the bedroom. But the turtle was not there and then the phone rang. It was my friend Wendell calling to tell me he would not be at work the next week because he had jury duty. As she was pulling away she said, 'Take care of my baby.'"

Smothermon said, "And that's the only time she's ever said that to you?"

"Yes."

"So what did you do next?" asked Smothermon.

"I was expecting Michael Taber any minute. He was supposed to be coming over to pick up a set of tires I was selling him. So I went outside to the garage, opened the garage door, because I was going to clean them, and then decided they were really dirty and had been sitting a long time, so he could clean them himself if he wanted them. So I went upstairs to round up some laundry. I knew from the morning that Whitney's basket was full. I cleaned off the kitchen counter and made some water."

Michael Porter began getting choked up, "Then it struck me how quiet the house was. I was not used to this house yet because we had just moved in. I had to walk around the sofa to turn on the television. That's when I heard the noise coming from the bedroom.

"That noise has gotten a lot of criticism. I don't know if it was an exhale, a guttural sound, but I know it was not natural. I ran into the bedroom and saw she was blue and was not breathing. I tried to resuscitate her by saying, 'Kelsey, what's wrong? What's wrong?' I went into the kitchen and called Gayla."

Smothermon asked, "Why not 9-1-1?"

"I can't say why I did what I did. But until you're holding a dead baby in your arms it's hard to explain why you do what you do. I told her something was wrong. She told me to call 9-1-1 so I did. I was trying to talk to 9-1-1 while I put her on the kitchen island. I was talking to her and the dispatcher trying to explain that Kelsey would not wake up.

"I have minimal CPR skills, but I tried to give her a couple of breaths. It did not work. There was a pull-up sitting on the counter. I didn't want anyone to see her like that, so I put it on her. I would have not wanted someone to see my own daughter like that. We went outside and Michael Taber pulled up to get the tires. Gayla pulled up and took Kelsey."

During cross examination Steve Huddleston stood and immediately attacked the District Attorney's decision to put Porter on the stand, "The

D.A. just told you he does not believe you, so basically he just allowed you to sit up here and lie."

Porter responded by asking, "Is that a question? I guess that's correct."

Huddleston spent the majority of his cross examination asking Porter about what happened the day Kelsey was murdered, "Okay, what do you say happened on October 11, 2005? You came home, Raye Dawn left. Isn't this where the nightmare started for you? This is where you started sexually abusing her?"

"That's absolutely not correct," said Porter.

"She started struggling?" taunted Huddleston.

"Absolutely not correct."

"She started screaming and you held her down and covered her mouth?"

"Absolutely not correct."

"Dr. Hawley says Kelsey was sexually assaulted."

"That's his opinion," replied Porter.

"In the OSBI interviews you told them you were circling the living room with Kelsey in your arms, why?"

"I don't know why. Until you have a child in your arms in that condition, you don't know what you'd do."

"That's because you were trying to figure out what to do?"

"That's not true."

"Because I've never sexually assaulted a child to death, you're right I don't know what that would be like," said Huddleston.

"Nor have I," said Porter.

"Why didn't you call 9-1-1 first?"

"I guess I didn't want to believe how bad it was. It was a mistake in hindsight."

"You put her on the kitchen counter?"

"Actually it was the island."

"You put her up there to clean her up didn't you?"

"No."

Huddleston told the jury when the OSBI went back into the house the water was running. He asked Porter why he defended his wife while OSBI was questioning him for murder, repeatedly saying Raye Dawn could not have beaten her child to death, "OSBI asked you over and over and you never said anything about it."

Porter replied, "I would have rather believed anything than that my ex-wife killed her."

"You never thought to tell them when they were questioning you for murder that she did it, that she abused her all of those times?" asked Huddleston, "What normal person in that situation wasn't going to tell about this abuse?"

"Most normal people probably would, but I didn't." Porter told the jury on July 10, 2007, that he was through lying for Raye Dawn.

Huddleston asked, "You had nothing to do with the death of this child?"

"Not directly."

"You agreed to take 30 years in prison? No one in this room would agree to that. It's ludicrous, really, that someone would take 30 years for Enabling. But that's not really what you did, is it?"

"I made a promise and I intended to keep it. And I did. I would never say I did something I didn't do," said Michael Porter. Moments later, deputies hauled Kelsey's step-father back to prison in the back of a squad car.

Wednesday morning, reporters asked Raye Dawn how she felt about her ex-husband's testimony. She stared straight ahead and walked toward the courthouse in silence. Her blonde hair shifted with a step of determination.

The prosecution called Ashley Gober, formerly Ashley Briggs, and later called her mom Teri Sigman. After going through tedious times and dates surrounding each major injury and DHS referral, Huddleston pointed out that it was odd she and her mother took countless pictures of Kelsey's bruises. Huddleston accused them of trying to build a custody case against Raye Dawn.

When Kathie Briggs took the stand, Huddleston accused her of breaking Kelsey's legs and inflicting the bruises that covered Kelsey's body in so many pictures. He questioned her about why three or four people would inspect Kelsey's body before going back with Raye Dawn. Kathie calmly responded to each accusation explaining her growing concern for Kelsey's well being.

After each of the witnesses, the prosecution reminded jurors of the same message. In the end, we now know Kelsey died on October 11, as a result of child abuse. Ashley Briggs was right. She was reporting child abuse to DHS time and time again. Kathie Briggs was right. As long as the Briggs family was inspecting Kelsey, calling DHS, and taking photos of the bruises, Kelsey stayed alive. When they were cut out of the picture, Kelsey died.

The Briggs family had not seen Kelsey since August 27, 2005. They did not go to the hospital because they knew they were not welcome. Royce's mom and dad tried to, but they were told to leave.

Kathie told the jury they did not have an open casket and she never saw Kelsey again. After more than four hours on the witness stand she was released by the Judge and finally allowed to listen to the rest of the trial.

Thursday morning, Raye Dawn wore a light blue sweater set and plaid skirt to listen to her former co-workers' testimony. Donna Gilbreth and Mildred Johnson told the jury they worked with Raye Dawn at Lewis Manufacturing. Donna was Raye Dawn's supervisor and would give Raye grips to braid. Donna says one day when Raye Dawn came over to her stand to get some more work, she noticed Raye Dawn grabbed the grips in a huff. Donna asked what was wrong and she says Raye Dawn told her, "That bitch (Kathie Briggs) is accusing me of child abuse."

Donna asked, "Well, did you hit Kelsey?" She says Raye Dawn admitted to beating Kelsey with a hairbrush through her diaper.

A couple of months later Donna noticed a sparkly diamond on Raye Dawn's ring finger. So she asked Raye Dawn how Kelsey felt about getting a step-daddy. She says Raye Dawn told her Kelsey did not like Porter. Donna advised her she needed to find out why Kelsey didn't like him because babies do not lie. Raye just brushed it off saying Kelsey was jealous that she was paying attention to someone besides her.

Then the prosecution called Matt Byers. Matt Byers used to work for the Meeker Police department and people around town speculate he used to date Raye Dawn. For two hours you would have never known Raye Dawn was on trial. Assistant D.A. Pattye High laid into Byers. She asked how he could have formulated the opinion that Kelsey fell out of the crib, broke her collarbone, and landed on a hairbrush bruising her rear.

Matt Byers explained he interviewed Kathie Briggs, Lance, and Raye Dawn. He did not feel it was necessary to interview Raye's mom or Michael Porter. In his official police report, Byers shared his opinion, a practice that is not customary. He told the jury he urged prosecutors to look at Kathie

Briggs as the perpetrator and believed it was a Munchausen's by proxy case. Meaning, Kathie was injuring Kelsey to draw attention to herself.

In the final minutes of his testimony Matt Byers revealed a nugget of information that explained so much in this case. High asked him if he met with Judge Key on June 16, 2005. He said when he met with the judge in his chambers, Key asked him his opinion on Kelsey's case. He told the jury that he advised the judge to give Kelsey back to Raye Dawn because he had to. In Byers opinion, Raye had completed her treatment plan and by law Key had to give her back. When questioned about what law he was referring to, Byers could not answer the question. In fact, he told the jury he still does not believe Kelsey was murdered.

Reporters swarmed Byers as he walked to his truck. They asked if he was an expert in Munchausen's and he turned the question around asking, "Are you?" He denied any relationship with the Smith family. That night Byers' ignorance was broadcast across Oklahoma. Despite two Medical Examiners' opinions, Byers told the television cameras he did not believe Kelsey's death was a homicide.

For the next day and a half DHS workers were questioned about each and every bruise reported in the confidential 6,000 page case file. One worker admitted DHS may have made a mistake by not contacting law enforcement to conduct a criminal investigation.

Prosecutors couldn't help but point out the lapses in communication among the DHS workers. Beyond all logic, the DHS workers naively believed Raye Dawn's stories. At the end of their testimony, High wanted to turn to the jury and sarcastically say, "Ladies and gentlemen, there you have it, the Department of Human Services."

The prosecution did not call Carla Lynch, Kelsey's CASA worker to the stand. Lynch later told Cherokee she would have testified that she went to Judge Key's office in September saying they had to get Kelsey out of that home. Lynch says she was basically cut out of the process because DHS thought the Briggs family had gotten to her.

Monday morning, as Raye Dawn walked swiftly into the courthouse for another week of testimony, reporters asked her how she spent her weekend. It would be her last free weekend for years.

Last up for the prosecution, two doctors, advertised as child abuse experts. OU Children's Orthopedic specialist, Dr. Sullivan, examined Kelsey's broken legs two years earlier. He told the jury it was undoubtedly a case of child abuse. In the midst of Huddleston's questions about the dates when the fractures could have occurred, Dr. Sullivan got frustrated and addressed the jury directly.

The doctor got choked up as he explained the case had caused him a lot of grief. He wanted to testify in person before Judge Key on June 16, 2005, but was not allowed. Only his video deposition was admitted as evidence. Sullivan says he would have told the judge to not, under any circumstance, return the child to Raye Dawn. Dr. Sullivan thought the authorities had been called when he contacted DHS about the broken legs. He was wrong.

The prosecution asked Dr. Block, a child abuse specialist out of Tulsa, to examine Kelsey's case file. After pouring over the file, Dr. Block said in no uncertain terms, Kelsey was a victim of child abuse. Block explained that any of the injuries on their own could have been considered accidents. But when compiled and looked at from a broad scope, Kelsey was being beaten and had been for many months. The evidence culminated on October 11, when Kelsey died as a result of child abuse.

Just before lunch, the prosecution rested and Gayla Smith prepared to take the stand. Gayla, like her daughter, wore a very matronly dress. It was long and tan with shoulder pads. Her hair was a shade grayer than her usual bottle blonde.

Gayla Smith answered every question Huddleston asked with flying colors. She told the jury her daughter was a good mother who loved her baby very much and was always surrounded by Smith family members.

Huddleston again used the signature calendars he referred to during cross examination of nearly every witness so far. The judge reminded jurors not to be tempted to fall asleep.

Gayla answered questions about who was taking care of Kelsey during each injury in question. The goal was to cast doubt that the injuries actually happened under Raye Dawn's watchful eye.

She talked about her concerns that Porter had lied to the family about graduating from college. After Kelsey died Gayla cleaned out the big house. She told the jury she found hot checks and a receipt saying Porter had cashed in his IRA and his house was going through foreclosure.

Before passing the witness, Huddleston pointed out that Raye Dawn gave several statements to OSBI without hiring a lawyer and had been completely cooperative throughout the entire criminal investigation.

Patty High stood and immediately put Gayla on the defense. Gayla knew the answers to all of Huddleston's questions, but she was not prepared for these.

High asked, "Those hot checks you mentioned Michael Porter wrote, when were those?"

"I don't remember."

"Were you there when they were written?"

"No."

"How did you find out about them?"

"I found them when I was going through the house."

"But they were written when your daughter was still Raye Dawn Porter?"

"Yes."

"So you don't know if your daughter wrote them?"

"No."

"How did you know about the IRA's he cashed in?"

"I seen the stubs of them," replied Gayla.

"But beyond seeing the stubs, you don't know anything more about why or whether your daughter was involved in that?"

"No."

"You said Raye Dawn would not have married Michael Porter had she known he was having financial problems. Isn't that your opinion?"

"Yes."

"Did you have any conversations with her about that?"

"No," answered Gayla.

High questioned Gayla about the abuse. She asked if Raye Dawn did anything to protect Kelsey. Gayla told the jury the flip flops Kelsey was wearing when she sprained her ankle at the zoo were purple and about three or four inches high. But when High asked her how Kelsey could get around in them, the grandmother admitted she had never seen Kelsey wear them.

As High shifted her line of questioning to the months before Kelsey died, when Raye Dawn had sole care of her daughter, Gayla's memory became a bit fuzzy.

High asked, "So the only mishap between June and October was the car accident?"

"Yes," said Gayla.

"Nothing else?"

"Nothing major."

"What else did you know about?"

"Well Michael Porter said a lamp fell on her head."

"Okay, Anything else?"

"Well there was the seizure activity."

"But you say you never saw one?"

"No."

"How about when she rubbed her eye raw; you didn't find that unusual?"

"No, Kelsey picked at things."

"So you say things got better when she went back to live with Raye Dawn. Were you aware she weighed less when she died than she did in March of 2005?"

Gayla quickly said, "She gained one pound at her last doctor's appointment."

"That's not the question I asked you; were you aware she weighed less when she died than she did in March of 2005?"

"She was also taller," snapped Gayla.

"Ms. Smith, I'm not trying to argue with you; but answer my question, were you aware she weighed less when she died than she did in March of 2005?"

"Yes."

High's next question caused jaws to drop, "Did Michael Porter tape Kelsey's eyes shut?"

"Seems like I remember that."

"How?"

"Raye Dawn told me."

"You told OSBI she was mad because Mike had put tape over Kelsey's eyes and mouth?"

"Yes, Raye Dawn was upset about it."

"Upset enough to call you?"

"Yes."

A wave of nausea came over Kathie. The story of Kelsey's life had been played out before a jury but this was one chapter she had never heard. She turned to Shirica, who had tears streaming down her face. Kathie put her head in her hands. The bench in front of her was the only thing holding her up as Kathie stared at the grandmother who could have saved her granddaughter. This was just one more piece of information she would have to break to Lance. The D.A. recommended Lance stay outside to avoid outbursts if lies were told.

"What did you tell her to do?" asked High.

"I asked if they were playing and I told her to watch him."

"Is that all you remember?"

"Yes."

"Did she call you to tell you Michael Porter said Kelsey fell down the stairs and got some bruises?"

"Yes, she was concerned."

"Why?"

"Because Kelsey was good at the stairs. We was starting to watch him."

"So why was Raye Dawn starting to watch him?"

"We just was."

Huddleston worked damage control by pointing out that the kids may have been playing when Michael Porter taped Kelsey's eyes and mouth shut. But as Gayla Smith walked off the stand toward her supportive family, the Huddleston's first and strongest witness may have destroyed Raye's defense.

The second and final day of the defense's case did not go much better. Huddleston called Rachelle Smith, Raye Dawn's sister, to the stand. Rachelle testified she spent nearly every day with her sister, even after Raye Dawn and Michael Porter got married. Rachelle claimed she never saw the bruises because Kelsey was with Kathie Briggs.

During cross examination Richard Smothermon said, "Mr. Huddleston asked you lots of questions about Mr. Porter. Let's talk about Raye Dawn, the defendant here. On January 14, 2005, she's accused of abusing Kelsey. Did you guys talk about that?"

"No," said Rachelle, "She didn't do it."

"What did she tell you happened?"

It was if a light bulb went off in the 21-year-old's head and she remembered somewhere she heard if you don't know the answer, the appropriate response on the witness stand is, "I don't recall."

"Did she ever tell you about bruising?"

"I don't recall."

"Wouldn't you say this was a significant part of her life and you guys are really good friends?"

"Yes."

"But you don't recall?"

"No."

The next witness, Miste Smith, Raye Dawn's sister-in-law, says she loved Kelsey like she was her own. Her memory was better than Rachelle's, at least during Huddleston's line of questioning. She could recall the flip flops she says Kelsey was wearing when she sprained her ankle at the zoo. She had a slightly different description of these elusive shoes, saying they were terry cloth, rainbow colored flip flops with quite a heel on them. Miste says after the bird show at the zoo, Kelsey said, "My foot hurt." So Miste called Raye Dawn at work and they took her to the emergency room.

The prosecution asked Miste a few more questions about the "sprained ankle" and referenced a statement Miste made to the OSBI about the incident.

"Let's talk about April 14, 2005. Isn't it true that Kelsey's foot hurt her on the 13th?" asked High.

"No."

"Isn't it true that Michael Porter brought her in the house that night and Kelsey said, 'My foot feel funny?'"

"It was asleep," responded Miste.

"Did you ever think, 'Oh my gosh, maybe there was something wrong with her foot?'"

"No, she could walk."

"Why did you tell the OSBI that?"

"It was a question they asked."

"But you didn't tell the jury that?"

In a defensive tone, Miste answered, "I have nothing to hide."

Miste told the prosecutor she knows Kelsey turned her ankle and her foot came out of her flip flops. Miste says she did not see it happen but was holding Kelsey's hand when her foot came out of the shoe.

Next, the defense called Pastor Charles Pearcy. Pearcy arrived at Prague hospital while emergency workers were trying to resuscitate Kelsey. He described what he considered Michael Porter's suspicious behavior in the minutes leading up to and the hours following Kelsey's death. The prosecution did not bother to cross-examine Pearcy or the Prague police officer who was also called to describe Porter's odd behavior.

Raye Dawn's cousin, Sarah Winters, testified that Raye Dawn jumped through hoops to get Kelsey back and did everything DHS asked of her. Huddleston specifically asked Winters questions about the hours following Kelsey's murder. She told the jury Michael Porter tried to commit suicide the next day.

There had been hours of testimony about Michael Porter's so called strange reaction to the murder of his step-daughter. Pattye High shifted the focus, asking Winters what she and Raye Dawn did the morning after Kelsey's murder. Winters told the jury, she, Raye Dawn, and Porter went to Chandler and the courthouse in Meeker before dropping Porter off at work.

"What did you do in Chandler?" asked High.

"We went to the courthouse and Raye Dawn got a VPO against Kathie and Lance," answered Winters.

"First thing in the morning?" asked High.

"Yes," replied Winters.

"What did you do at Meeker City Hall?"

"Gave the police the paper work to serve them."

"So the petition for the VPO's was filed at 11:02 a.m.?"

"If that's what it says," said Winters.

High pressed on, "So that's the first order of business for the day? Why? Did you think, by golly the Briggs were responsible for her death, even though they hadn't seen her in months?"

"No one said the Briggs were responsible for her death," snapped Winters.

"Was it that she was afraid of the Briggs? Or that she didn't want them to come to the funeral?"

"She never needed to say that," said Winters.

"It was assumed?"

"Yes."

"In the end, little Kelsey had two separate funerals?"

"Yes."

Huddleston, once again doing damage control, pointed out that an agency involved in the case suggested Raye Dawn file the VPO's. He also explained the other order of business at Meeker City Hall was to purchase a burial plot.

Janet Gragg, Raye Dawn's sister was the defense's final witness of the day. She told jurors that Kelsey was awesome and she was very close to her sister. When Huddleston asked how Raye Dawn disciplined Kelsey, she told the same story Gayla shared.

Raye Dawn would count. Before she could get to the number two, Kelsey would finish saying, "two three" and Raye Dawn would laugh forgetting about whatever it was Kelsey had done.

The night Kelsey was murdered, Raye Dawn and Porter stayed at Janet's house. She told the jury Porter ate two sandwiches and some chips while he watched television. At the time she admitted she did not find it odd but in hindsight she thought it was important to mention.

Janet claimed to be "very close" to her sister, but she says Raye Dawn did not call her to tell her Porter had taped Kelsey's eyes and mouth shut.

"Did she call and tell you Michael Porter says Kelsey fell down the stairs and she didn't believe it?"

"No."

Janet told the jury she would have turned Raye Dawn in, had she suspected her sister was abusing Kelsey.

Jurors later referred to that day of testimony as, "Alzheimer's day" because no one from the Smith family could recall the answers to questions from anyone but Huddleston.

Wednesday, July 18, 2007, Britten spent her 26th birthday covering the last day of the trial. Raye Dawn wore a tan skirt suit and entered yet another door. Again she tried to avoid the television cameras; however, there were more of them than her.

Every camera would get a shot of her in handcuffs, sobbing in the back of a squad car later that day.

The defense called Brandon Watkins as its final witness. Brandon was Kelsey's guardian ad litem, her lawyer, during many of the court battles. He told the jury Raye Dawn always cooperated. In September, he initially recommended the state drop the deprived case against Raye Dawn and Michael Porter. There were no reports that concerned him; however, he withdrew the recommendation because the six months required by law had not passed.

The six month statute was created after a boy named Ryan Luke died as a result of abuse. The intent was to allow the state to ease out of the child's life, as opposed to an abrupt cut off. The prosecution reminded jurors Kelsey did not live through that six month time period.

Prosecutors showed Watkins the stack of pictures of Kelsey with bruises. Watkins told jurors no one showed him any of those pictures at the time. The young lawyer explained he made the best decision he could at the time with the information he had.

By 9:15 a.m., the defense rested its case.

A few minutes later, Pattye High stood, wearing the same pink suit she wore on the first day of trial, to address the jury for the final time. She began as a teacher, calmly instructing her twelve students to take their common sense to deliberations.

And then she unleashed the anger that had been building for eight days of trial; the anger over charges that had not been filed; anger over a dead two-year-old.

High's neck became beet red as she began the most moving closing argument reporters in the room had ever heard.

High told jurors to look at the evidence in front of them because, "The one person who could not come into this courtroom and tell you what happened is Kelsey. But she left behind her broken, battered body as evidence for you. Look at what happens when you don't look at the evidence. Brandon Watkins, he didn't know the evidence.

"You have hindsight. Kelsey should not be dead. We have all of these pictures, pictures of what she should be doing, going on 4 wheelers, playing at birthday parties."

High generally raises her voice during closing arguments. This time she began shouting over Raye Dawn's sobs, "Do not make the mistake everyone else did. Do not believe every bizarre repetitive excuse Raye Dawn Porter has told you. Believing Raye Dawn Porter is what killed Kelsey Briggs. Those tears are worthless here. Kelsey is dead and she's responsible for it. This is that child's mother. Do NOT let her tears in this courtroom dissuade you."

High pointed out that Dr. Sullivan said Kelsey's legs were not broken by accident. She asked whether jurors believed it was willful when Raye Dawn took a hairbrush to Kelsey's butt, "This mother reasonably chose to do nothing. We are accountable for the choices we make. If you want to believe she is not the abuser and that Michael Porter did it, then she knew. A mother does not have the right to choose her man over her baby. A mother has to choose to protect her child. When you come home and your baby's eyes are taped shut, maybe you think it's a joke. But she didn't. She called her mother to tell her. OK, bad choice Raye Dawn, we'll give you that one. But how about the time Kelsey had fallen down the stairs? Remember when Gayla Smith told you, 'We were watching him.' Really? What are you watching him do? Really? She watched him beat her child to death.

"Now is the day of accountability. Now she's dead. No one had a better opportunity to save this child's life. And that's if you believe Michael Porter is the killer."

High held up two pictures, one of Kelsey smiling on the courthouse steps after Raye Dawn and Porter got married, the other from the autopsy table, as she said, "How do you go from this to this? How do you go from playing at the courthouse to the morgue?

"I heard this quote once, 'All that is necessary for evil to flourish is for good people to do nothing.'

"The doctor, the Meeker Police Department, the CHBS worker, you can get all worked up about what they did or did not do. But this jury is not here to decide if DHS screwed up; if Judge Key made a good decision. There will be another jury on another day to decide that.

"Your job is on her mama. What responsibility does she have for the death of her child? None? She didn't know?

"A long line of good people in this case have done nothing. All of the sympathy in the world will not save Kelsey. She's gone. I submit to you those bruises on her buttocks, her legs, and her face. And this woman's story is that she never saw them.

"Who pays the price? Kelsey Shelton Smith-Briggs.

"On and on people doing nothing. Don't do nothing. It's clear she is guilty beyond a reasonable doubt of both. But you've got to speak to her with your verdict. Tell her today the evil stops. Find her guilty."

The Briggs family wiped their eyes with tissue. Reporters blinked away tears. The judge told everyone to take a bathroom break before Steve Huddleston made his final plea to find Raye Dawn not guilty.

Huddleston began by thanking the jury and ensuring them that doing their civic duty was the most important thing they would be asked to do in their lives. Then he began taking a personal stab at the other lawyers in the room. The lawyers prosecuting his client for either abusing Kelsey or allowing her to be abused.

"This case from the state, from start to finish, is full of doubt. The state said we are going to have some unanswered questions. Questions lead to doubt. I still have them.

"There are a lot of photographs, but are they of the same incident. I believe they are. They have put up everything to pile it on. Don't have tunnel vision.

"What about the soap in the eye? The tape? I can take each person in here and take pictures of all of your child's injuries and it would look like the kid got beat up. Think about someone taking pictures of all of the bumps. Click. Scrape. Click. I can twist it and turn it, make every truth I want to about it, but when the tables are turned, the truth comes out.

"October 11, 2005 my client was not home. That is the day Kelsey died. Jean Bonner says Kelsey was playing and laughing before Porter got home. These pictures of Kelsey on the autopsy table do not belong in this trial. They should be in Michael Porter's murder trial.

"Make no doubt, Michael Porter murdered this little girl. Do you have any doubt? If you don't have any doubt, think about the DA saying, 'I think you committed the murder of this child.' It should be done. Dr. Yacoub says they were fresh injuries. Then we heard how Kelsey was sexually assaulted. Every time I stood up and said Michael Porter murdered and sexually assaulted Kelsey, did you hear that? Why didn't they object?

"Why wasn't Dr. Hawley called to testify? They exhumed the body. They flew him down here to do another autopsy to put this child through another autopsy. I didn't hire him. Why didn't they call him? Because he would say Kelsey was sexually abused and that didn't fit here. What is that all about? Is that fair? Is that above the board? Is that the way we should prosecute this case?

"I have no earthly idea why they put Porter on the stand when the D.A. knew he wasn't telling the truth. It seems bizarre. I didn't even write down the dates of what he was saying because this whole incident he kept saying Raye Dawn was the greatest mom. OSBI told him he murdered this little girl and he says now's the time to stand up for my woman? He bellied up to the bar and took 30 years. Why would you plead to 30 years? He's a liar.

Why the DA didn't prosecute him for the murder of Kelsey I don't know. The evidence was there. We weren't even putting on Porter's case but we proved it to you.

Huddleston held up an autopsy picture of Kelsey's private parts when he asked, "Why didn't he introduce this into evidence? Every one of those autopsy photos goes with Mr. Porter, not us."

"Tape on the eyes? We've gotten to that point. Throw everything at them and by God just get a conviction. DHS, CASA, CHBS, the police, now they want to charge her. Mistakes were made but they want to try her with their mistakes. Sometimes you can't stop a sexual predator. Every one of them said Mr. Porter was a good guy. Now she should have known. I'm tired of it. Sick and tired of it. Every single little thing. They couldn't prove murder, abuse, they come up with tape at the end. She told the OSBI way back about this and told them it was not a big deal. When everything else is crumbling, bring on the tape!

"I started thinking this morning, what would it be like to be Raye Dawn? She finds out the person she married raped and murdered her child. Then the websites and the media start hounding her. Did you kill your baby? Did you kill your baby? She's chased down the hall. Then they filed on her. She's looking at life in prison. They're still looking at her. Is she faking those tears or not faking?

"She's been through enough. It's time to draw the line in the sand and say it stops here. I need you to stand up for her. It's time the jury verdict be unanimous. Stand up, stop it, stop this stuff. It's time. Find her not guilty of every charge and you know why."

Everyone in the courtroom went to lunch. High and Smothermon escaped to the library across the street. Smothermon wandered off by himself to think about his closing arguments. After lunch, Smothermon's wife slipped in to the courtroom to listen as her husband made his final comments to the jury.

He began quietly, "I'm glad there was a lunch break, because when Mr. Huddleston finished his closing arguments, I was angry. They chose a style of attacking and they attacked me personally. I wanted to defend every accusation they made toward me and my office. But at lunch I really thought about it, and realized that's not what this was about. It's about Kelsey. Not about me.

Smothermon promised to answer every question they had, after the verdict. He promised to tell them why he pled Michael Porter.

"But that's not what this trial is about. I want to talk to you about Kelsey; I've lived this case since October 12, 2005."

His voice cracked as he said, "I want to be the voice of Kelsey today.

"There's a reason I sent Michael Porter to prison for 30 years. I hate him. Take him for whatever value you deem appropriate. They were going to put him on trial regardless. That was their defense.

"Who is on trial here? This is the state versus Raye Dawn Smith. The defendant misses the entire point and it's not the first time. The reason she's not charged with murder is because I don't believe she committed that crime. This defendant wants you to think Michael Porter did those injuries. Kelsey had a really, really bad life. Those injuries are only the final chapter in Kelsey's life.

"Michael Porter said one thing on this stand that you should remember. He said, 'Me not doing anything to stop it makes me as bad as had I did it.' He's never said any truer words.

"Her mother told you she knew. They'd be the first to watch him. Not the first to report it. They want you to believe because everyone was watching them, she couldn't have abused her. But that only works if there was no further abuse. We know there was further abuse. What do you do when someone says perpetrator unknown? Did she do anything differently? No.

"People were watching her, but they never had the benefit of the truth. She did everything. That's what they want you to believe, and this is very telling. I met with Raye Dawn and her mom immediately following Michael Porter being charged with murder. She says she has done everything; well, she didn't. She never told me about the tape over Kelsey's eyes; she never told anyone about Porter saying Kelsey fell down the stairs. That would have been real helpful to know when you're putting together a murder investigation.

"Gayla Smith says they were starting to watch him. At that point Raye Dawn's guilty of enabling child abuse. It's not enough to watch. The law requires action.

"You can't wait for him to break her legs.

"You can't wait for him to confirm your suspicions.

"You can't wait until she's murdered.

"If you choose that path you can't hide behind DHS, the D.A.'s office, and Michael Porter. They want you to think Michael Porter was hiding in the shadows. Who's hiding in the shadows now? She's hiding in Michael Porter's shadows.

"This defendant abused her child and watched as her child was abused over and over. She either did it or let it happen."

Raye Dawn again began sobbing as Smothermon continued, "What do you do about it? Hold her accountable through her tears. Tears do not absolve you of your accountability. I've sent a lot of people to prison crying.

"The path of no action caused Kelsey Shelton Smith-Briggs to be murdered.

"Kelsey Briggs died. She died. She died. She's dead.

"This child was murdered because her mother allowed it to happen."

At 2:45 p.m., the jury began deliberating.

Each television station rushed multiple crews to Bristow to cover every courthouse exit. Reporters and photographers devised strategies to get interviews with jurors as they walked out one door. If she was found guilty the primary goal was to get video of Raye Dawn as she was ushered into the squad car. Finally, reporters needed to get on the air live with the verdict.

Within the first hour the jury asked lawyers whether DHS confirmed abuse against Raye Dawn in the January 14, 2005, incident. Judge Vassar told them he could not give them any additional information, explaining that was discussed in detail during testimony.

The families that had been divided since Lance and Raye Dawn's divorce sat divided during these final hours. The Briggs family gathered in the empty courtroom down the hall; the Smith family sat near the center entrance to the courthouse. At least 50 yards and several walls separated the families.

Inside the courtroom where the Briggs family was waiting, Richard Smothermon warned the family to be prepared for either verdict. Smothermon said the judge was not kidding when he ordered everyone not to show any emotion after the verdict. Britten sat with the Briggs family at a table at the front of the courtroom. The air conditioning made it a cool spot to curl her hair and put on her make-up in case she would be breaking into afternoon programming with a verdict. Kathie rested on the floor behind the jury box trying to gather her thoughts before Raye Dawn's jury returned.

When the jury was still deliberating into the 5 o'clock hour, the Briggs family began to get anxious. They were concerned Judge Vassar might send the 12 decision makers home for the night.

During the 5 o'clock evening newscast, one station reported a second question from the jury. Jurors asked if the decision on punishment had to be unanimous or if majority could rule. Smothermon did not share that question with the family for fear it would get their hopes up the jury had reached a guilty verdict.

Just before 6:00 p.m., reporters learned the jury had reached a verdict.

With nervous anticipation family members, reporters, and witnesses filed through the metal detectors and into the courtroom. The last people through security had not sat down when the jury handed the judge the verdict. Smothermon's wife held Jeanna's hand as the verdict was read:

"We the jury find Raye Dawn Smith guilty of enabling child abuse. We sentence her to 27 years in prison."

Raye Dawn's sister Rachelle screamed.

Raye Dawn looked to her mom and said, "Help me."

Raye Dawn immediately began sobbing saying she did not understand.

Deputies ordered her to take off all of her jewelry.

People in the crowd began looking around, asking if they heard the verdict correctly. Lance thought it might have been two years, or maybe seven, but could not believe the jury returned a sentence of 27 years in prison. Kathie had to sit down. She stared at the D.A. in shock. She had prepared herself for a five year sentence.

Britten ran to the front lawn where a photographer was standing by ready for a live shot. Breathless, she grabbed the microphone and listened for her cue. She was so winded she had to catch her breath on live television. She reported the verdict and Raye Dawn's reaction, promising more details later in the evening. Nearby, Cherokee and the other reporters began cutting into programming as well.

Outside the courtroom photographers were positioned in the garage, where a squad car was waiting to escort Kelsey Smith-Briggs' mother to the Creek County Jail to wait for her formal sentencing. Photographers could hear Raye Dawn sobbing as deputies led her down the hallway. When she reached the garage she looked at the cameras. Seemingly on demand, the young mother screamed, "I don't understand, I loved my baby." She buried her head in her hands as deputies shut the car door, silencing her tears.

Outside, the Smith family snuck out the back door of the courthouse, avoiding reporters who were eager to get "their side" of this dramatic end to the story.

The Briggs filed out of the courtroom, hugging each other and their cell phones as they shared the verdict with others.

Microphones from all over the state waited for the family to respond to the verdict. Lance's voice echoed in homes across Oklahoma that night. "I am relieved," he said, "What this was, right here today, was justice for my daughter. The horrible, horrible part is she could have prevented it. She's over there crying when they read the verdict. She could be out playing with Kelsey right now and not in handcuffs."

Shirica could not stop picturing Raye Dawn looking toward her mom for help. Fitting, because Shirica knew that is what Kelsey must have thought as she looked to her own mom for help.

In the days that followed Raye Dawn was given an opportunity to explain to the judge why the jury got the case wrong. Ultimately, the judge hands down the official sentence. In her pre-sentencing investigation, officers with the Department of Corrections read Kathie's impact statement and interviewed Lance, Gayla, and Raye Dawn herself.

In a written statement, Raye Dawn said, "I have always felt this was a conspiracy against me. I also believe that there are people guilty of things running free. This entire ordeal has been ongoing far too long and I have never been treated like a mother who lost her daughter. I did everything I knew possible to do. I worked with DHS, the best to my ability and knowledge.

"I never, ever thought Mike would've hurt Kelsey. If I would have thought that I would've ran w/her and left everything else behind. Then I would've turned him in.

"Kelsey was my best friend in the entire world and it hurts so bad for people to say the things they do. Kathie Briggs knows I didn't hurt Kelsey and she knows I didn't sit back and let it happen. When Kelsey was having night terrors and possible seizures, I thought they were being triggered by something she was dreaming about that had happened while she was w/Kathie.

"If I could have seen into the future I never would've dated Mike Porter. I would love to see my son and one day try to live a normal life again, although I will never see my beautiful daughter again."

From prison, the officer says Raye Dawn continuously repeated, "I don't understand."

Raye Dawn promised if the judge gave her the opportunity to go home, she might take classes on public speaking and begin to write her book. Raye Dawn told the officer she needed to speak about the "situation". She wanted to talk to others about marrying the wrong person more than once, "I feel like I have to do this."

Gayla told the D.O.C. officers the jurors who convicted her daughter were "inbred" and had their minds made up before trial. Gayla said, "The jury has no idea who she was. They do not know our family."

Before sentencing, the judge can consider a victim's impact statement. Kathie wrote about happier times:

"The past two years have been consumed with things that went wrong in Kelsey's life. I would like to share some memories of happier times. Kelsey loved an audience, and at the age of 13 months, she won the title of Miss Personality in a baby pageant. If something did not go quite right, she would hit her hand against her forehead and exclaim, "Oh man." Kelsey wanted to be independent. If you offered her help she would say, "I do it." If you offered again, she would give a stronger, "I do it." She had very good phone skills and loved talking to her daddy while he was deployed. She would say, "Daddy a soldier. My daddy in Army." She had conversations with him when no one was on the other end of the line. Kelsey lived 33 months and we were cheated out of the first four and the last four. All we have are the memories. Raye Dawn saw to it, our family would live a life of grief because of her actions.

"The day Kelsey went back into Raye Dawn's home, my attorney looked at me and stated, 'The next time you see her, she will probably be dead.' We saw her once more seven weeks before her death, for five hours. Her body was frail, bruised, and even worse, her spirit was gone. As I was leaving that day, I looked back and said, 'Kelsey I need you to know that I love you and I will see you again.' I never dreamed the next visit would take place in heaven. We now have to live wondering if Kelsey thought our family abandoned her? Did she think her daddy didn't love her anymore? Did she think she was being punished when placed back into an abusive home?

"Mothers all over the world grieve the loss of children due to illness. They would trade places with their child or make any sacrifice to have them healthy again. Kelsey's mother allowed her child to suffer while deliberately covering up lies to protect herself. Raye Dawn was given two opportunities to love and protect her child, God gave her the first one, Judge Key gave her the second. She did not have to be a great mother. She did not have to be a good mother, according to DHS policy she only needed to provide adequate care and she failed. Raye Dawn does not have the ability to think of anyone other than herself. She had the opportunity to remove Kelsey from this situation and she made the conscious decision to let her live in fear, be tortured for months, and eventually murdered.

"We will never know what happened October 11, 2005. Some members of our family believe it was Raye Dawn who dealt the final blow. What we do know is Raye Dawn could have prevented it, regardless of the perpetrator. We have been given a life sentence, as we now have to live without Kelsey. We have wiped away many tears from Kelsey's cousins. Two of them were heard on the playground, talking about their own safety and were trying to figure out which one killed Kelsey. We spend each December 28, visiting a cemetery instead of watching Kelsey blowing out her birthday candles.

"We sat in the courtroom as the verdict was read. Raye Dawn exclaimed, "I don't understand," my thought was neither did Kelsey. If Raye Dawn does not understand after watching this horror story unfold, she obviously does not take responsibility for her part. I pray Kelsey's little brother can find peace in his life knowing one of his parents murdered his sister and the other parent allowed it to happen.

"This jury listened to seven days of testimony and finally someone 'got it'. Our faith that the system can work, has been restored. We are satisfied with the sentence the jury has handed down. It is our hope Raye Dawn is sentenced to the 27 years the jury recommended.

A two-year-old child should not be dead, but she is, and her mother is responsible and should be held accountable.

Kelsey's life will not be forgotten and once again, I want to say how blessed I feel that God chose our family to know and love this little angel."

Complete strangers. A man and woman, from the Department of Corrections, who spent just a short time talking to Raye and her family also, "got it". The officers recommended the judge uphold the jury's 27 year sentence saying, "The perpetrator who caused Kelsey's death has not been determined. Smith denies culpability in this offense. She denies she allowed Kelsey to be abused. Instead, Smith attempts to diminish her responsibility for the abuse of her daughter and projects blame to others who were the only individuals who took actions to protect Kelsey. Because of Smith's denial of responsibility it is unlikely that Smith will display a willingness to change her behavior. Through her actions and omissions, Smith has shown she poses a serious threat to any children or minors in which she has been entrusted for their care."

The judge had nearly two months to pour over all of the reports and make his final ruling on Raye Dawn's sentence.

Downpours made the drive to Bristow slow that September morning. The news crews nearly had to pull off the Turnpike. They could not see anything but the wave of water attacking the windshield.

Lance said he had not lost a minute of sleep since Raye Dawn was found guilty. He was confident Judge Vassar would uphold the jury's recommendation of 27 years.

Kathie was nervous. The system failed her once and it could happen again.

No one was prepared for what happened in the courtroom that day.

Raye Dawn got out of the back seat of a squad car wearing a pin striped pant suit and handcuffs. Gayla was waiting nearby for a moment with her daughter. Raye Dawn lifted her cuffed hands over her head to hug her mom's neck. They walked inside the courthouse side by side.

Raye Dawn waited patiently for her new lawyer, Stephen Jones. Jones represented Timothy McVeigh in the Oklahoma City bombing trials. The controversial lawyer walked briskly through the door, his blue leisure suit and thick glasses speckled with rain.

Raye Dawn and her lawyer covered their mouths and whispered as reporters tried to discern what was being said between the lawyer and his client. When words were not appropriate, Jones walked up to the files sitting next to the bench and pulled out blank documents as scratch paper.

A small wooden wall separated the inmate from her family. The right side of the room blushed different shades of pink. The Briggs family wore Kelsey's favorite color to watch deputies haul Kelsey's mom off to prison.

Raye Dawn's minutes outside prison walls were extended by a few. Pattye High walked into the courtroom about seven minutes late, still wet from the thunderstorm. The lawyers met in the judge's chambers before the bailiff asked the courtroom to stand.

Jones asked the judge if Raye Dawn could have an opportunity to address the court. Judge Vassar told Raye Dawn she could make a short comment. Reporters braced, frantically flipping to a blank page in their notepads. People in the courtroom held their breath. She was going to speak? What would she say? Would she apologize?

Raye Dawn whispered to her lawyer, "Should I stand?" And she did. Raye stood, turned toward the "pink" side of the courtroom. Her eyes passed Lance and focused on Kathie Briggs. The young mother said, "Kathie, I forgive you."

The courtroom chuckled in disbelief.

The judge sentenced her to the full 27 years.

Before deputies could escort her into the squad car, reporters had one last chance to ask Raye Dawn questions for the camera. As soon as she spotted Raye Dawn, Britten shouted, "Raye Dawn what do you forgive Kathie for?"

Cherokee asked, "Are you ready to go to prison?"

As Raye Dawn reached the door to the car, she froze as Britten asked "Raye Dawn, who killed Kelsey?" Raye Dawn glared at Britten and the camera. For a moment Britten thought Kelsey's mother might answer the question. As their eyes locked, Britten asked again, "Who killed her?"

Seven seconds passed as the two stared at each other, Britten, waiting, hoping for an answer to the question that still haunts her dreams.

Raye Dawn ducked into the squad car. No excuses. No answer. Just silence.

Michael Porter

"I don't want to see you have a heart attack," said Garrett.

"I just lost my daughter. And now me and my wife are being accused of killing her."

"Yeah that's true. One of you two are going to be responsible for this deal. And I admit that would make me a little nervous too."

"It's not nervous. It's just heartbreaking."

"Yeah, it's sad. But you know what else is sad is Kelsey will never see her third birthday."

"I have told you everything that I know that happened, everything that happened. And I don't know what else I can tell you. So I'm at the point where I guess I'm going to have to talk to a lawyer."

"Well, the truth is what would be good."

"I told you," Porter finished.

Raye Dawn Smith

Under the watchful eye of the same camera that gazed at Porter, Raye shook her head as she told her mom, "I mean I didn't tell them, but I've sat here all day long and I've told them the same thing over and over and it's the truth."

"Stick with the truth," replied her mom.

"I was going to stay here and tell them I don't know. I didn't get up to pee; I haven't ate anything. I was going to sit there, and I'll stay here until they listen to me, but I did not hurt my daughter. She was fine when I left. She was eating raisins and telling me, 'Mommy I love you so much.'"

When Garrett came back in from his conversation with Porter he told her, "Somebody is going to catch it for this deal."

Raye replied, "I understand, because, like I told you over and over, I want to know what happened to my baby."

So does the rest of Oklahoma.

Only three people know who killed Kelsey that October day.

Two are in prison.

The other is in heaven.

Three years after Kelsey's murder, her cousin Eryn asked her mom for a piece of paper and a few minutes alone at Kelsey's grave. Eryn wrote...

Dear Kelsey,

I love you and miss you so much.
More than you can ever imagine.
I wish you were here.
My life has been miserable without you.
Your the best.
If you have been watching me I've been doing great in dance.

Love, Eryn

EPILOGUE

RAYE DAWN SMITH IS SERVING A **27** YEAR PRISON SENTENCE FOR ENABLING CHILD ABUSE. The judge denied her motion for a new trial. The Department of Corrections reports Raye Dawn still has her four leaf clover tattoo.

Mike Porter is serving 30 years for the same crime. He filed for a reduction in sentence; the judge refused to hear his case.

Kathie Briggs is actively involved in her nine other grandchildren's lives and is the founder of Kelsey's Purpose, a grassroots organization designed to raise awareness about child abuse and reform Oklahoma's Department of Human Services. Kelsey's Purpose has 35,500 members who log in from all over the world. The Briggs family founded The Kelsey Briggs Foundation and will give a memorial scholarship every year.

Lance entered rehab for alcohol addiction. In 2009 he settled the $15 million lawsuit against the State of Oklahoma for $625,000, the maximum amount the state can pay out in a case like Kelsey's.

Richard Smothermon won several awards for his handling of Kelsey's case. Pattye High is now in private practice.

Porter and Raye Dawn's baby, Blaine Smith, is living with one of Raye Dawn's relatives.

Raye Dawn's original attorney Greg Wilson lost his license to practice law for a year for mishandling another case.

Judge Key was voted out of office.

Despite thousands of television news stories about Kelsey's case and the system that failed her, none of Kelsey's caseworkers has been fired. One got a promotion.

The Oklahoma law named after Kelsey, designed to protect other children, did not protect the 5 children who have died in state custody since Kelsey.

For more information on Kelsey's story visit: www.kelseyspurpose.org

BRITTEN FOLLETT

On Fox News Network, Britten reported, "Last night I cried myself to sleep after watching Kelsey's story on YouTube. 6 million people have watched it. Kelsey should not be on YouTube. Her death could have been prevented." Since that report, the number of views has gone up to 37 million. As a television reporter, Britten has covered Kelsey's case since the day after her death.

Britten's dedication to uncovering corruption within Oklahoma's Department of Human Services, has prompted parents and grandparents to call her daily reporting problems with the system. Due to confidentiality laws, many of those stories will never be told; however, Britten has spent the last year investigating the intimate details of the back room deals and negligence behind Kelsey's story. Because Kelsey's dead, her story can be told.

Britten's television reports have earned her three Emmy nominations along with six state and regional broadcasting awards, including Oklahoma's 2005 Best Investigative Report. She graduated Summa Cum Laude from Southern Illinois University-Carbondale, where she was an award winning Division One volleyball player.

Two of her fiction stories have been published in literary journals. Britten is no stranger to the book business. Five generations ago, her family founded Follett Corporation.

In Britten's spare time she enjoys reading, singing karaoke, working on her scrapbook, shopping, and building her Barbie doll collection.

CHEROKEE BALLARD

Cherokee's career in television news began 25 years ago. She earned national recognition as Oklahoma's 2008 Woman of the Year. Her 2002 weekly series, "Cherokee's Journal: Lessons in Living with Cancer," took viewers on her personal journey through changes and challenges when cancer presented itself, from diagnosis, chemotherapy, to hair loss, radiation and finally, recovery.

Cherokee is a University of Oklahoma alumnus and worked as a professor at the School of Journalism, instructing its "Writing for Broadcast" classes.

Cherokee grew up in Oklahoma City and is native Cherokee Indian. She is part of a small community of Native Americans within the United States who are television news anchors. Cherokee was honored in a 2001 photographic exhibit at the Smithsonian Museum in Washington, D.C. called, "Cherokee Nation: A Portrait of a People." It depicted contemporary Oklahoma Cherokees.

In 2002, she won the Cherokee Nation Medal of Honor Award and in 2001, the IABC Central Oklahoma Excel Award. She has also won the Staff Peabody Award and a Regional Emmy Award for her coverage of the Oklahoma City bombing.

CPSIA information can be obtained at www.ICGtesting.com
Printed in the USA
BVOW061835310512

291509BV00002B/29/P